Making Certain It Goes On

The

COLLECTED

POEMS *of*

RICHARD HUGO

Also by Richard Hugo

A Run of Jacks

Death of the Kapowsin Tavern

Good Luck in Cracked Italian

The Lady in Kicking Horse Reservoir

What Thou Lovest Well Remains American

31 Letters and 13 Dreams

The Triggering Town: Lectures and Essays on Poetry and Writing

Selected Poems

White Center

The Right Madness on Skye

Making Certain It Goes On

The

COLLECTED

POEMS of

RICHARD HUGO

W. W. NORTON & COMPANY

New York / London

The text of this book is composed in Janson, with
display type set in Horizon. Composition by Vail-Ballou Press, Inc.
Manufacturing by The Hadden Craftsmen, Inc.

First Edition

Library of Congress Cataloging in Publication Data

Hugo, Richard F.
    Making certain it goes on: The collected poems of Richard Hugo.
    I. Title.
PS3515.U3   1983   811'.54   83-8016

ISBN 0-393-01784-2

W. W. Norton & Company, Inc., 500 Fifth Avenue, New York, N.Y. 10110
W. W. Norton & Company Ltd., 37 Great Russell Street, London WC1B 3NU

1 2 3 4 5 6 7 8 9 0

. . . Believe you and I sing tiny and wise
and could if we had to eat stone and go on.
—from "Glen Uig"

PUBLISHER'S NOTE

In accordance with the author's wishes before his
untimely death, *Making Certain It Goes On: The Collected
Poems of Richard Hugo* contains all the poems that
appeared in book form during his lifetime, with the
exception of two from *Good Luck in Cracked Italian*. It
also restores "December 24, Alone" to *What Thou Lovest
Well Remains American*, and concludes with all the new
poems written since *The Right Madness on Skye* that he
wished to include. The new poems were arranged in
their present order by Ripley Hugo and Matthew
Hansen.

CONTENTS

A Run of Jacks   [*1961*]

Trout   *3*
Near Kalalock   *3*
Bass   *4*
West Marginal Way   *5*
Lone Cheer from the Stands for a Bitter Crane   *6*
Underwater Autumn   *7*
La Push   *7*
The Gull Hardly Explained   *8*
Triangle for Green Men   *9*
Beachthieves   *12*
North   *12*
Or Another Place   *13*
Resulting from Magnetic Interference   *14*
Alki Beach   *15*
Meridian   *15*
Keen to Leaky Flowers   *16*
Antisocial Easter   *17*
Back of Gino's Place   *18*
A Troubadour Removed   *18*
Ocean on Monday   *21*
Snoqualmie   *21*
A District in the City   *22*
Schoolgirl at Seola   *23*
A Map of the Peninsula   *24*
Gooseprairie   *25*
Argo   *26*
Ballad of the Upper Bumping   *27*
Centuries Near Spinnazola   *29*

Cape Alava   *30*
Skykomish River Running   *32*
Mission in Carmel   *33*
Kapowsin   *34*
Graves at Mukilteo   *36*
A Chapel Further West than Most   *37*
Politely like Snakes in the Oats   *37*
Name the Mystery Fin and Win a Doll   *39*
1614 Boren   *39*
Bassetti's Lions   *41*
Memoirs   *41*
Lecture   *43*
Neighbor   *44*
Duwamish   *44*
Holy Family   *46*
Northwest Retrospective: Mark Tobey   *47*
Digging Is An Art   *48*
Orcas in the Eyes   *49*
The Way a Ghost Behaves   *50*
No Bells to Believe   *51*
Two Graves in a Day   *52*
At the Stilli's Mouth   *53*
The Way a Ghost Dissolves   *54*

Death of the Kapowsin Tavern [*1965*]

DUWAMISH, SKAGIT, HOH

Introduction to the Hoh   *59*
From the Rain Forest Down   *59*
Between the Bridges   *60*
Duwamish No. 2   *61*
Bad Vision at the Skagit   *62*
Plunking the Skagit   *63*
Hideout   *64*
Duwamish Head   *65*

OTHER WATERS

Tahola   *69*
Cape Nothing   *70*
Lone Lake, Whidbey   *71*
Sweet Piece from Fontal   *71*
Dancer at Kozani's   *72*
Index   *73*
The Anacortes-Sydney Run   *74*
Mendocino, Like You Said   *75*
The Colors of a Bird   *76*
Lake Byron, Maybe Gordon Lord   *77*
Road Ends at Tahola   *78*

MISSION TO LINZ

LIMITED ACCESS

Eileen   *85*
What the Brand New Freeway Won't Go By   *86*
December 24 and George McBride Is Dead   *87*
Antiques in Ellettsville   *88*
The Other Grave   *89*
Houses Lie, Believe the Lying Sea   *89*
First South and Cambridge   *90*
In Stafford Country   *91*
For a Northern Woman   *92*
Port Townsend   *93*
Fort Casey, without Guns   *93*
One by Twachtman at the Frye   *95*
Bouquets from Corley   *95*
The Squatter on Company Land   *96*
The Church on Comiaken Hill   *97*
The Blond Road   *98*
Pike Place Market   *99*
Graves at Coupeville   *101*
Death of the Kapowsin Tavern   *102*

Good Luck in Cracked Italian   [*1969*]

WHERE ALL DOORS OPEN IN

Docking at Palermo   *105*
Napoli Again   *106*
The Bridge of Sighs   *106*
Galileo's Chair   *107*
Morning in Padova   *108*
S. Miniato: One by Aretino   *109*
Tiberio's Cliff   *110*
Brueghel in the Doria   *111*
Castel Sant'Angelo   *112*
Kennedy *Ucciso*   *113*

SIDE TRIPS BACK

G.I. Graves in Tuscany   *115*
A View from Cortona   *116*
Eighteen Days in a Tuscan Wood   *117*
Viva La Resistènza   *118*
April in Cerignola   *118*
Tretitoli, Where the Bomb Group Was   *120*
Where We Crashed   *121*
Spinazzola: *Quella Cantina Là*   *124*
Note from Capri to Richard Ryan on the Adriatic Floor   *126*
The Yards of Sarajevo   *127*
Paestum   *128*
Galleria Umberto I   *129*

MARATEA

Maratea Porto   *131*
The Picnic in the Saracen Ruin   *132*
Maratea Antica   *133*
One Son North to Naples   *134*
Maratea Porto: The Bitter Man   *134*
Cantina Iannini   *135*

Pizzeria S. Biagio *136*
Maratea Porto: The Dear Postmistress There *137*
Maratea Porto: Saying Good-bye to the Vitolos *138*
Last Words from Maratea *139*

REMOTE OR STONE

South Italy, Remote and Stone *146*
Storm in Acquafredda *147*
The Park at Villammare *148*
Why Sapri Will Never Be Italian *149*
Beggar in Sapri *150*
Sailing Dalmatia *151*
Remote Farm on the Dubrovnik-Sarajevo Run *152*
Spinning the Sava *153*
Christmas with Shepherds in Brefaro *154*
Italian Town Abandoned *155*
Montesano Unvisited *156*
With Anna at Camaldoli *157*
Sailing from Naples *158*

The Lady in Kicking Horse Reservoir [*1973*]

MONTANA WITH FRIENDS

A Map of Montana in Italy *165*
The Milltown Union Bar *166*
Where Jennie Used to Swim *167*
Where Mission Creek Runs Hard for Joy *168*
Graves at Elkhorn *169*
St. Ignatius Where the Salish Wail *170*
Bad Eyes Spinning the Rock *171*
Dog Lake with Paula *172*
To Die in Milltown *173*
Pishkun *174*
Reclamation at Coloma *175*
Helena, Where Homes Go Mad *176*

Silver Star   *177*
With Kathy in Wisdom   *178*
Indian Graves at Jocko   *179*

TOURING

Drums in Scotland   *181*
Chysauster   *182*
Walking Praed Street   *182*
Somersby   *184*
The Prado: Bosch: S. Antonio   *184*
The Prado: Number 2671, Anonimo Español   *185*
At Cronkhite   *186*
Upper Voight's, to All the Cutthroat There   *187*
Taneum Creek   *188*
The Gold Man on the Beckler   *188*

TOURING WITH FRIENDS

Cataldo Mission   *190*
Montgomery Hollow   *191*
The End of Krim's Pad   *192*
Old Map of Uhlerstown   *193*
A Night with Cindy at Heitman's   *193*
Point No Point   *194*
Cornwall, Touring   *195*
Shark Island   *196*
The Tinker Camp   *197*
Cleggan   *198*
Crinan Canal   *199*

MONTANA

The Lady in Kicking Horse Reservoir   *201*
Ovando   *203*
Driving Montana   *204*
Montana Ranch Abandoned   *205*
2433 Agnes, First Home, Last House in Missoula   *205*

Ghosts at Garnet   *207*
A Night at the Napi in Browning   *208*
Camas Prairie School   *209*
Missoula Softball Tournament   *210*
Phoning from Sweathouse Creek   *211*
The Only Bar in Dixon   *212*
Dixon   *213*
Hot Springs   *214*
Bear Paw   *215*
Degrees of Gray in Philipsburg   *216*

What Thou Lovest Well Remains American   [*1975*]

A SNAPSHOT OF THE AUXILIARY

A Snapshot of the Auxiliary   *221*
Saying Goodbye to Mrs. Noraine   *222*
A Good Day for Seeing Your Limitations   *223*
The House on 15th S.W.   *224*
A Snapshot of 15th S.W.   *225*
December 24, Alone   *226*
Remember Graham   *227*
A History of the Sketch   *228*
Why I Think of Dumar Sadly   *228*
Time to Remember Sangster   *229*
Again, Kapowsin   *230*
Flying, Reflying, Farming   *231*
Last Day There   *233*
Places and Ways to Live   *234*
What Thou Lovest Well Remains American   *235*

STRANGERS

Goodbye, Iowa   *237*
Farmer, Dying   *238*

Living Alone   *239*
Turtle Lake   *239*
Late Summer, Drummond   *240*
Reading at the Old Federal Courts Building, St. Paul   *241*
Ode to the Trio Fruit Company of Missoula   *242*
Old Scene   *243*
Landscapes   *244*
Reconsidering the Madman   *245*
The Cripples   *246*
Invasion North   *247*
Cattails   *248*
The Hilltop   *249*
Changes in Policy at Taholah   *250*
Indian Girl   *251*
The Swimmer at Lake Edward   *252*
Ghost in a Field of Mint   *252*
Iowa Déjà Vu   *253*
The Freaks at Spurgin Road Field   *254*

LECTURES, SOLILOQUIES, PONTIFICATIONS

Plans for Altering the River   *256*
Three Stops to Ten Sleep   *257*
On Hearing a New Escalation   *258*
Announcement   *259*
For Jennifer, 6, on the Teton   *260*
Approaching the Castle   *261*
Listen, Ripley   *262*
Graves in Queens   *263*
Starting Back   *265*
Keokuk   *266*
Topographical Map   *268*
My Buddy   *269*
The Art of Poetry   *271*

31 Letters and 13 Dreams [1977]

Letter to Kizer from Seattle   *275*
Letter to Bell from Missoula   *276*
Letter to Sister Madeline from Iowa City   *277*
In Your Fugitive Dream   *278*
Letter to Simic from Boulder   *279*
Letter to Matthews from Barton Street Flats   *280*
In Your War Dream   *281*
Letter to Ammons from Maratea   *282*
Letter to Hanson from Miami   *283*
In Your Bad Dream   *284*
Letter to Annick from Boulder   *285*
Letter to Mantsch from Havre   *286*
In Your Young Dream   *287*
Letter to Reed from Lolo   *287*
Letter to Peterson from the Pike Place Market   *288*
Letter to Stafford from Polson   *289*
In Your Small Dream   *290*
Letter to Hill from St. Ignatius   *291*
Letter to Wagoner from Port Townsend   *292*
Letter to Bly from La Push   *293*
In Your Blue Dream   *294*
Letter to Libbey from St. Regis   *295*
Letter to Logan from Milltown   *296*
In Your Hot Dream   *297*
Letter to Gale from Ovando   *298*
Letter to Welch from Browning   *299*
In Your Racing Dream   *300*
Letter to Snyder from Montana   *301*
Letter to Scanlon from Whitehall   *302*
Letter to Wright from Gooseprairie   *303*
In Your Wild Dream   *304*
Letter to Haislip from Hot Springs   *304*
Letter to Mayo from Missoula   *305*

Letter to Levertov from Butte   *307*
In Your Dream on the Eve of Success   *308*
Letter to Kathy from Wisdom   *309*
Letter to Goldbarth from Big Fork   *310*
In Your Big Dream   *311*
Letter to Birch from Deer Lodge   *312*
Letter to Oberg from Pony   *313*
Letter to Blessing from Missoula   *314*
In Your Dream after Falling in Love   *316*
Letter to Gildner from Wallace   *317*
Note to R. H. from Strongsville   *318*
In Your Good Dream   *319*

White Center   [*1980*]

Museum of Cruel Days   *323*
After a Train Trip, One Town Remains   *324*
Doing the House   *325*
Scene   *327*
Second Chances   *328*
With Ripley at the Grave of Albert Parenteau   *329*
With Melissa on the Shore   *330*
The Ballpark at Moiese   *331*
Wheel of Fortune   *334*
Open Country   *335*
The Other Beaverbank   *336*
At the Cabin   *336*
Birthday   *338*
Repairing the House, the Church, Restoring the Music   *339*
Leaving the Dream   *340*
Beaverbank   *341*
The Towns We Know and Leave Behind, the Rivers We
   Carry with Us   *343*
Fort Benton   *345*
High Grass Prairie   *346*

Brief History   *346*
Medicine Bow   *347*
Overlooking Yale   *348*
Imagining Delaware   *350*
A Good View from Flagstaff   *351*
Port Townsend, 1974   *352*
Getty   *352*
The Small Oil Left in the House We Rented in Boulder   *354*
At Our Best   *354*
Graves   *355*
Dwelling   *356*
Changes at Meridian   *357*
Guns at Fort Flagler   *357*
Fairfield   *358*
To Women   *359*
How to Use a Storm   *360*
How Meadows Trick You   *361*
Snow Poem   *362*
The Carnival Inside   *363*
From Altitude, the Diamonds   *364*
Bay of Sad Loss   *365*
Bay of Resolve   *366*
Bay of Recovery   *367*
The Sandbanks   *368*
The River Now   *368*
Sound Track Conditional   *369*
Belt   *370*
Bone Hunting   *371*
Houses   *372*
White Center   *373*

The Right Madness on Skye   [*1980*]

The Semi-Lunatics of Kilmuir   *379*
A Snapshot of Uig in Montana   *379*

A Map of Skye   *380*
Clachard   *381*
Greystone Cottage   *382*
The Clouds of Uig   *383*
Graves in Uig   *384*
Hawk in Uig   *385*
Uig Registrar   *386*
Piping to You on Skye from Lewis   *387*
The Clearances   *387*
Glen Uig   *389*
Sneosdal   *390*
Kilmuir Cemetery: The Knight in Blue-Green Relief   *391*
Kilmuir Cemetery: Stone with Two Skulls and No Name   *393*
Duntulm Castle   *394*
Mill at Romesdal   *396*
Druid Stones at Kensaleyre   *397*
The Braes   *398*
St. John's Chapel   *399*
Trumpan   *400*
Langaig   *401*
Ayr   *403*
Ferniehirst Castle   *404*
Culloden   *405*
The Standing Stones of Callanish   *406*
Ness   *407*
Carloway Broch   *408*
The Cairn in Loch An Duin   *410*
St. Clement's: Harris   *411*
Letter to Garber from Skye   *413*
Villager   *415*
The Right Madness on Skye   *416*

New Poems

Last Words to James Wright   *423*

STONE POEMS

Green Stone   *425*
Gold Stone   *426*
Gray Stone   *427*
Red Stone   *427*
Brown Stone   *428*
Blue Stone   *429*

MAKING CERTAIN IT GOES ON

Where the House Was   *430*
Elegy   *431*
O-Mok-See at Nine Mile   *432*
Tony   *433*
Distances   *434*
Here, but Unable to Answer   *435*
Salt Water Story   *436*
Ashville   *438*
Confederate Graves in Little Rock   *440*
Bannerman's Island   *441*
George Stubbs at Yale   *442*
Pishkun Reservoir   *443*
Poem for Zen Hofman   *444*
Death in the Aquarium   *445*
Making Certain It Goes On   *446*

Index   *449*

A Run of Jacks

[1961]

Trout

Quick and yet he moves like silt.
I envy dreams that see his curving
silver in the weeds. When stiff as snags
he blends with certain stones.
When evening pulls the ceiling tight
across his back he leaps for bugs.

I wedged hard water to validate his skin—
call it chrome, say red is on
his side like apples in a fog, gold
gills. Swirls always looked one way
until he carved the water into many
kinds of current with his nerve-edged nose.

And I have stared at steelhead teeth
to know him, savage in his sea-run growth,
to drug his facts, catalog his fins
with wings and arms, to bleach the black
back of the first I saw and frame the cries
that sent him snaking to oblivions of cress.

Near Kalalock

for Barbara

Throw sand dollars and they sail alive.
One dead salmon slides to immediate maggots
and the long starch of his side begins,
the chunk of belly gone in teeth

beyond the sonar stab, in green too thick
for signals from our eyes. Tan foam tumbles
and we call the bourbon in us wind.

We put this day in detent with a pastoral
anxiety for stars. Remember when our eyes
were ocean floors and the sun was dissonant
and cold, unlike today. Scream at waves
go back you fools or die, and say once
light was locked in a horizoned hunger.

A crack wind breaks the driftwood's white
from stark to cream. East is lost
but serious with lines: defeated slant
of grass, the cirrus pointed and the sudden
point of sun, the lean of ocean
on our throats, bacon-baited knocks
of sea perch in our palms.

Now the shore is speared by ancient orange,
let a trickle say a beach is bleeding.
Tonight the sea will come like the eyes
of all cats in the world stampeding.

Bass

On his sides are recreated reeds,
shadows of a log or pad,
parts of an ambush pattern:
his green-black fusion
with the well-adjusted lily bed.

The broadness of him and his fins
and sadist mouth are legends
in the lives of darting fry.

Where shade extends
panic is prerequisite to size.

Evening clicks with oars and reeling skills.
A nylon nymph is twitching in the water
so alien to lazy scales
he bangs with blazing hunger,
head high in the world to display a meal.

West Marginal Way

One tug pounds to haul an afternoon
of logs up river. The shade
of Pigeon Hill across the bulges
in the concrete crawls on reeds
in a short field, cools a pier
and the violence of young men
after cod. The crackpot chapel,
with a sign erased by rain, returned
before to calm and a mossed roof.

A dim wind blows the roses
growing where they please. Lawns
are wild and lots are undefined
as if the payment made in cash
were counted then and there.

These names on boxes will return
with salmon money in the fall,
come drunk down the cinder arrow
of a trail, past the store of Popich,
sawdust piles and the saw mill
bombing air with optimistic sparks,
blinding gravel pits and the brickyard
baking, to wives who taught themselves

the casual thirst of many summers
wet in heat and taken by the sea.

Some places are forever afternoon.
Across the road and a short field
there is the river, split and yellow
and this far down affected by the tide.

Lone Cheer from the Stands
for a Bitter Crane

Fly, crane—your wing assumes no weight—
and, swerving slightly, shear
waves flat. Fall. Float.
Climb, with no more effort, air.

Your graceful rage is from the rude
space lacking any frame or frown,
not caring as you darken in
the baric shade of cloud.

No sun spotlights you. Salt
does not applaud. There is no stage.
Yet the edge
of day is bruised by your abrasive flight.

Fly, crane. From the weight
of darkness others fall. Space in gray
fatigue and water flat
behind you cancel day.

Underwater Autumn

Now the summer perch flips twice and glides
a lateral fathom at the first cold rain,
the surface near to silver from a frosty hill.
Along the weed and grain of log he slides his tail.

Nervously the trout (his stream-toned heart
locked in the lake, his poise and nerve disgraced)
above the stirring catfish, curves in bluegill dreams
and curves beyond the sudden thrust of bass.

Surface calm and calm act mask the detonating fear,
the moving crayfish claw, the stare
of sunfish hovering above the cloud-stained sand,
a sucker nudging cans, the grinning maskinonge.

How do carp resolve the eel and terror here?
They face so many times this brown-ribbed fall of leaves
predicting weather foreign as a shark or prawn
and floating still above them in the paling sun.

La Push

Fish swim onto sand in error.
Birds need only the usual wind
to be fanatic, no bright orange
or strange names. Waves fall
from what had been flat water,
and a child sells herring
crudely at your door.

The store has a candy turnover
amazing to the proprietor.

He expected when he came
a Nordic rawness, serrated shore,
a broken moon, artifacts
and silence, large sales of corn.

Smelt are trapped in the river
by a summer habit, limit
of old netting rights ignored.
Who but an officed lawyer
far away has read the treaty,
his sense of rightness rounded
in a bar? The broker's pier
is measuring the day in kings and jacks.

Your land ends at this border,
water and stone, mobile in tide,
diffuse in storm, but here.
The final fist of island rock
does not strike space away. Swim
and you are not in your country.

The Gull Hardly Explained

He crossed the country like a wire.
Crowds came to find detachment
in the way he climbed
when shocks of cliff evolved
in fog or skimmed the sudden roofs.

He curved the profile of a thigh
above the sea, hung fleet in spray,
trailed by serious fans.
When high sharks sensed a frantic meal
he tore clouds open for the octant's arm.

•

Over the Azores he hovered like a lord,
surveyed the stone old fences, the basket
on the farmwife's head, the vineyard,
then circled without pose or swerve
and left at the proper moment.

He came to Rome no foreigner,
his sharp flight a dagger
latent in the Forum, his beak a claw
applauded in the Colosseum,
he photoed well between two columns.

Record in rock that brutal day
filled with those who followed him to Athens,
each a brute, and he ignored the ruins,
laddered the sky, his dorsal view
a rigid fire in a marble face.

Triangle for Green Men

1

He would hoard this hill, this salal
and this air hard as alder,
mallards in a naïve wedge slit south.
Dark from distance three gulls
cut three trails of burn in leather clouds
and were not things to know, nor ferns
that rattled from a bird or beaver,
the sudden brook and cress in marathon.

He had heard of other countries
in the east, with no indignities:
specks of pepper on a tablecloth,
a punctured screen, the wrong
place for a picnic.

What choice had he been forced to
by the subtle days, chaos scratched
on a convenient slate, a mumbled hymn?

For the moment he chose the familiar,
where he had learned to hate, and moved
in hate along the unpaved street
where lamps jammed black to black
to make night thicker. Twice
the tricky liquid of his eyes
canonized the street-lamp shine.
Once he fractured darkness like a rough moon.

As he slept, ice increased.
A fir fell.
A new fir grew.
Steelhead ran.
A little water leaked in on the sill.

2

The storm started with slight warnings,
the first movement of low grass.
He followed the journey's finger
where it points, down the dead color
of pavement to the hill that flares
white leaves in wind. The wind
grew tall. The power
of his calm was glee at earth
about to be knocked, the mountain
blunted by wind, pines to be bent,
rivers turning on their sides in shock.
He knew a secret of ground,
how it assembles into sand or clay
and is, even under floods.

A mountain is also ground
where it is not rock or rock
becoming ground beneath snow

feeding roots at timberline,
never succumbs to a wind bigger
than mountains, faster than rivers
fall when earth falls sharply below
what had been sedate current.
Even when wind caves the ribs of a fawn
the mountain, braced by blueness, is not stunned.

3
Not one angel will ever arch in the sun
nor the cannon roar for us. Calm day
passed him gently. Wind touched
his temple with a slight hand.
Hills were a language
he could only hear. Clouds were white
and taut, tape covering an old cut.
Like any search this ended
in a home-made swamp.

Surprised he could be this passive
without pose, his hate released, bent
grass faintly in a way he could not see.
Birds hung and did not seem to fly.
Movement was alien to him
or he to the moving day.

His knuckles burned in thin red wind
and the day, though calm, was never organized
in any exact manner. He was traveler
and compact ghost. Three gulls
are often four and sudden water
is electric, cress and water magic.

Note over note a pond receives the rain.
A song explodes on fatter ponds.
A wiser wedge of mallards
slaps the morning dumb with wings.

Beachthieves

Waves policed the sand to call
me criminal. I played their game: stole
shells for my table, climbed the stones
with loot. Weed hands obliged. Salt
stung my knuckles pink with guilt
but laws like moon and slant prevailed.

One bird above me, shell in hand
(no shell I'd mount for smiles, yet,
loaded as it was with ooze and meat,
a famous jewel), circled in a raid,
his wing acknowledging I'd run
from tailing tides in tribute to his greed.

These to him were crucial:
aim and height, hard target, his corkscrew fall
to where the take lay broken for his meal.

No sound of water fought my social
claim: a dipping wing when he, black
felon, aimless dropped his felony on rock.

North

He will bomb the final town
with questions of beyond. What trail
is open now? Does he need a gun?
He will be too vague about the gold
and leave too many clues
and be remembered well by Eskimos.

He will go where grass is gesture only
and the tricky wind

will amplify his breathing to a roar.
His sacks of extra weight
will be forgotten by the stone
he thinks he won't forget.

He will think strange things
toward the end: that he is welcome
anywhere or a pygmy prince,
a master of the avalanche
beginning in the stars
he flicked into the sky when king.

He will die as warm grays take
the snow and his eyes in leisure,
hearing the border beating
with patrols, and somewhere
not for him, the grief exploding
where the law attenuates the sea.

Or Another Place

Ugly women loud in public,
ribs of cattle and the thought
of living in this room become
one feeling. You and the afternoon
are left, the stained calendar
of 'thirty-five, home sweet home
embroidered on linen. If a stage,
the glass across these boards
could have a diamond meaning.

Something ought to happen. A bell
should bang beyond the meadows
or a car go by, a swallow rise
from no nest hidden in the corner,
a ghost remark on the weather.

Something ought to scuff the scene
too focused for attention.

One window rations light
that does not scatter. Here,
perhaps, a world took alien
dimension, glaciers burned
and flowers, as in photos,
broke from the spectrum.

Resulting from Magnetic Interference

These are strange shores. No sand.
No oysters. No slant to the earth
yet the water ends.
It is shore only because there is water
and land.

Stars are Asiatic, a dove stark.
We hear the leaves become bizarre
and nothing is in flight:
old gull symbol of a one to one dream,
a dull wren.

We can see the tragic forming
hurricane and victim;
and a man comes like a cat
to wait by the colorless forest,
his blue hands stuttering welcome.

Alki Beach

Clams and barnacles clatter
black and white in the first feet
of a new tide. By old piles
perch gleam, slide by flexing
men o'war. Bathers urge
the summer to their skins
and water climbs in air
to hurt their eyes. Gulls
echo in two-note screams to the south
of pioneering winds, the moment
a ferry spawns waste.

Where whites first landed
is forgotten. Spray,
abandoned, falls from the statue
by the marked-off, unused picnic grounds.

A love begins: a beer can, tossed,
stops rolling where the waves
can barely reach. And a love is ended
or it never started: one man,
his coat too dark for the day,
where waves will never reach, remembers
what descended where the bubbles are.

Meridian

When I came here first the lake was full,
coves formed slowly and land rolled
into the water with arcs expected of birds
and the middle seemed raised from the shores.

To keep the lake a size, the rate of rain
played to the speed of vapor
and the absorbing silt. I saw the faint tides,
and clouds faded first in the water.

Ales and doctors and dispersing girls
paced the shoreline changed by slides
that left no trace. High Slavic lakes
will be erased by fill dirt and collapsing stone,

and every perch go cannibal in coves
where the moon is thorny on altering floors.
I come only when cold claims the senile,
and water rolls to the shores like surly ground.

Keen to Leaky Flowers

To know expanse I read thin books
on spruce and buffalo, and sailed
where ice and bears are serious.
I rose when the sun broke wild
and blinding on the field, walked
to the bay made famous
by old Indians and now the sun.

Why track down unity when the diffuse
is so exacting—crocodiles give clouds
a candy meaning in the manic frame.
The world should always pour on us
like this: chaos showering,
each thing alone, dependent as a dream.

I bent with every local contour then.
A buttercup erupted. Aspen leaves
in summer on the stillest day

and hedge tips in the wind moved savagely
and strange. Geology had grace.

To turn is to go. To see a weed
from other angles, learn its name,
preserves it more, its battle
with the grass. Transpierce
a perfect diamond with the shadow of a fly.
I am keen to leaky flowers,
how they con devotion from a bee.

Antisocial Easter

These graves never fit a standard hymn.
Notes in air decay.
Each stone is heavy with a name
and ground has learned the way.

Tomorrow will be neither quaint nor pearl,
nor strange skies valuable.
These graves are driftwood drained of blood
by green aggression and the sucking tide.

Concerning sin, the rise and fall,
what anodic questions can be asked?
Was it stain or shadow cast
by music on the wall?

Your mouth will find a hundred troughs where laughter
flows for feed.
You will juggle during time's suave slaughter
a stack of silver and some trillium seed.

Back of Gino's Place

Most neglect this road, the concrete torn
and hunched, purple boxcars
roasting in the wind or in the sun,
both direct as brass. Only smoke
from two shacks and a scratchy radio
prevent abandonment from falling
on this lateral bare area like fog.

In the winter what clean nightmare
brought a sketcher here
to risk his hands, the loss of line
in this much light? Not the poverty
alone, but other ways of being,
using basic heat: wood brought in
by the same sea that is blaring
wealthy ships to a freshly painted port.

He was right to come. Light
in this place cannot kill the lines
of the charred boat, the rusted net,
the log-boom beached and slanted
waiting for a tide. Not when a need to die
here, just to be an unobtrusive ghost,
takes from mud and wood the color of the day.

A Troubadour Removed

He planned his course on Orinoco charts.
Past Barrancas snoring, odors of the journey,
named the flowers native in his bones.
And fed by ivory mandolins and wine
copper wives were peeling on the shore.
He had been here like a bird before.

•

At night he navigated by the toucan's blare.
Day was blinding, but a dragonfly
hung steady in his octant like a star,
and riprap nudged his boat around the turns.
Where waterfalls denied a water course
a wild brown girl was waiting with a horse.

She trotted out in front. The trail broke
far too far in sunlight, way beyond
the sunny terror he was using for a joke.
She said there are some castles in such altitudes
the golden walls can limit condor weaves.
A bandit drum kept rolling through the leaves.

He followed her through tribes with faces
of the pregnant painted blue and tribes
with celebrations of the nearby cliff,
the excellence of one long sandy dive.
He climbed above the fading of his guide,
and castles came with a golden roar through clouds.

He entered fat to dance through those luxurious days,
attended by the berry girls in courts
of fluid carpeting, where marble sprung
like moss beneath his country toes.
In every lime-dark corner lovely outlines moved.
He alone was hardness in a world of give.

Where towers toss off gold the golds deflect
and sky is weak from light. The blinded
condors coat their wings in gold and fall
and moan a liquid warning to the pastoral:
holes in mud mark where all birdies go.
Now see the bird bones sharpen on the hoes.

The castle and the girls, the music pouring
down green halls to feed the garden dancers,

a throne available for nightmares
and the king a king who does not intervene—
he loved these in a way that is not German.
Against the walls a lemon wing was beating

and then the walls were gone. Above the steam
of primitive meat he strung on poles to dry,
a dead bird turned black wings
to silver in the sun and flew away
and had no lime or luck for pilot aid,
no toucan droning signals from the shade.

Leaves and water organized the sun
against his swelling sight. He took wrong trails
to waterfalls and horses, tame and tan.
A drum defined the rolling of his eyes.
(Sing with effort what he sang was easy:
spinning songs to rock the seagulls dizzy.)

And he never loosened slowly like a caravan
when afternoon is spread to see there are no thieves.
Rice and idols foxtrot in the distant towns
and monster flies are chanting on their knees.
Clever girls are stomping out their wisdom.
Private boys provide the stomp a rhythm.

He died where shade remains a tyrant problem.
Every light will play along his bones
arranged like rivers and meridians
where castles kiss the condors out of sky.
His ear will tint the travelogs of children,
the Orinoco flowing and Barrancas sleeping by.

Ocean on Monday

Here at last is ending.
Where gray coordinates with nothing
the horizon wrinkles in the wind.

These will end: shrimp a mile
below, blue shark, sole,
rocks alive as crabs in shifting green,

patent bathers, barnacles, kelp that lies
in wilting whips, jelly-
fish that open lonely as a hand,

space that drives into expanse,
boredom banging in your face,
the horizon stiff with strain.

Snoqualmie

There is no decision. Nothing final
though the day is rifle hard
and fields assume a second green.
Frost, broken by the noon, slips
down slanted ages of the dirt
to feed the river. There is summer
hinting on your back and your hunt
for winter, for the latent face
that is seldom one year older.

A leaf falls easily. The river
has an ease. Southless birds
decline to sing. If bad glass,
space or bone are states of change,

there is still the large dispersal—
too long for a lens and too thin
even for an eastern gaze.

To know it you recall crayola odors,
first fields away from home,
the constant stranger. Where could he go
after being funny, the world so stocked
with preferential clowns
to break the autumn limits of the water?

A District in the City

People say his painting caught so much:
"A sarcous image wrapped in black canal."
He came hungry for the lines
of wintered trawls, poles like bleak sticks
in a burned field. But above him
on the high bridge, autos poured
a Sunday monotone. The day was sunless,
so the shadow on the district came out stain.

Line and color, yes—the frantic white in black;
but not the building dated 1903 in stone
and jammed between canal and hill,
the man who saw each jumper pass
the lumber mill. The man in 'forty
yelled, and just last August
or the year before, that nurse went
with her skirt puffed like a chute.

He should have come here for no reason
or for silly reasons: to eat bad food
or learn the way to break a heavy load
from the foreman high on muscatel

and beer. There is no mayor,
no council. No group is planning change.
The high bridge will insist tomorrow
and the black canal is moving like a month.

Schoolgirl at Seola

*"Why teach youth the past or terms of change
when they learn so rapidly in the immediate day?"*
MIMO SHRIGLEY

She came to alter sky with glass
that has no edge, to hear the shells
that sound like famous wars
and find odd stones. If you spoke
to her of contraband and the pier
she cannot reconstruct from stumps
of piles, the hermit no one saw,
famous for his cruelty to boys,
she would only think you strange.

To her a store has never been lethargic
or built without dural.
Why should she believe the road
she came on was not always road,
the swimmers' sand once hard in wind
and steep, or where those proud homes
post high value in a lawn or child
who never swears, an adult idiot
played with stiffening eels?

Between the naïve movement of a crab
and what a snipe implies
in gratifying arcs the lag
is lunitidal. Sky is changing color
seen through day. Her face browns
as scheduled by the sea, and night is wide.
A skate is spread to surface in the dark.

A Map of the Peninsula

See this arm, the rivers have good names—
Dosewallips, Sol Duc, Bogachiel.
This map is right, they pioneer from hills
but at this bend and this, the boom
of cornered water kills the cry
of sea-run cutthroats and the hammering
lost cedars pouring to the sea.

Paint it grand with mountains, but the scrub
some gypo left, the one-o-one in ruts
from constant rain, shabby meadows
elk create, fog that fakes the ocean's
outer rim will smear your canvas, turn
your art as savage as the Indian
who bums you for a muscatel in Forks.

What is harsh is the bone-infecting,
sound-deranging, forest-brooding damp;
moss that hangs on maples like disease.
And there is drama in the annual run
of kings, though recently some bones
were left to testify they spawned
while we were tracing glaciers on the map.

These contour lines and layered browns
are mountains, this cartographic line
of blue that picks up thin blue streams,
a river dying in the ocean's far
too democratic green. Soak the map
in rain and when this cheap dye runs
only glaciers and the river names remain.

Gooseprairie

for Jim, Lib, and Franz

Water bumps and bounces white
above the level of the land to hang
in air in motion here and there
like unrelated clouds. Fast birds
get their reputation from the wind.
Flight, a stream, creation need
both daylight and a lie. See
before the dawn a flock of aspens
shake creating morning, and the river chips
a word we cannot say in stone.
Let that log jam break and run
and the latest maps are obsolete.

That girl along the stream, blonde
and sleek with speckles on her back—
would she sizzle if we threw her
in the pool, or grow a gill
and swim and reappear in fall,
a Dolly Varden at the spawning grounds?

Our cabin comes complete—a man
to hate, the water cold for bourbon
even in July. Drink all day.
Five elk trot too proudly
into evening's sanctimonious brown.

Mountains are constructed by the moon.
The snow we saw was dirty in the day
is stark white now. Moonlight. Snow.
All the luxuries of yesterday returned—
death by poison roses or a broken
heart. The air was colored

with crayola when we crossed the pass,
and now our throats are stinging
from those ninety years of looking for hard lines;
and all that time
the secret of the world was slide.

Our midnight laughter alters A
to O and trails off in the gorges.
Time, geography, our incomes say
forget that drunken meadow
and the man we hate, the girl or trout.
O is seldom glacial. The bellow
of the elk, a rough O in the mountains
starts a slide of igneous and snow.

Argo

In the dark a boxcar grinds
to a free stop. Locomotive smoke
and a dove flock fan and lift
to where the white kite hangs,
string slanted to the willow clump
where hobo fires burn. Sound and light
on schedule leak into the yard.

A doggy mile-long freight pulls out
certain of clear track and ample siding.
Doves are scattered and the kite is down,
the fires lost in dawn.

Day and the eastbound train
curve in. The switchman's wave
gives east a special distance,
an early eater hope of being—
like a map, of finding girls
and wisdom waiting in Dubuque.

The swamp means little, blurring by
in green and brown. Perhaps the dead
trade places underground.

Some are major travelers
who never wave and know each stop
and always where they are,
smiles relaxed at tangents
and faded from the strain of grades.

Ballad of the Upper Bumping

In the pounding white is a man to kill,
vague in spray, hidden under the fall,
aware of roots convenient for descent
and the intentional guns,
and gone like cones in the pour
before the gunners can aim.

Easily the gunners' coming has a core.
Here was a castoff widely hunted king
convinced these commoners would not climb down
shale scared gray by the roar.
They see him clawing moss spun out in foam
and the fern snap off in his hand.

The river screams release from run-off snow.
His plunge converted to the natural
by glacial green and the blurred bed
magnified in May.
He thought the kingdom waters loyal,
and rivers know where royalty can go.

Hermits dance the news to jubilant cities.
Leaders shout he will be found in August
blue where dollys spawn.

His gems will glow outrageous in the pool
like teeth reported in his smile;
our queen turned slightly from the flogger's jest.

The king is dead. Long dance the queen
with a withering hermit down the streets
where gunners return to some girls.
Kisses sting at stories of the gorge,
roots that held in slipping shale,
the gun-impounding roar.

Water strands relax and water fades
from hands and moving water needs
old noises like the hum
of rats in stranded silt.
The river void of noise, the silent
whitefish slip to sucker colored rocks.

Pools are scanned by the paid incisive eyes
of camping children, every riffle checked,
each log and large stone poked
and no king turned.
Now absolutist beavers clog the stream
and every ponderosa hides a breathing king.

A poet said the force of flowing years
beat those noble bones to a petty size
to string them with the normal skeletons
of autumn on the sand.
Look. Today we call these salmon kings.
He was hanged for gross imagining.

Gunners see him every May in the white,
and never seeing him, shoot through rainbowing spray.
Gone like cones in the pour—
and what can the gunners say.
The queen is thin in a cave removed from summer.
And wet light rolls through the hermit sleep of a hunter.

Centuries near Spinnazola

This is where the day went slack.
It could have been digestion or the line
of elms, the wind relaxed and flowing
and the sea gone out of sight.
This is where the day and I surrendered
as if the air
were suddenly my paramour.

It is far from any home. A white
farm, tiny from a dead ten miles
of prairie, gleamed. I stood on grass
and saw the bombers cluster,
and drone the feeble purpose of a giant.

Men rehearsed terror at Sardis
and Xerxes beat the sea.

And prior to the first domestic dog,
a king of marble, copper gods,
I must have stood like that and heard
the cars roar down the road,
the ammo wagon and the truck,
must have turned my back on them
to see the stroke of grass on grass
on grass across the miles of roll,
the travel of my fever now, my urge
to hurt or love released and flowing.

A public yes to war. A Greek will die
and clog the pass to wreck our strategy.
There will be a time for towns to burn
and one more sea to flog into a pond.

Cape Alava

1

At this west-most U.S. point
I try to see that Orient beyond,
a red canoe a hundred men
are pumping past a shrine
they build to the unusual
(a fir bent oddly or a stone
stained yellow by some animals)
to celebrate the void.
West of here the only west is water,
tight horizon and the glare of sea
the wind drives tyrant in my eyes.

Wind is friend to herons
as they halt to spot that single
dart of silver that betrays
a million smelt. Birds that play
are lying to the sea, slanting,
serious with beaks
above the games of hate
in green too thick for green
or anything but black.

Ling and bull cod stranded
and merganser trapped by wind—
my eyes are north and south with weather
trying to destroy and climb,
sweeping flint to detonate July.
West of here the only west is failure,
candlefish in sun, the heron's flight
from symbol into common air.

2

Where fields are vertical and hard
music tries like snow to be remembered,

flakes and notes outnumbered by the bells.
Who believes the pears were skinned by rain
or holly pounded blunt by February's mauls,
the promise of a girl with tiny hands?

The wall is air and cannot echo pain.
The hill is flat and I am free to sweat.

Now I must abandon
rumors of a mountain goat in flames,
trout shot from a gun, layers of refrain
in layered firs along the river
named for Indians who gathered elegance
by trapping dogs. Hard to think that swamp
had owners and was sold, the stunted tree
once flared, the moon was ever red.

I will not clatter of the land behind.
Day is tight as hide. The ocean beats at day
but cannot break the daily flow of rolls
begun some prehistoric Monday
when the sea and sky were trading grays.

3
Day is forever strange. The rolling sea
was really sliding, and the heron
told a joke before he dove in hunger.
Relaxed, the black is green again
as sun unpiles the sea, fathoms back
to six feet each, white caps nothing
but the foaming tips of waves.

At this west-most point I sail a stone
against the wind and watch it climb
and hang—time of flight increased
when air is moving counter to the toss.
West of here the only west is future,

alien and warm. The Oriental stream
on schedule, each merganser streaks
to find a temple like a homeless clang
and the stone hung long enough to be a star.

I build a shack and wait for candy odors
in the wind, a current from Rangoon.
Ships go by on radar, but a withered clown
can fix position on a rock in air.

Skykomish River Running

Aware that summer baked the water clear,
today I came to see a fleet of trout.
But as I wade the salmon limp away,
their dorsal fins like gravestones in the air,
on their sides the red that kills the leaves.
Only sun can beat a stream this thin.
The river Sky is humming in my ear.

Where this river empties in the sea,
trout are waiting for September rain
to sting their thirst alive. If they speed
upstream behind the kings and eat the eggs
the silvers lay, I'll pound the drum for rain.
But sunlight drums, the river is the same,
running like old water in my ear.

I will cultivate the trout, teach their fins
to wave in water like the legs of girls
tormented black in pools. I will swim
a week to be a witness to the spawning,
be a trout, eat the eggs of salmon—
anything to live until the trout and rain
are running in the river in my ear.

The river Sky is running in my hair.
I am floating past the troutless pools
learning water is the easy way to go.
I will reach the sea before December
when the Sky is turning gray and wild
and rolling heavy from the east to say
late autumn was an Oriental child.

Mission in Carmel

for Frank, Olive, and Tom

No sense of past. Did Serra
beat the labor from the Indians
with whips to build this church?
Were the troughs they ate from
pine or live oak? Today is known:
seals that fatten on the herring
Spaniards throw from piers in Monterey,
the silly trumpet tree,
our war of flick with holy water
and our praise of slaves who built
the window wrong (twisted
some dead monk might say
on purpose or from quakes).

Come, Hun, ruin with crude arrows
grace and idols. Pyramids still grunt.
In Greece the temples sweat and cry
and Roman viaducts have broken backs.
Tears should have the credit for the lovely,
but the tearless women breathe so well.
Here the cactus and the limes do badly.

The interior will be remembered brown
whatever color, and the frowning

statue red. Despite our jokes today
none of us is cold about the dead.
I believe the bones in any tomb
have moving parts, and something runs
unnamed across the altar
when candles dwindle and the church is dark.

To some a bell rings out a threat
on Sunday: build a church and eat.
No bells are here to summon back
the savage with his tools and stare.
Junípero is long gone, man. Successful.
Dead. We know two cats of stone
who have no purpose but to purr
and fail and look wise while the cars
go by. No bells around their necks,
no meaning but the meaning of a cat:
wisdom takes the credit for the lovely,
and the lack of trees in Egypt meant
the ocean waits to spay the deity.

Let's drive away from Serra and the slaves
and know the hatred native to eclectics.
Our mission is that hill we have to cross,
brown and from the quakes not quite symmetric.

Kapowsin

Black from sun and the stain of hemlock bark
and nowhere deep, this lake could mask a town.
The town beside it died in 1908
and these remain: a man gone dim—
a girl is swimming in his dead Tokay—
a woman who gets pregnant from a song,
the tavern always filled but never loud.

•

A bass cracks out of shade to scatter fry,
and perch are watergrass. Two sunfish
tumble (lily pads cut loose). Five bubbles
and a murmur mark the trout's retreat.
Say Kapowsin (Indian for lake-of-stumps)
and you strand a doll's canoe on snags
some blasters left. Water cried and climbed
the day they blew the cedars from the lake,
and women stopped a picnic to applaud.

Heat is hoarded by this black lake,
but summer light is driven north
and cracked on stone by tribal wives—
their amber eyes immune to glare,
their dark skins hiding what must burn
or cruise to Africa like autumn clouds
this steam became. Ask the man in mud
with lilies in his claw, how water tries
to race December twenty-first. To count
the ducks divide the guns by five.

The town that barely is. That queen in wine.
Past and present violence in water.
The faint skip of a careless crane.
Poison chunks of bark that knock the eyes.
These facts I claim for my rasorial past
though I came here only yesterday from harm.

Today, I troll a spoon that offers
sky for bait. Rowing, I might argue
no defeat is total, but a rainbow hooked
on hunger climbs the heron's wind,
his gill collapsed in anger, his dorsal fin
extended, still no wing. The wake is chaos
and the town is loud with light
this lake selected before the day went north.

Graves at Mukilteo

We come for nothing but we read the stones—
Laroway and Wong, the baby, Rose,
"Budded On Earth To Bloom In Heaven."
If we dug and if the last thing
to survive, the bones I guess,
were bones instead of dirt,
we'd find the stones are all mixed up.
Those aren't Rosie's bones, they're Japanese.
That's too big a bone for Lila's thigh.

This lot can't be used in standard art.
True, the grass is growing on the graves
the way it should in poems, but sky is sliced
in blue rectangles by some power lines
and the sea is never wild between these islands.
No dolphin herds. No blackfish
or convenient danger. The names engraved
could never dignify an allegoric song.

The town has plans to put the stones in order,
cut the grass, reinforce the mortar;
but the offspring of the dead are scattered
and their O.K. hard to get.
Rosie's doll is rumored in Tibet
and Lila's hoard could make a pack of trouble
no matter where they are or who.

It's so out of way. Here
the sheriff might find a stolen car
abandoned. A boy will get his first
in the tall grass back of Laroway
and Wong where maples screen
the moonlight from the house next door
while markers spall and the mayor regrets
the dead can be this derelict.

•

Their disease was motto and the gold beyond—
ours what fifty years have done to dying.
Today we come for nothing
but we read the sea and wait.

A Chapel Further West than Most

Sung badly hymns are loaded with remorse
singers on the cross
their music peeled the paper from the walls
I hear that dissonance in waves today
the ocean thick with commerce and debris

She was way off key that girl of farms
old from hoeing stone
and farming soil the worms and crows ignore
she sang loud enough to be alone
hitting notes that only dogfish hear

That book was black and white with Luther's grief
Sola on the leaf
the ocean protestant with tide
and elegance abandoned in the foam
four hundred years of idols with no blood

Now the church is rich
I still hear those twenty-odd bad voices
though hired voices clean the sea with tones
walls are varnished teakwood and the windows
stained by far-off artisans

Politely like Snakes in the Oats

Who appreciates the fingers cramped
from effort, or the water shocked by sound

to rise and live in oblique beds?
Who appreciates a farm for simple reasons:
food, the female green of lettuce rows,
the sharp red of a beet against the brown
dirt or a yellow pan? Who is stunned
by raw simplicity? Perhaps a few.

The statue of a saint is derelict in wind.
A cave is home. Past the elms, the cliffs
that could be English in a song
but are American, beyond the sea
that clowned for centuries
to be this blue, a State decides
what monuments will outlive words and weather.

Talent comes to know all words as freaks
and spends a lifetime looking for a cure,
a special oil, a new drug, anything to shake
the memory: you say the toucan jumped—
you feel a guilt—hear a crash in dreams—
no home today but caves—there it is
at last—parricide in the aviary.
The caves of course symbolic: primitive escape.

What stings politely is the snakey thought
that art is always failure. The pyramids,
though gross to liberals and saints
who can't erase the image of a slave
dying as he climbs, his back bent under stone,
a whip his only motive, still clearly state
by shape and bulk, a northern need—
the color elegant from weather, as if the rock
had skin. For dying kings—geometry in sky
where now the distant hum of bombers
only makes a camel want to sleep.

Name the Mystery Fin and Win a Doll

No shark, the fin that scars a circle
on the sea. Pastoral and neat
and even curving—gull in wind—a harm.
A real gull climbs beyond the threat.
No creature, eel extended, dolphin flung
upwind with gills for wings can get
that high. And no one, bird or we
can name that cruising dorsal fin.

Or name it: flag of a nation lost
nine centuries and looking for a land.
The sea has monsters, why not monstrous
towns, valleys full of salty cows,
stores the girls swim through,
barnacles on crosses, starfish stuck
to statues of the kings who won the wars,
limp prophecies of a wet 900 years?

Sunlight names the fin a fin. A dark form
darker than the dark green water, sleek
and derelict, looks for Mozart's grave.
Coax it raging with a name: Torpedo!
And it dives in silver energy.

1614 Boren

for Guy Tucker

Room on room, we¹ poke debris for fun,
chips of dolls, the union picnic flag,
a valentine with a plump girl in a swing

who never could grow body hair or old
in all that lace (her flesh the color
of a salmon egg), a black-edged scroll
regretting death: "whereas—Great Architect—
has seen it fit—the lesser aerie here—
great aerie in the sky—deep sympathy."
Someone could have hated this so much . . .
he owns a million acres in Peru.

What does the picture mean, hung where it is
in the best room? Peace, perhaps. The calm road
leading to the house half hid by poplars,
willows and the corny vines bad sketchers used
around that time, the white canal in front
with two innocuous boats en route,
the sea suggested just beyond the bar,
the world of harm behind the dormant hill.

Why could room 5 cook and 7 not?
These dirty rooms were dirty even then,
the toilets ancient when installed,
and light was always weak and flat
like now, or stark from a bare bulb.
And the boarders when they spoke of this
used "place" and "house," the one with photos
of Alaska on his wall said "edifice."
This home could be a joke on the horizon—
bad proportions and the color of disease.

But the picture, where? The Netherlands
perhaps. There are Netherland canals.
But are they bleached by sky, or scorched
pale gray by an invader's guns?
It can't exist. It's just a sketcher's whim.
The world has poison and the world has sperm
and water looks like water, not like milk
or a cotton highway. There's a chance

a man who sweated years in a stale room,
probably one upstairs, left the picture here
on purpose, and when he moved believed
that was the place he was really moving from.

Bassetti's Lions

These two cats guard the grapes. Their claws
are harsh as ancient mobs. Their stone eyes
fix on thieves through moonlight
and their voices shake the vines.
They bleed at harvest. In their limbs
the stone veins swell with memories
of Africa unpicked. Bluebirds
take a big chance pecking at the heads.

From here, the bay, even with a fresh tide in,
is always brown and rippling with fur.
Where the bay is blue, Oriental ships
roar in with flags and shouts of "fang"
that could mean "port" in Singhalese. Clouds
have manes and water turns to grass in wind.

Leoni. Vi festeggio oggi.
This wine your keeper offered me
is red as a lion's tongue, dry
as your scorn when, from the highway,
cats, abandoned from the passing cars,
come to sleep beneath your bellies
purring sweetly and oblivious to rain.

Memoirs

Once I changed my name to race the rich
on those expensive lakes where girls are gold

from living and their legs and bellies brown
with threats of garden love. I flew to fake
my arm into a wing, circled clouds
until my face was green, and shouted
"Look! I'm volitant. Ice along my brows."

But some believed my flight. When it snowed,
crumbs were issued over frozen sills
and I was forced to fly and find a role
where actors crack applauding for the crowd.
When I say my teeth are made of wood,
policemen warn the animals away.
The cleric wears a hornet in his ear.

In the flowers seeds explode and flow,
the meaty fade, and only altitude
remains, sting of air when soaring.
I flew from feathered roles to those of fur,
then back to wings and beak. No lines of white
or rules are in the air to limit play,
snap and slow roll and a split S out.

Hey, the cirrus tickled but the rain
slicked down my arms until I fell.
My application for a face is filed.
My repertoire is loaded with disdain.
I can play a lizard with this skin,
with makeup be a paca or a teal,
anything directors dare to name.

I admit the wealthy win the water.
I am me. All my roles are over.
That night I faked a limp into a name,
said I shot the fat bird from the wire—
cheap, theatric snort. Behind this bleat,
beneath this fur and sweat, I spin
along the ground like dandelion seed.

Lecture

Now rockets pierce the limit of our air,
our plans to grow potatoes on the moon
are near. Forget those poems about the woods
a little north, where pools of rain, you say
stare like eyes of silver giants, fallen
in a storm (symbolic war). The day
is ready for a poem about the stars.

Not the stars of Keats. Not far-off stars
that help us with our girls. Not patterns
of stars, the various bears and galaxies
of cats, certain only to astronomers.
I mean the actual stars, the burning gasses,
those erupting hunks of solar matter
changing red to blue, complete with hisses.

I don't mean ignore the stellar forms.
There are squares of stars and star rectangles,
stars that form the points and arms of stars,
a starry brontosaurus and the shark that dives
through midnight and the planets turned to stars
by secondary rays. These and constellations
I may never see are ready for a poem.

It's all yours now. Write the poem from notes
you take first hand—you younger ones
are sure to travel space before you die.
At my age I can only stroll in woods
a little north, suggesting to the girls
who come to learn about poetic form
the wind creates a star in pools of rain.

Neighbor

The drunk who lives across the street from us
fell in our garden, on the beet patch
yesterday. So polite. Pardon me,
he said. He had to be helped up and held,
steered home and put to bed, declaring
we got to have another drink and smile.

I admit my envy. I've found him in salal
and flat on his face in lettuce, and bent
and snoring by that thick stump full of rain
we used to sail destroyers on.
And I've carried him home so often
stone to the rain and me, and cheerful.

I try to guess what's in that dim warm mind.
Does he think about horizoned firs
black against the light, thirty years
ago, and the good girl—what's her name—
believing, or think about the dog
he beat to death that day in Carbonado?

I hear he's dead, and wait now on my porch.
He must be in his shack. The wagon's
due to come and take him where they take
late alcoholics, probably called Farm's End.
I plan my frown, certain he'll be carried out
bleeding from the corners of his grin.

Duwamish

Midwestern in the heat, this river's
curves are slow and sick. Water knocks
at mills and concrete plants, and crud
compounds the gray. On the out-tide,

water, half salt water from the sea,
rambles by a barrel of molded nails,
gray lumber piles, moss on ovens
in the brickyard no one owns.
Boys are snapping tom cod spines
and jeering at the Greek who bribes
the river with his sailing coins.

Because the name is Indian, Indians
ignore the river as it cruises
past the tavern. Gulls are diving crazy
where boys nail porgies to the pile.
No Indian would interrupt his beer
to tell the story of the snipe
who dove to steal the nailed girl
late one autumn, with the final salmon in.

This river colors day. On bright days
here, the sun is always setting or obscured
by one cloud. Or the shade extended
to the far bank just before you came.
And what should flare, the Chinese red
of a searun's-fin, the futile roses,
unkept cherry trees in spring, is muted.
For the river, there is late November
only, and the color of a slow winter.

On the short days, looking for a word,
knowing the smoke from the small homes
turns me colder than wind from
the cold river, knowing this poverty
is not a lack of money but of friends,
I come here to be cold. Not silver cold
like ice, for ice has glitter. Gray
cold like the river. Cold like 4 P.M.
on Sunday. Cold like a decaying porgy.

•

But cold is a word. There is no word along
this river I can understand or say.
Not Greek threats to a fishless moon
nor Slavic chants. All words are Indian.
Love is Indian for water, and madness
means, to Redmen, I am going home.

Holy Family

Here, the nuns are rumored cruel. Beat
in the name of Jesus. Scratch the voices
of the choir with those poison thorns.
The Dugans know theatrics, clip at least
four inches from the ruler's stroke. Wince
and clown and say yes ma'am enough,
hail a hundred Marys and you're safe.

Money buys a secondary Christ. Blood
and pain, the best. Rap me, Sister,
I have violated eels. All you kids
be kind to mother, do as daddy grunts.
You should be grateful for this day-old bread
and for the birds and trees. All the saints
who died for us take beads on what we say.

Hey, there's Jesus coming down the road.
Look, no whip. No terrifying word.
I swear it, Sister, swear—He's dancing
in the dust with Dugan's worst, and dressed
in corduroy and silk. When visions break,
what remains in summer? Melted nuns,
a clown not quite eternal in the heat.

Northwest Retrospective: Mark Tobey

What life is better—stone and stone?
Freaks are honored in the East with shrines,
even marked and worshiped, even painted
if some color amplifies the strange.
In the market men are selling color
cheap as fruit. On canvas what faint
line extending, splits and lives,
returns and multiplies, and never ending
stiffens like a fighter's wrist, becomes
a net and traps our eyes with salmon,
or is silk and floating, or is quiet
like a map? What drums are driving
migratory ants through charming lakes,
and if beholders weep, what painter
needs their tears to mix tomorrow's oils?

That's where harmony was contraband,
and later where the loot was owned,
and later where the cirrus circled
Mars and left white trails of pain
that hung for centuries. (A line
of poetry is not a painter's line,
and in museums flight is not allowed.)

Beyond Van Allen rings, the stars
don't glitter, arrogant as moons.
When did we start? Light-years ago.
Why did we come? No matter. We
are not returning to that world
of ditch and strain, the research terms:
cryogenic fuels, free radicals,
plasma jets, coordinated fusion.
Only the last, in all this void, applies.
A universe is fusing in our eyes.

•

Why return to air and land, when
free from weight and the weight
of hope, we float toward that blue
that kisses man forever out of form.
Forget the earth, those images and lies.
They said there'd be no wind out here,
but something blows from star to star
to clean our eyes and touch our hair.

Digging Is an Art

Now they bury her and the clouds run scared.
Elms and the cemetery hedges whine.
Sky shakes in the Bible and the coffin swings.
Now dirt raps on the coffin until wind
and the indifferent cars rip away the choir
from our eyes. Pour the dirt on, digger.
Shovel faster. Sink her where she lies.

For she was harsh as dirt. Her voice crawled
down the garden like a weed, and yet
potatoes bloomed, the beets and carrots
shoved their greens beyond her hymn.
The rock of ages crumbled into soil.
Then the corn came, swaying like her dream
of daddy hanging from a harness in the barn.

At nine on Sunday, those magnetic chimes
five blocks away, her only decent dress,
her rapid stride as if the world would burn,
her envy of the latest cars that passed—
her husband was a failure and the bells
made up for all the luxury she missed.
But he had been defeated by her voice.

Bang the Bible hard in broken rhythm.
She fertilizes soil despite her coffin.
That grass is lucky growing near her stone,
the marker of an enemy of growth.
Shovel, digger. Seal the day forever.
Wet the dirt. The weight will shut her mouth.
A midget spade is digging for a man.

Before I run forever down that dark long wind,
killed by bells, my head split open
by ingratiating clangs, I'll worm my way
into that ground no digger recommends.
Plant the headstone anywhere between champagnes
and drink until you sweat. The wind will bring
you money and the choir keep you clean.

Orcas in the Eyes

for James McGarrell

I can't name those birds, black with height.
Let's call them Spaniards and their circles
typical of hunger. Between the San Juans
blackfish roll their fins through tourist eyes.
North and south the islands flare with names.
Shafts of mainland try to break for Asia
and in the Strait of Georgia, Birney trailed a seal.

Winter here is not grim city winter.
Summer tugs the water from the air
to cool the meadows where the sheep eat grass
in leisure, and wind travels
over the grass in urbane waves of light.
If your rage needs targets, here, you die,
turn mystical or kind, or think the in-tide
will deposit women, sleek and friendless on the shore.

•

Call those high birds Spaniards and the Spain-
faced girl in the café a vicious winter
when she strolls. Certainly those hills
hide mariners, and cows are fat with dropsy.
Call those high birds hungry and your vision meat.

The Way a Ghost Behaves

Knock or none, that woman hears a knocking,
runs to the door, ready for a friend—
only frost in moonlight and the dog
she cannot stand.

She believes that God is in the trees,
perched like a bird, waiting for the crumbs
she scatters on
the snow for definite robins.

Love to her is mystery and pain.
Her children died
and winter puts a creaking in the house
that makes her sing and grin.

Her garden works
because, early on the first warm day
while others wait the official end of winter
her hoe is ringing rocks away.

Deaf or not, that woman hears me knocking,
runs to the door, ready for a friend—
only rain and darkness and a man
she'd love again.

No Bells to Believe

When bells ring, wild rain pelts the river.
Who rings bells in the abandoned chapel,
once a school, once a shed where hide
was stored? The painter painting reeds
a private color, poppy farmer,
and the seiner folding autumn's nets—
they hear the bells and don't look up.

Mad Sam, the nutty preacher rings the bells.
He remained despite that mess, twelve
years back—the squaw—the poisoned wine.
Not Sam. He drowned beneath a boom.

No bells. Even when Mad Sam went mad
with God each Sunday and the women wept
to hear their imperfections yelled across
the river while a drum knocked Jesus
senseless and the tugboats tooted home.
No bells then. None now. What rings here
is something in the air unnamed.

The wild rain rings. The painter's reeds
run down the canvas in a colorful
defeat, the seiner's nets gain weight
and poppies wash away. The women told
Mad Sam before he ran out on the logs,
you must accept the ringing like the day.

Two Graves in a Day

Now I break the mask, repeal those years
of forging any other face until
my name is mine. Now I can regret
that one of these two graves is not among
the hawks that circle in their cackles,
the rocky goats, the hunter's pant
that cracks about the gorges like a shot.

There is a woman rots and laughs down there.
In the earth her bones are long and soft
as whips in air. In a dream a whip
is coiling in the wormy water
where I dive to set my face on fire
from the flint and granite chips that hang
unmoved by wind, in any diver's air.

I feel the sticks. With fumes and shaggy hair
I'll leave the town, the rules
for my survival planted in the horns
that blast the passes open to the north.
And I am Indian enough to grow the corn
and crow will ambush if a cedar
crowds the alder to insure his plan.

I am also thief. See this silver tooth
is blaring like (my mouth is turned to sun)
a trumpet. I know her granite name
will never climb funereal despite my song
of decent birds that drift and cry Alado,
come with all your hair and bake your arms
where beaver ponds are steaming to be clear.

At the Stilli's Mouth

This river ground to quiet in Sylvana.
Here, the quick birds limp and age
or in flight run out of breath and quit.
Poplars start and then repeat the wind
and wind repeats the dust that cakes the girl
who plays a game of wedding in the road
where cars have never been. The first car
will be red and loaded with wild grooms.

August rain says go to blackmouth,
violate the tin piled derelict against
the barn and glowing like the luck
a fugitive believed until he found
this land too flat for secrets
and the last hill diving on him
like a starved bird. The crude dike,
slag and mud and bending out of sight,
left gray the only color for the sky,
wind the only weather, neo-Holland
printed with no laughter on the map.

That hermit in the trailer at the field's
forgotten corner, he has moments, too—
a perfect solo on a horn he cannot play,
applauding sea, special gifts of violets
and cream. In bed at 5 P.M.
he hears the rocks of children on his roof
threatening his right to waste his life.

With the Stilli this defeated and the sea
turned slough by close Camano, how can water die
with drama, in a final rich cascade,
a suicide, a victim of terrain, a martyr?

Or need it die? Can't the stale sea tunnel,
climb and start the stream again
somewhere in the mountains where the clinks
of trickle on the stones remind the fry
ending is where rain and blackmouth runs begin?

Now the blackmouth run. The Stilli quivers
where it never moved before. Willows
change to windmills in the spiteless eye.
Listen. Fins are cracking like the wings
of quick birds trailing rivers through the sky.

The Way a Ghost Dissolves

Where she lived the close remained the best.
The nearest music and the static cloud,
sun and dirt were all she understood.
She planted corn and left the rest
to elements, convinced that God
with giant faucets regulates the rain
and saves the crops from frost or foreign wind.

Fate assisted her with special cures.
Rub a half potato on your wart
and wrap it in a damp cloth. Close
your eyes and whirl three times and throw.
Then bury rag and spud exactly where
they fall. The only warts that I have now
are memories or comic on my nose.

Up at dawn. The earth provided food
if worked and watered, planted green
with rye grass every fall. Or driven wild
by snakes that kept the carrots clean,
she butchered snakes and carrots with a hoe.

Her screams were sea birds in the wind,
her chopping—nothing like it now.

I will garden on the double run,
my rhythm obvious in ringing rakes,
and trust in fate to keep me poor and kind
and work until my heart is short,
then go out slowly with a feeble grin,
my fingers flexing but my eyes gone gray
from cramps and the lack of oxygen.

Forget the tone. Call the neighbor's trumpet
golden as it grates. Exalt the weeds.
Say the local animals have class
or help me say that ghost has gone to seed.
And why attempt to see the cloud again—
the screaming face it was before it cracked
in wind from Asia and a wanton rain.

Death of the Kapowsin Tavern

[1965]

DUWAMISH, SKAGIT, HOH

Introduction to the Hoh

Nearly all the rivers color like the sky
and bend in other places after extra pour.
This blueness is high ice. Cartographers
are smiling at the curves that will recur.

See the white in spring, the milk flow
high enough to run the smaller aspens down.
See there is no urge to lay the sun
across your going like a greasewood patch.

Think of stark abundance, a famous run of jacks
the vanished tribe at the mouth once bragged about.
Think of hungry Mays, the nets reversed
to snag what rot the river washes out.

Glacial melt and tinge are slight in autumn.
Cutthroat backs and pools retain the blue.
Remember famine as these broken leaves
ride away like Indians from you.

From the Rain Forest Down

Click and clatter. Water off for heaven,
loose on bends and bending out of anger
and the fat man groans. Water turns
again and keeps the fat man guessing,
splits the pines and hustles for the open.
Water home to water, free. The fat man
rots all May.

•

One man was a statue of despair.
Concrete turned the water dirty gray.
A willow grows where an arm should be
and here's the river, shooting for the end,
the statue bobbing by. On the bank
the fat man tips a beer to worldly
river play.

This fat man plays a vicious clarinet
all night, takes food through his eyes,
believes his music makes the current
permanent and warm. He blows a storm—
blows the forest nothing in the rain.
He lives to learn his music only drove
trout upstream.

Now the river slams him with its noise.
His breath comes phony. Worms are crawling
through his clarinet. To the river
he admits he came to stop the flow.
The river laughs his feet away.
The fat man runs to join the marble
in the sea.

Home. The word is dirty. Home is where
the dirty river dies. Dogfish come
to eat the fat from the fat man's eyes.
His clarinet is floating past Marseilles.
In the woods a slender girl decides
to cast herself in stone; for music, whistle
silently.

Between the Bridges

These shacks are tricks. A simple smoke
from wood stoves, hanging half-afraid

to rise, makes poverty in winter real.
Behind unpainted doors, old Greeks
are counting money with their arms.
Different birds collect for crumbs
each winter. The loners don't
but ought to wear red shawls.

Here, a cracked brown hump
of knuckle caved a robber's skull.
That cut fruit is for Slavic booze.
Jars of fruit-spiked bourbon bake
on roofs throughout July; festive tubs
of vegetables get wiser in the sun.
All men are strong. Each woman knows
how river cod can be preserved.

Money is for life. Let the money
pile up thirty years and more.
Not in banks, but here, in shacks
where green is real: the stacks of tens
and twenties and the moss on broken piles
big ships tied to when the river
and the birds ran painted to the sea.

Duwamish No. 2

Mudhens, cormorants and teals take
legal sanctuary in the reeds,
birds and reeds one grey. The river
when the backed-up tide lets go
flows the only north the birds believe.
North is easy: North is never love.

On the west hill, rich with a million
alders and five hundred modern homes,
birds, deep in black, insist the wind

will find the sea. The river points
the wrong way on the in-tide
and the alders lean to the arid south.

Take away all water. Men are oiling
guns beside ripped cows. Wrens have claws
and clouds cascade with poison down
a cliff mapped badly by an Indian.
Tumbleweeds are plotting to stampede.
Where there is no river, pregnant
twice a day with tide, and twice each day
released by a stroking moon,
animals are dangerous as men.

When the world hurts, I come back alone
along the river, certain the salt
of vague eyes makes me ready for the sea.
And the river says: you're not unique—
learn now there is one direction only—
north, and, though terror to believe,
quickly found by river and never love.

Bad Vision at the Skagit

When hills give out, the river loses power.
It started slowing near the State Asylum
and before Mt. Vernon turned into a slough.
Shacks of migrants on the diked bank—
children playing house—male or stark
the wind reminds the farmer and the worker:
soil is rich with men; man ultimately poor.

No lovers love in grass along the shore.
The corn is often stunted. There's some hope
in churches, outlined clean on hills behind
the town. But what design. In stores,

prices climb each payday. The artist
ends up weakly painting buckeye cows.

Mexican and Serb—bending backs and sweat—
European cursing in the grove—wages weak
as yesterday's manure: I should see injustice,
not slow water and the beating birds
that never move a foot against the sun.

Plunking the Skagit

It's mystery, not wind, the men
endure. Steelhead drew them here
where tons of winter drive above
them north and fires start the day
along the bar. A hundred feet
of nylon settles on the river
and the wait begins. Each line slants
tight from an upright rod to water
and underwater to the pencil lead.
A flat south: wind will hammer
water from their eyes, wind and water motion
faking knocks of steelhead in the bells.

These men are never cold. Their faces
burn with winter and their eyes
are hot. They see, across the flat,
the black day coming for them
and the black sea. Good wind
mixes with the bourbon in their bones.

A real name—steelhead—rainbow
from the sea. He runs in summer, too
but that is undramatic, the river
down and warm. No pour to push against.

No ice to snap his fins. No snow
to lay him on for photographs.

Men keep warm with games. The steelhead
is a Burmese spy, a hired gun
from Crete. He comes to mate, not die
on some forgotten sand like salmon.
He rides the river out in spring
planning then his drive for next
December, when big rains bring him
roaring from the sea with fins on fire.

This near the mouth, the river barely glides.
One man thinks the birds that nick
the river mark the fish. Birds believe
the men are evergreens. Above
the guess and ruffle, in the wind—
steelhead to the spawning ground.

Hideout

In the reeds, the search for food by grebes
is brief. Each day, inside the shack
the wind paints white, a man keeps warm
by listening to ships go by, keeps sane
by counting European faces
passing north in clouds. Tugs deposit
miles of logs outside. A tax collector
couldn't find this place with holy maps.

When salmon crowd each other
in the river, and the river boils
with re-creation's anger, what tall man
re-creates too clearly domes of mills
downstream, and the gradual opening
as if the river loved the city

or was crying loudly "take me" to the sea?
What odd games children play.
One shouts himself into a president.
Another pins the villain salmon
to the air with spears. A rowboat
knocks all night against a pile.

Morning brings a new wind and a new
white coat of weather for the shack.
The salmon moved upstream last night
and no bird cuts the river, looking
for a smelt. Ships sail off to Naples
and the bent face bobbing in the wake
was counted in another cloud gone north.

Duwamish Head

1.

That girl upstream was diced by scaling knives—
scattered in the shack I licked her knees in
where she tossed me meat and called me dog
and I would dive a dog at her from stars,
wind around my ears—violins and shot.

With salmon gone and industry moved in
birds don't bite the water. Once this river
brought a cascade color to the sea.
Now the clouds are cod, crossing on the prowl
beneath the dredge that heaps a hundred tons
of crud on barges for the dumping ground.

My vision started at this river mouth,
on a slack tide, trying to catch bullheads
in a hopeless mud. The pier was caving
from the weight of gulls. Wail of tug
and trawl, a town not growing up

across the bay, rotten pay for kings—
these went by me like the secret dawns
the sea brought in. I saw the seaperch
turn and briefly flare around a pile
and disappear. I heard bent men
beg a sole to look less like a stone.

Beyond the squatters and the better homes
stars were good to dive from. Scattered
in the shack I licked her knees in.
Diced, the paper said, by scaling knives.

2.

River, I have loved, loved badly on your bank.
On your out-tide drain I ride toward the sea
so deep the blue cries out in pain from weight.
Loved badly you and years of misery
in shacks along your bank—cruel women
and their nervous children—fishhooks filed
for easy penetration—cod with cracked necks
reaching with their gills for one more day.
Last year's birds are scouting for the kill,
hysterical as always when the smelt run thin.

Jacks don't run. Mills go on polluting
and the river hot with sewage steams.
In bourbon sleep, old men hummed salmon
home to mountains and the river jammed
with blackmouth, boiled in moonlight while the mills
boomed honest sparks. October rolled
with dorsal fins and no man ruled the runs.

When I see a stream, I like to say: exactly.
Where else could it run? Trace it back to ice.
Try to find a photo of your cradle.
Rivers jump their beds and don't look back
regretting they have lost such lovely rides.

I could name those birds, see people
in the clouds. Sight can be polluted
like a river. When this river asks me:
where were you when Slavs gave up their names
to find good homes on paved streets west of here?
I talk back. What are you, river?
Only water, taking any bed you find.
All you have is current, doubled back
on in-tide, screaming out on out.
I am on your bank, blinded and alive.

3.
Where cod and boys had war, a bolt plant roars.
Sparks are stars. Next Sunday, when I die
no drunk will groan my name in spasms
as he vomits last night from the dock.
I have memories of heat upstream.
Her arms and eyes had power like the river
and she imitated salmon with a naked roll.

My vision started at this river mouth
and stuck here (bullhead in the mud)
a third of what could be a lifetime.
The city blares and fishermen are rich.
Tugs and trawls repainted slide to ports
and perch found better color in the sea.

My fins are hands. The river, once
so verbal drifts with such indifference
by me I am forced to shout my name:
backing up on in-tide, screaming out on out—
river, I have loved, loved badly on your bank.

Scattered in the shack I licked her knees in—
beyond her, nothing, just the Indian
I use so often infantile in dreams
of easy winters, five-day runs of silvers,

festive bakes, the passing of the jacks
to sand pools promised by the rain.

To know is to be alien to rivers.
This river helped me play an easy role—
to be alone, to drink, to fail.
The world goes on with money. A tough cat
dove here from a shingle mill on meat
that glittered as it swam. The mill is gone.
The cat is ground. If I say love
was here, along the river, show me bones
of cod, scales and blood, faces in the clouds
so thick they jam the sky with laughter.

OTHER WATERS

Taholah

Where sea breaks inland, claiming the Quinalt
in a half saltwater lake, canoes turn gray
waiting for the runs. The store makes money
but the two cafés, not open, rot in spray.
Baskets you can buy are rumored Cherokee.
When kings run wild, girls use salmon oil
to stain a doll's face real. The best house
was never envied for its tile. Cars
and philosophic eyes are coated by the sea.

Whites pay well to motor up the river,
harvest blackmouth, humpbacks, silvers,
jacks and sea run cuts. Where rain assaults
the virgin timber and the fishpools boil,
the whites pry stories from the guide
with bourbon. Sunset, and they putt downriver
singing. But the wind, the sea
make all music language, dead as a wet drum.

When whites drive off and the money's gone
a hundred mongrels bark. Indians
should mend the tribal nets in moonlight,
not drink more and hum a white man's tune
they heard upstream. What about the words?
Something about war, translated by the sea
and wind into a song a doll sang
long ago, riding a crude wave in.

Cape Nothing

The sea designed these cliffs. Stone is cut
away odd places like a joke.
A suicide took aim, then flew out
in the arc he thought would find the sea.
He came down hearing "sucker" in the wind,
heard it break at "suck-" and all the time
tide was planning to ignore his bones.

Far out, the first white roll begins.
What an easy journey to this shore,
gliding miles of water over stars
and mudshark bones that laugh through tons
of green. You can time that wave and wind
by tripling your memory of oars.
The sea will con the gold from our remains.

Foam is white. When not, no dirtier
than bones gone brown with waiting for the sea.
When wind deposits spray on bone
bone begins to trickle down the sand.
Now the bones are gone, another shark
abandoned to the sea's refractive lie.
The moon takes credit for the boneless rock.

Bones don't really laugh beneath the sea.
They yawn and frown through green at time
and lie in squares to kid the moon
and drive stars from the water with the gleam
of phosphorus gone mad. Now a diver
poses on the cliff for passing cars
before he flies out singing "water, I am yours"

Lone Lake, Whidbey

for Dave Wagoner

The sun, the warm man renting boats
and warm farms slanting to the lake
decide the wind is warm. Our numb
hands fight the anchor rope. We drift
to a wobbly stop in lilies.

That green crud (algae) makes this lake
look stagnant every May. Chorus-
girls could strut along that shore
or a king replace the farms he burned
with castles, but the blackbird
on the reed that bows defeated
will remain, his red ignited
by the wind. A reel is singing nylon
down the guides, and in that second sky
a line is moving, terrified.
Blood and rainbow sides are also red.

Underwater, the farms go on.
Catfish graze like cattle in the weeds
and trout fly over the catfish
like those high birds without form
or name, flying the morning away.

Sweet Piece from Fontal

My darling we are trolling Lake Fontal,
slipping by the snags that jut from moss,
skirting beds of pads. Two trailing spoons
flash a sneaky hunger to the trout.

Guess what monster levels on the gleam—
five pounds in the oven, losing oil
and sizzling with fun, grinning in his heat.
That's a fishhawk frowning from the pine.

We came here on a slow and dirty road.
Now we slide on glass, trusting clouds
to braze the surface, blur the sight of trout.
I wheel the boat and never cross our lines.
Rainbows nick our spoons. Behind the boat
the trout that bends your tip is jumping,
spitting out your hook and going.
That's a fishhawk frowning from the pine.

Other lakes are roasting in those hills.
Their steam will never singe a pine,
cannot bake a fishhawk though we hate him.
Highland lakes so high only condors
find them, rage alive with rainbow
fatter than a day with thirty days.
That's a fishhawk frowning from the pine.

That's a fishhawk frowning from the pine.
Let him frown. That crank can't fly or drink
or know what trouble drove us to this lake.
Clouds are years gone north and wind is playing
light about your face. Let's troll until
we take a double creel, then row for home,
our hunger pounding and our fishing rods broke down.

Dancer at Kozani's

Through the white chiffon that covered her
we whipped her with our eyes until
she crawled the floor in heat.
When she got up, disrobed and shook

the wall got wet. The lute
that led her shimmy stung her thighs.

Swish of red hair on the floor, twitch
of buttock, breast line clean in shake—
she danced us into war and back
and when the fiddle tied her to a rock
she wiggled free. Her legs were wild
as pillars to a Persian lost in wind.
When far strings tore her from our sight
what vain trout circled in our wine?

We swam out into the smothering night
praying for rain to wash the smoke away.

Index

The sun is caked on vertical tan stone
where eagles blink and sweat above
the night begun already in the town.
The river's startling forks, the gong
that drives the evening through the pass
remind the saint who rings the local chime
he will be olive sometime like a slave.

Screams implied by eyes of winded eagles
and wind are searing future in the stone.
The cliff peels off in years of preaching water
and the cliff remains. The saint is red
to know how many teeth are in the foam,
the latent fame of either river bed
where trout are betting that the saint is brown.

Flakes of eagle eggshells bomb the chapel
and the village ears of sanctuary dumb.
In a steaming room, behind a stack

of sandbagged books, the saint retreats
where idols catch a fever from his frown.
The saint is counting clicks of eagle love.
The river jumps to nail a meaty wren.

And April girls enlarge through layers
of snow water, twitching fish and weeds
and memories of afternoons with gills.
If a real saint says that he could never
see a fiend, tell that saint to be here,
throat in hand, any Friday noon—
delirious eagles breed to tease the river.

The Anacortes-Sydney Run

In my best dream I have crossed the border
and my coins are wrong. Without the tongue
I gesture, sweat and wake aboard this boat.
Ladies in their staterooms write bad poems—
mountains in the distance evidence of God.
Maps are hard to read. Two nations own
these islands. The shade of green on one
could be Canadian, but firs and grebes
are mine. The latest run of Springs
are far too international to claim.
Yet they use our rivers for their graves.

The law protects the San Juans. No bilge here.
Gulls still trail the ferry but go hungry.
You can buy an island. In my worst dream
I am living here, contented and alone.
That house is mine. The blue smoke rising
means I'm cooking. Constant knock of water
means I'm drunk, enjoying private jokes
and bowing as the walls begin to roar.
The Coast Guard breezes by my door.
They haven't stopped to chat in twenty years.

•

In no dream I am standing on this deck
admiring the sheep on what turns out
to be the final island before landing.
I woke up dead among these islands—
this boat chugging in a bad direction—
the north I go, my wake already fading.

Mendocino, Like You Said

for Robert Peterson

From China contra-boom-bang water
jars the cliffs, spray above the roofs
of homes on stilts. Boats and hotel rot.
Russians doubt a profit from the road
or sea. Water cracking fathoms
into sky, the grass that moves by green alone
when wind is gone, say be alive.

We say die. We say catch the world
without the neon, only iron, wood
and clay and dated. See how the sad
is best reflected in a face when albacore
are weighed. Despite old poems and songs,
women on the shore are far too tough
to be there simply waiting for the men.
The boats are in but no one plans a dance.
No two talk an hour after anchor.

The sea's a band. A far-off clarinet
is coming on. The ocean blows the grass.
Birds are driven landward close enough
to claim. We know we're weak and wrong
but music and another knee
refill our eyes with a keen butane.

The Colors of a Bird

A bird sails from the hole in that high stone,
circles once and glides down, humming
with his wings. He seemed white half-
way up, but green now as he ticks
the river. No one doubts the water.
It will eat the best men from the sky.

Gold. Not gold, but blue. The tan bird
in and out of sunlight hugs the stream.
Now he uses cedar bark for amber,
takes the color of a hostile man.
He has no taste. How satisfied he seems
anywhere he flies throughout the spectrum.

He found shades of pink in Italy.
Man can give one color only,
promise birds a perfect afternoon:
trout and worm, a coy girl brought to answer
in the grass. The bird will never brown
hoping for the sun this river flicks.

The red bird sweeps the evening water flat.
Picnics never work. The army
separates in current as they drown.
Now the laughing black bird draws
a hectic line of nothing on the air
and drives relieved into the rocky dark.

Lake Byron, Maybe Gordon Lord

for Patt Wagoner

Deep in that black water where you tossed a book
of Byron, trout have read Don Juan
and are fighting mad. Madness like the mushroom
pushing rocks aside to rise is latent
in your past. Despite the wealthy cabins,
owls you spot are right for disapproving.
You are right for loving birds with scowls.

Only wars without a name have meaning.
Byron died for nothing. What rare hawk
reduces you to meat with perfect circles?
How easily you draw him as a woman—
coy lids fallen, head half turned away—
"You can't mean me." You know the problem.
How to earn a talon. You earn yourself
by showing birds a way to be afraid.

I'm no stranger to the darker waters.
True, they half disown me, but the stars
are bound to stutter when the crappie ripe
with gold assemble and you paint them.
Not really well, but saying fish are birds
and birds are stars and keep your head down.
Don't think too much when young about the heavens.

Byron must be rotting in the mud.
I don't know what water does to paper,
but it must be awful, like one human
to another. You're a hawk's authority
on what it takes to die and then recover.

Road Ends at Tahola

My nostrils tell me: somewhere *mare nostro*.
Here the wolf-fish hides his lumpy face in shame.
Pines lean east and groan. Odors of a booze
that's contraband, are smuggled in by storms.
Our booze is legal Irish and our eyes
develop felons in the endless spray.
Mare nostro somewhere, and eternity's
a law, not a felony like here.
That derelict was left for storms to break.

One ship passes denting the horizon,
creeping down the world. Whatever gave us pride
(food en route to Rio) dies. The wake could be
that wave we outrun laughing up the sand.
Night comes on with stars and years of dead fish
lighting foam with phosphorus they left.
All day the boom was protest, sea against
the moon. *Mare nostro* somewhere and no shame.

Remember once, a scene, a woman naked
clowning in the sea while armies laughed.
Her man, a clown, had courage and he came
and hauled her (both were sobbing) up the stones.
If I were strong, if wolf-fish didn't dive
beyond the range of scorn, you'd be alive.

I can't say *mare nostro*. Groaning pines
won't harm you, leaning east on galaxies.
I know I'm stone. My voice is ugly.
A kelp bed is a rotten place to hide.
Listen. Hear the booming. See the gleam,
the stars that once were fish and died.
We kiss between the fire and the ocean.
In the morning we will start another stare
across the gray. Nowhere *mare nostro*.
Don't claim it and the sea belongs to you.

MISSION TO LINZ

1

If you look at the sky
north, there where it ends
as if finite or breaks its northern orange,
in a vacuum of time
you might suddenly know this:
that the sky where it ends does not end
and you will pass its horizons.

You must know it before
you can think of it, speak of it;
it must come on you more sudden than flare
before you identify yourself with the power:
the olive with yellow band death in the bay,
the Pratts, the Hamilton Standards,
the Norden, turrets of fifty calibers.

It must seem weird, incommunicable
the desire for ozone
cold and the unremembered terrible.

You could realize an angel in orange
between the Alps, blue in summer, and the spray of cirrus
but that is visual and will not do
and besides it is remembered beautiful.

Or you might hear the rotation to come,
the thunder of revolving iron,
the padded burst blackening under the nose,
sound of the almighty sickening
but that is auditory and will not do
and besides it is remembered terrible.

You can see the gunners smoking
on the morning stones.
The navigator tugging his harness.
The pilot who checks everything twice.
The good-natured bombardier
or co-pilot swearing.
They too could look at the sky
north, there where it ends
as if finite or breaks its northern orange,
and in that moment of no time know it:
where they will be in hours
of rotation and revolving iron
before they can think of it,
speak of it.

It must seem weird, incommunicable
the desire for ozone
cold and the unremembered terrible.

You can know it.
It will come on you quickly.
But even if you can say it,
once the engines have started nothing is heard.

2
Nothing is heard in the north,
and the northern temperatures grow cold with the height.
There is the stark crack of voice
taking oxygen checks and the sharp static answers.
You are beyond birds, a season called summer.
There are places away from the world where the air is always winter.

Nothing is heard in the north.

The engines pound out their particular fever
a sound that has a silence of its own.

There is the control of needles and gauges, green
and showing the speed, the degrees and the climb,
and the six boxes of six shudder and rock
where the sun goes pale in the thinness of air
above the Adriatic. Fifties are tested,
checked in
with the stark crack of six voices
and the seventh replying with a sharp static answer.
And the engines pound out their particular fever
a sound that has a silence of its own.

No one can call this movement
though Europe wavers and falls back to the south
and a needle says one-fifty-four. The air
is ten centuries of waiting. A flange
is your breathing and the throat says nothing
behind the tight mask, and the mask,
the silent engines are all your loss of self.

The sterile Alps, blue in summer
swing up, pass for an hour underneath,
fall harshly into their brown valleys
and the grey one-rail towns of vertical protection.

But what do you think
while Europe wavers and falls back to the south
in a way that is not called movement?
While the flange breathes for you
and the needles swing to other numbers?

Europe wavers and falls back to the south,
the silence rotates your life in the roar
and you think this:
that out of thirty-six we stand a chance
(statistic) to lose three at the most.
Twenty minutes before the wide turn

you will say it over and over
where the air is twenty centuries of tension
and the sun goes pale in the thinness of air
you will say it: three at the most.

But the engines pound out their particular fever.
A silence of its own.
There are places away from the world where the air is always winter.
Nothing is heard in the north.

3
You fly north to a point, swing slowly
to the east, open your belly and brace
before the eight-minute course, planned
on violet maps a smile before, but now
Linz opens like a flower below your nose
and the silence drives louder airs into the bay.
The dagger black explodes and the praying increases
until the over-ripe melon of day, cracking its hide
shows the red-moist fear just back of your brows.

A plane evaporates so quickly,
silently, it might have been
from magic were it not your fear
knew ten reduced molecular.
There is the silence and the waiting
in eight-minute vacuum, and black puffing
thick as enormous dark rain,
some, the close, sounding, a few
the very close, jolting.

Out of the thirty-five still airborne
there was a moment, one
your dreams will lose, stopped in tiny fire,
flipped dizzily away,
a wing peeled back like a sudden unloosening arm
fluttered down five miles of sky as paper,
and you didn't hear a thing.

•

And the moment
when the sky split open, allowed
the lazy tons of yellow-banded children
to fall in forty-second wonder, converge
in a giant funnel. Now you
who, so high, can only see
the puff like a penny dropped in dust
at your toe on a country road, rack up
and out, down with a speed
that strains the blueprint—until
noiselessness, the level back
into clean sky.

Of all this, this, and only it:
you can forget, and will, the degrading prayer
when the sound is gone, only this:
you feel good to your own touch,
you remain.

4
Summer is heard in the south,
and the southern temperatures grow warm as you drop.
The speed is easier, the brain
warmed by the sound of insult,
and you defend yourself by making fun
of others' fear, of your own prayers.
You come into birds, a sun that is warmer.
There is land away from the sky where the sound is
    always summer.

There is the needle control, the green gauges
showing the speed, the degrees and the fall.
The engines sing you to the home of men,
the earth, and think of it; its brownness,
its solidity, its greenness. You can build
warm rooms on its hills, love on it,
and if you die on it you remain
long enough to be lied about, buried in it.

Anyone can call this movement.
Europe speeds back to the north. The Adriatic
glimmers its blues to the brown shores of summer
and the engines sing you to the home of men,
the earth, and think of it.

If you think of it you know soil
is its own loveliness and you want to be on it
to drink, speak and study friends' faces.

If you think about it for a long time
the mind, like engines, will sing
you to the home of men,
where concerts carry
fast in summer wind.

LIMITED ACCESS

Eileen

Why this day you're going so much wind?
When you've gone I'll go back in alone
and take the stillest corner in the house—
the dark one where your dark-eyed ghost
will find me whipped and choking back my rage.
I won't show my hatred to their food.
I have to live here with these shaking hands.

Find a home with heat, some stranger
who's indifferent to your dirty dress
and loves you for that quiet frown
you'll own until you die or kiss.
The wind is drowning out the car
and raising dust so you can disappear
the way you used to playing in the fern.

Some day I'll be too big for them to hit,
too fast to catch, too quick to face the cross
and go away by fantasy or mule
and take revenge on matrons for your loss
and mail you word of faces I have cut.
Be patient when the teasers call you fat.
I'll join you later for a wordless meal.

Then I'll stroke the maggots from your hair.
They come for me now you're not here.
I wax their statues, croak out hymns
they want and wait for dust to settle

on the road you left on centuries ago,
believing you were waving, knowing
it was just a bird who crossed the road
behind you and the sunlight off the car.

What the Brand New Freeway Won't Go By

The block is bare except for this five-story
ugly brick hotel. Perhaps the bulk
frightened stores and homes away. Age is clear
in turrets and the milk on window sills.
The new name and the outside coat of paint
must have raised the rent. As you drive by
the rooms seem yellow and the air inside
is stale because a roomer, second floor,
in underwear, unshaven, fries a meal.

To live here you should be a friend of rain,
and fifty with a bad job on the freights,
knowing the freeway soon will siphon
the remaining world away
and you can die unseen among your photos—
swimmers laughing but the day remembered cold.

Rooms have gas. The place was in the papers.
Police have issued statements about cancer
and the case is closed, but not the jokes
passing boys are drilling through the walls.
Top-floor renters look down floors of sweat
to traffic that might stop were they to go.
Some rooms are paid for in advance with shock.

If, when the freeway opens, a man
afraid of speed still takes this road,

the faded Under New Management sign
might mean to him: we are older too—
live here—we'll never treat you badly again.

December 24 and George McBride Is Dead

You a gentleman and I up from the grime—
now wind has shut your dark, dark eyes
and I am left to hate this Christmas eve.
Christ, they're playing carols. Some crap
never stops. You're dead and I'm without
one goddam Wagner record in the house
to play you up to what for some must be
behind the sky with solid orchestration.

Rest in your defeat, you stupid jerk,
so fat your heart gave out, so sweet
you couldn't help but hear the punks.
"One gulp. The whole quart, Mac." That town
you died in—so unlikely—vineyards,
sunny valleys, stark white missions
and the pale priest summoning
brown sinners from the olive grove.
I'll not know your grave, though I believe
our minds have music that can lead us
through the tangle to the lost stone of a friend.

I get along, write my poems. Essentially
a phony, I try my feelings now
and know I fail. George, it's Christmas eve
and bells are caroling. I'm in the kitchen,
fat and writing, drinking beer and shaking.

Antiques in Ellettsville

for Ann McGarrell

That nine-foot doughboy, were the sculptor good,
would be at war. What bayonet, what snarl
can win against the shade of pleasant oaks,
the road that makes an open store seem closed?
On that plate, a rose survives the cracks.
Faces crack with age. The owner
leaves her beans to brag about the pewter.
Miss Liberty is steadfast in an oval frame.

Fun to laugh the past away—silly words
etched lovingly in gold—eyes so tough
and ignorant the photograph went gray—
a farm that might still be—a Clydesdale team.
Now we trade-in chrome to hide the wear
or hide behind next year, afraid of Hoosiers
waving old hellos from older porches.

Our problem is the value of the old,
the value of the cruel. A sadist thinks
a bruise is just a rose. Pyromaniacs
would bruise this town to cinder
had they not gone big-time in the east. Out west
the oldest thing is neon. Here, the antiques
warn us to be tolerant of dust.

Let's run and love the old and know tomorrow
whatever trails our running leave in air
a tiny crone will price and call antique.
Why not a giant soldier for your lawn—
his bayonet as level as your frown
when salesmen come, their baskets heavy
with those bullets armies wouldn't buy.

The Other Grave

Long and smelling good, the cemetery grass
could be a kiss. You failed a field
of Ypsilanti wheat. Below your stone
you never try to touch her there beside you.
I used to blame your failure on the moon.

When old, you needed words like "lake."
"Lake" I'd say. Your eyes began to farm.
Horses took you and a friend where coves
were wonderful with bass—bluegills
clowning for your rind below the log.
Catfish ran five pounds. See my picture.
See my mustache then. Any photo fades.
You remain in yellow with your catch.

I'd like to sing you, point each word
about you up and shoot. Wasn't gold
too easy for your maps, or love
too simple for your brilliant arms?
I said a British wind was in your face—
only blue the undertaker planned.
The tunes you hummed were so unknown
I told a dog you were a fine composer.

Why am I afraid or sorry you are dead?
My hands paid contraband to be this still.
My mouth rotted with the truth
to be as tough as wheat before your stone.

Houses Lie, Believe the Lying Sea

Forget the keep-off sign. That cow
is no detective paid to guard this house

and the barricade is rot. Inside
the stove is moldy. Sunlight rays
through slits to spot the dust we breathe.
Rooms are sick for light. That male doll
fractured in the corner means
the rage of children went remote
in sea light and the humming flies.

The well still works. Pump, and water
coughs out brown. Did a father weep
and shout at weeping children: we are poor?
And when they moved without a buyer,
did the mother turn Chinese with shame?
An empty house can teach a rat despair.

Decay is often moss, green when grass
is dirty, tan or dying. Someone's due
to tend the cow. The meadows slant
a way they didn't when we entered.
Those rooms will be remembered vaguely
years from now in Greece. Who's for loving
on those rags, that broken glass?
Let's go loving where the ocean
scatters on the rocks to die like homes.

First South and Cambridge

Sandbanks climb and curve until
a stadium. Brief bones gleam
in grey-brown bars of periods
that end in -cene. Say monster
and the wind roars animate
about the walls. A sparrow pecks
at 70 A.D. The jaw you dig
is just a dog, no scientific coup.

•

The banks have Indian voices
or turn Sicilian in the heat
or promise over the top, green
hills spread out for lovers
and a brook no man has seen.
But there, salal, though green
is far too stiff for romance
and Hitler left his rubbers in the creek.

When sand is covered over (alders
grow in sand) you might hope
for another end—banks exploding,
robins caught in tiny slides, each
grain a boulder Indians roll down.
But these banks, once so urgent
in their Sunday need-to-be
pace their end a little slower
than you fight the end of sand.

In Stafford Country

No hills. Raw wind unchecked, brings word
of death from Texas. No shade. Sun bruises
the oats gold. With homes exposed
no wonder people love. Farms absorb
the quiet of the snow, and birds
are black and nameless miles away.

Without a shield of hills, a barricade
of elms, one resorts to magic, hiding
the joker well behind the gesturing hand.
Childish wars continue in our minds.
Paint is the gray it was in Carthage.

•

Where land is flat, words are far apart.
Each word is seen, coming from far off,
a calm storm, almost familiar, across
the plain. The word floats by, alive.
Homes are empty and the love goes on
as the odor of grain jumps in the wind.

For a Northern Woman

I reach for you. You smile and I am male.
Mornings when we stroll this pale canal,
past these poplars factories turned brown,
yet with height and swing insisting
they are green, your eyes say what north
you're from. They call me man. Your hair
is orphan as I break it in my hand.

Lady, I control you. On command
you kiss some old stream south to home.
Let's name what's warm along this quay:
the trawl that pounds desire for the sea,
pregnant cats, fishing men who need
no fish, the ancient hanging wash.
My plan for you is cruel: to roast you
in the light I steal from your blonde form.

Smile me male again. Or never smile
by this canal gone gray from waste
or from that early sky the northern know.
Poplars stretch so far above us, branches
tick the sun. I know that aching bark.
I ache to cast you hot in northern stone.

Port Townsend

On cliffs above the town, high homes disdain
what is not Victorian below
but Indian or cruel. A plaque declares
a chapel older than the town.
(Many worship God before they're born.)
The Keystone ferry sails without a car,
a passenger, not even trailing gulls.
The pulp mill shoots bad odor at the sun.

Arriving here is feeling some old love—
half a memory—a silly dream of how
a war would end, a world would settle down
with time for hair to gray before you die.
The other half of memory is sight.
The cliffs will hold another thousand years.
The town is rotting every Sunday night.

A novel fakes a start in every bar,
gives way to gin and talk. The talk gives way
to memories of elk, and elk were never here.
Freighters never give this town a second look.
The dead are buried as an afterthought
and when the tide comes glittering with smelt
the grebes have gone to look for meaty ports.

Fort Casey, without Guns

for Rae Tufts

The iron doors we shut on ammo rooms
slam like a heart attack. Had the guns remained,
grass would still be busted by July to straw
and riptides groan as current doubles back

in hatred. Concrete walls were hopes
of pioneers, one shade deeper gray each spring.
From these emplacements, ten-inch cannons tracked
fifty years of freighters down the strait.
The sea shot out the gunners' eyes with light.
The army moved to Coupeville in defeat.

What's left to save, the riptide will protect.
We joke our way through battlements,
dim powder huts, the corridors where words explode
and we are skeletons, trapped by a mistake—
the wrong door closed, a turn we didn't make.
We claw at rungs to take us into sky.

Straw bales on the muster ground deny
a need for war. The farmer doesn't care.
The strait can go unguarded, pagan ships
sail in with slave girls and a threat of fun—
the Stars-and-Stripes torn down—the Constitution
used to start a fire for the wienie roast.
Only harvest matters. Here, the army
harvested no enemy. Even boredom cracked—
contraband steamed down in 'twenty-eight—
the bootleg wink—rum for rotting men.

Best to come here when the picnics peter out.
On dark days, gulls are shells (man will not disarm)
and we can play our war. I am a captain.
Make that cloud salute. The Olympics
bomb the strait with shadow. In the meadow
where October green begins, cattle eat
and children point their space guns at us,
crying boom the booming sea can't hear.

One by Twachtman at the Frye

The flags beyond those dunes are roaring.
Carnival here. Freaks for the fun of children.
Taffy and games. Beyond the din, the sea
compounds the joy. Ships go by,
plenty of fuel and no destination.
Beyond the sea, you feel, people are living,
happy and loving, no hymns or diseases.

You cannot cross that sand to the fun.
That friendless grass prohibits what chance
you might have to shake phantoms of lust—
two women fighting over your body,
the loser to love you, the winner to die.
They always fight dirty in dreams.
You always hear the games in the wind.
You are never closer, forever held back by the sand.

Someday you'll cross it, enter the gate
of the gayway, win all the money,
eat yourself sick and come back relaxed
to these dunes, and here find your bones
friendless as grass, covered with laughter
and flags the seawind tore from the poles.

Bouquets from Corley

Are these flowers paint? Back of each bouquet,
behind the eyes of good men, odor beats.
It's not the fault of some damn cow we knew
that our hands go slowly blue from work.
Flowers will be ruined by a storm or painted.
Roses flare in ancient loams of thieves.

That Friday everyone is born on
slides into a weekend for our leisure—
walking streets and sensing Ward's bouquets—
rage in the composure, regret in color
fading back into a childhood weather—
oil diluting rain to save the garden.

In hills where hate began, cows are flowers.
Udders swing and seem remote in gray.
Outside the gallery, roses are composed
by rain and killed. Paint does not wash off.
In painting, roses have the sense to be afraid,
knowing it's not the fault of an old cow
that a flower, like a man, left one weather
for another long ago to live.

The Squatter on Company Land

We had to get him off, the dirty elf—
wild hair and always screaming at his wife
and due to own our land in two more years—
a mud flat point along the river
where we planned our hammer shop.
Him, his thousand rabbits, the lone goat
tied to his bed, his menial wife: all out.

To him, a rainbow trail of oil might mean
a tug upstream, a boom, a chance a log
would break away and float to his lasso.
He'd destroy the owners' mark and bargain
harshly with the mill. He'd weep and yell
when salmon runs went by, rolling
to remind him he would never cheat the sea.

When did life begin? Began with running
from a hatchet some wild woman held,

her hair a gray cry in alfalfa
where he dug and cringed? Began in rain
that cut the light into religious shafts?
Or just began the way all hurt begins—
hit and dropped, the next man always righteous
and the last one climbing with a standard tongue?

In his quick way, swearing at us pressed
against the fence, he gathered rags and wood
and heaped them in the truck and told his wife
"Get in," and rode away, a solid glare
that told us we were dying in his eye.

The Church on Comiaken Hill

for Sydney Pettit

The lines are keen against today's bad sky
about to rain. We're white and understand
why Indians sold butter for the funds
to build this church. Four hens and a rooster
huddle on the porch. We are dark
and know why no one climbed to pray. The priest
who did his best to imitate a bell
watched the river, full of spirits, coil
below the hill, relentless for the bay.

A church abandoned to the wind is portent.
In high wind, ruins make harsh music.
The priest is tending bar. His dreams have paid
outrageous fees for stone and mortar.
His eyes are empty as a chapel
roofless in a storm. Greek temples seem
the same as forty centuries ago.
If we used one corner for a urinal,
he wouldn't swear we hadn't worshipped here.

•

The chickens cringe. Rain sprays chaos where
the altar and the stained glass would have gone
had Indians not eaten tribal cows
one hungry fall. Despite the chant,
salmon hadn't come. The first mass
and a phone line cursed the river.
If rain had rhythm, it would not be Latin.

Children do not wave as we drive out.
Like these graves ours may go unmarked.
Can we be satisfied when dead
with daffodils for stones? These Indians—
whatever they once loved or used for God—
the hill—the river—the bay burned by the moon—
they knew that when you die you lose your name.

The Blond Road

This road dips and climbs but never bends.
The line it finally is strings far beyond
my sight, still the color of useless dirt.
Trees are a hundred greens in varying light
as sky breaks black on silver over and in
the sea. Not one home or car. No shacks
abandoned to the storms. On one side,
miles of high grass; on the other, weather
and the sea reflecting tons of a wild day.

The wind is from Malay. Tigers in the wind
make lovers claw each other orange. Blond
dirt rises to recite the lies of summer
before the wind goes north and cats rip
white holes in the sky. Fields are grim
and birds along this road are always stone.

•

I planned to cheat the road with laughter.
Build a home no storm could crack
and sing my Fridays over centuries of water—
once more, have me back, my awkward weather—
but the land is not for sale. Centuries
are strung: a blond road north and south
and no man will improve it with macadam.

The road is greased by wind. Sun has turned
the blond dirt brown, the brown grass
black and dark ideas of the ocean
silver. Each month rolls along the road
with an hour's effort. Now the lovers
can't recall each other or identify
that roar: the northern pain of tigers.

I know that just a word I'll never have
could make the brown road blond again
and send the stone birds climbing to their names.

Pike Place Market

In many tongues, hawkers scream our fingers
off the fruit display. All day, we never see
the rows of lightbulbs shining. Rages faked
by blinding grapes and pears make eating
cosmopolitan. In *The Athenian*
Negro faces do no better than the white
against the sea outside. A prude might wait
long enough to see the U.S. Fleet pull out.
Voyeurs keep dark islands in reserve.

Behind their eyes, old men are shooting moons
with yellow guns. Solly cleans a carp
with carvings doctors and a thug would envy.

These market skills go back to deep in Egypt,
deep in dynasties of dirt, in minds
of cats who hug the market in a storm.
Here, it is assumed all things have value.
The world will not wear out. Best-selling
paperbacks with covers bruised by grease:
one dime. No bargaining, though produce
can be talked down sharply after five.

Who plans to tear this market down?
Erect a park? Those militants who hate
the old and odd, and dream of homes where lawns
are uniformly green. Who gloats at space for rent,
stalls abandoned, fire that destroyed
those baskets Indians will never weave again
and turned a case of rump roasts into char?

Let the columns rot, progressive mayors deny
a city has a private right to be.
Let the market slide into the sea.
The sea has meat, is derelict and kind.
Snapper, red from failure, live on sun.
No bass ever knew another, and the pompano
like men arranged to be alone.

Market. In November, drink the darkness in
and make the dark your closing. Burlesque
rows of lightbulbs that were lit all day,
shine for the first time, glinting
off a pigeon and the rinsed cement
and women poking in the garbage for a meal.

Graves at Coupeville

When weather shouted at us: vagabond
we looked for weathered towns where men are strange.
Our clothes were older than these stones where words
erased by moss are silly said aloud.
We had idols that the light deranged.
Last night's strangers could have been our friends.
The dead were singing slogans in our blood.

Think of walls your insufficient fist bounced off,
walls your face ran down and couldn't stain
and I was turned away by smiling aides,
couldn't find a job. Why a car so old?
Why the world so new, the men so knowing?
Don't the wounded find a use for mold?
We need no introduction to these plots.

That's the captain—lost his head to knives
of Haidas. That's a smuggler and that
a sentimental fool. Read his epitaph:
Mary. We love one another still.
I'll go first. You mark my stone with lines
the south wind often writes on zany days.
Dump me in a river roaring for the sea.

We joke back across the strait at islands.
Men are islands. Haidas live in carvings
in stockades men turn into museums.
We never give old guns another glance.
Taste your tears, the lime of them, the liquor.
Give the foolish dead a second chance.
The weather hates our poses
but the sun deranges men with laughter.

Death of the Kapowsin Tavern

I can't ridge it back again from char.
Not one board left. Only ash a cat explores
and shattered glass smoked black and strung
about from the explosion I believe
in the reports. The white school up for sale
for years, most homes abandoned to the rocks
of passing boys—the fire, helped by wind
that blew the neon out six years before,
simply ended lots of ending.

A damn shame. Now, when the night chill
of the lake gets in a troller's bones
where can the troller go for bad wine
washed down frantically with beer?
And when wise men are in style again
will one recount the two-mile glide of cranes
from dead pines or the nameless yellow
flowers thriving in the useless logs,
or dots of light all night about the far end
of the lake, the dawn arrival of the idiot
with catfish—most of all, above the lake
the temple and our sanctuary there?

Nothing dies as slowly as a scene.
The dusty jukebox cracking through
the cackle of a beered-up crone—
wagered wine—sudden need to dance—
these remain in the black debris.
Although I know in time the lake will send
wind black enough to blow it all away.

Good Luck
in Cracked
Italian

[1969]

WHERE ALL DOORS OPEN IN

Docking at Palermo

You can't weep like them, can't pound the rail
with love for this or any land.
You never understood a cloudy north
so how these tears or that syllabic sun?
This rock that came at you for hours
came at others twenty years ago
in dread. You pass the bay
where they invaded, saying it was wrong.
On either side a cliff and raining guns.

The dolphins had their fling and now
Palermo comes. Blue dots on your right
are welders welding ships. Other dots
are neon just turned on, others
faces strained from waiting on the dock
and now the son is old and home to die.
If you went home a bear would turn away.

For them, the gangplank's down. For you
a cheating cabby waits. Learn the names
of streets or give them names to fight.
You have five hours here. If here before
with hate, you walk a street called war
and beg a man who was a beggar then:
now I have no gun, show me how to cry.

Napoli Again

Long before I hear it, Naples bright
with buildings trumpets from the hill.
A tugboat toots *"paisan"* and I am back.
That dock I sailed from eighteen years ago.
This bay had a fleet of half-sunk ships.
Where those dapper men are drinking wine,
a soldier beat an urchin with a belt.
Fountains didn't work. I remember stink.
Streets and buildings all seemed brown.

Romans hate such recent ruins,
bombed-out houses you do not repair.
Better pillars one must work to date.
Forget the innocent cut down,
cats gone crazy from the bombs
waiting down those alleys for delicious eyes.
Here, the glass replaced in *galleria* roofs,
cappuccino too high priced, it's hard
to go back years and feed the whores for free.

I'll never think of virgin angels here.
Did I walk this street before,
protesting: I am kind. You switch the menu,
gyp me on the bill. Remember me? My wings?
The silver target and the silver bomb?
Take the extra coin. I only came
to see you living and the fountains run.

The Bridge of Sighs

That's our last look at the green canal.
Now the steps go down. Our life
is stone and chain. Moments back

we passed the Tintoretto mural
and saw our judgment screamed:
life in a rheumatic cell.
Jails today have thinner walls
and better air. Judges are the same.

Here we see a claw mark of despair
ripe as those mosaic walls outside.
We hear the sobbing of a mind gone wrong
from years of hearing water pound
on stone, unseen, ten feet away.
Guards are fun. We tell them jokes
and they remove our chains for meals.

Giants paint what kings require.
Uniforms ablaze. Glory of our time.
Multicolored spears. Sweet ax
come down and save the state from shame.
This son took the throne and so on
while you and I went white with pain.

And now we've won, let's paint one torment
only: dungeon where a king still begs for food
and smiles. Mix black with black to get that gray
of stone that tells him, age, but never die.

Galileo's Chair

In gold light here a small guard
warns me not to cross the velvet chain
or climb the stairs that might break down
beneath my modern bulk. Galileo's telescope
was not the first but first toward
the sky. The milky way's not milk
and Venus circles in and out of light.

Take air away and even fire falls—
a voice through this tan air, across
these tiers, seducing men to think.
Star without parallax, he measured time
by weight, like men, and moons of Jupiter
were cause for wine. Sagredo warned
of Roman hate so heavy it can crack
the latest lens. No Pope honors proof
we move about the sun. God is weight
enough to bend an unrecanting knee.

He may be wrong. The sun may circle men.
The stairs might hold me but his chair,
inelegant and worn, is the odd star
fixed beyond my chain. The brown wood
turns this hall a darker brown
each year. We'll give in too and air
will darken in Peking. Outside, pigeons
called by bells of Padova
to fan about a tower, highest point
for miles, the first and last to catch
the sun, won't fly or will fly blind.

I never cross the chain. The small guard
tries to talk but my Italian's stuck.
Was the dungeon black? The one he went to
when he'd lied to God, and where he said
eppur si muove and it did.

Morning in Padova

Market this morning where dazzling rows
of tiny birds skinned pink, the heads left on,
tell my foreign eyes this scream for raw life
from the death of things may be less abstract
and more Italian than I thought.

Bright tiers of fruit scream too, and meat,
the chestnut hawker and his fire. The world
is screaming, "Don't starve, I'm
a starving farmer" at the world.

This variety of food and in Saint Anthony's,
bones that trumpet from the pillar
loud without a sound, validate man's
weird interior, his hoarded silver,
how he kneels in terror where the lid went down.
We eat good food. We name our body parts.
The skeleton still blows his windless horn.

Padova, I'm proud our Clinton grape
helped save your failing wine. Is your time
coming too? Galileo left and Venice
sinks four inches every hundred years.
You hid all your Jews in 'forty-four.
The ghetto's just a name. We need a name,
not Jew or man but something not so old
formed wild downstream. I hate to bargain
but I bargain for the Giotto yellow
of a pear before bells send the farmers home.
I remain with pigeons, cats, the first bite
of my pear important in my teeth.

S. Miniato: One by Aretino

Applause and wondrous gazes of love
for the Saint retrieving the hoe. Farms
will prosper now. The miracle will toll
from the chapel high on the mural
where two monks chat, while to the right
a hunter chases two deer, whatever they were—
hounds after hare—up a bare hill
that breaks at the apex, spilling what's male,
animal, hunger or hate from the world.

Other males persist. One beats his ass
in the ass with a stick. Another, not here
but in the chapel next door, dabs at his eyes
while Latin chanted locks him down tight.
A peasant hacks at stone he must rent
and must hack until rain turns it to soil.

Most male of all, the red fisherman
focused mad as a lover on trout
the Saints stirs to hunger, is central.
Won't go to church, just piles up his catch
from the lake painted so oddly
it seems a map of the lake. Next door
the wedding is over. The fisherman
concentrates harder, ignoring the Saint
and his gang, dressed in uniform white.
Only the pole and line and dark trout
curving through green really matter.
Monks can go to their bell rope, deer
or dogs and the hunter tumble to doom,
the ass move on, olives flare from the stone.
His adamant eye and red robe mean
the fisherman knows retrieving a tool
is no miracle, not when the lake
has no depth and your halo is gold.

Tiberio's Cliff

Tiberio was kind according to the guard
left over from a recent war. Seven seconds down
his enemies went pulp on rock.
The stone I throw hangs where its arc ends
then goes down screaming Latin no one hears.
It disappears. No final click. No foam.

•

Virgins ragged from a violent week of use,
war hostages and inept clowns
fell clawing for a wing. Tide has taken
all remains away, blood, bone and broken hair.
Only gray straight down to boulders
and the guard turned mean. Sharks have gone
two thousand years without a decent meal.

I'll never stare this cruelty away.
Far out, five trawls are flat and peaceful
where three temperatures of sea ally
antagonistic streaks of blue. Below
the sea tugs green and female at my hands.

Brueghel in the Doria

It's a rare Brueghel without people.
Perhaps they cower on the maindeck
as the cannons bang. I see a few
but tiny on the dock, no doubt fans
of naval battle, maybe shouting whee.
What war was this? The ships seem grimly
similar, or did Brueghel know
when war begins the enemy dissolves?

The sea and sky are serious. The sea
is tortured by maneuvers though
its green is rooted in some memory
of toy, anchored solidly
to the lower frame. The sky
is yellow, moving right and back
away from fight toward the dark
behind Vesuvius, the private war of sky
always far away from what you are.

•

For me, the city counts. Even then
it climbed, and sky above it
opened to receive it, as the two arms,
docks, open to receive the traveler
who slides toward it on this heavy green,
old boats inside him playing out
the war he must not win, and strangers
on the dock, his money in their eyes,
saying this is Naples. Welcome.

Castel Sant'Angelo

for Agostino Parise

Piles of rock balls used for ammo then
could still be fun, or rooms where guards got drunk,
stone mugs and tough wood tables still intact.
We order coffee made with a machine
that gleams the name of some firm in Milan.
Had Tosca jumped from where they claim,
she would have splatted by that taxi in the street.

Banquets lasted days, meat roasted black
to gnaw on after girls and endless wine.
When gluttony and love had turned them mean,
they brought the sadist and the virgins in.
Where they dropped the bores in the canal
is grated, and a horny guard points out
the best of the pornography above.

Popes came puffing down that wall to hide
where cruelty and orgy used to blend
before they locked the drawbridge down,
burned invitations, charged admission,
found if everyone came in that no one
had a knife or thought, or was interesting.

They fired guards and opened dungeons
so touring girls from Iowa can peek.

Cruelty is what a land endures before
it's clean. Years of torture here
fan out from us, brown miles of monument
and dome, pigeons rising pink in haze
and broken women scattered on the stream.
We stand on stone and holy violence
of men, and even late in afternoon,
Rome seen from a parapet is always dawn.

Kennedy Ucciso

Don't scream at me you God damn' wops,
nine at night. I know what the headline says.
Blasted by some creep in Dallas.
Don't ask me who Johnson is.
Don't ask *racismo, comunismo?*
I don't know. That fountain lit
and flowing over naked ladies, fish,
animals and birds, is blurred. You and words
in giant print keep banging at my head.

I voted for him, not my kind of man.
My kind could not be president,
just a target for the cold. You slip in
noisy knives of why. *Un gran uomo?*
Certamente. I know, here this very year.
Yes, a Catholic. Yes. Yes. Very rich.
A man who put some sixty million lives
on some vague line and won.
I'd vote for him again. But here
in the *piazza* where the fountain
makes wet love to ladies and stone swans
I want your questions and my hate to end.

•

The fountain runs in thighs of lovely stone.
Ladies do quite well, subduing swans
and lizards, giving in to fish. You Romans,
quite *simpatici*. Someday we'll be you.
I weep in the *piazza*, perfect wop.
Take your questions to a sainted star.
My Italian fails. *Come si dice:*
He was not afraid of what we are.

SIDE TRIPS BACK

G.I. Graves in Tuscany

They still seem G.I., the uniform lines
of white crosses, the gleam that rolls
white drums over the lawn. Machines
that cut the grass left their maneuvers plain.
Our flag doesn't seem silly though plainly
it flies only because there is wind.

Let them go by. I don't want to turn in.
After ten minutes I'd be sick of their names
of the names of their towns. Then
some guide would offer a tour
for two thousand lire, smiling the places
of battle, feigning hate for the Krauts.
I guess visitors come. A cross here and there
is rooted in flowers. Maybe in Scranton
a woman is saving. Maybe in books
what happened and why is worked out.

The loss is so damn gross. I remember
a washtub of salad in basic, blacktop acres
of men waiting to march, passing three hours
of bombers, en route to Vienna, and bombing
and passing two hours of planes, coming back.
Numbers are vulgar. If I stayed
I'd count the men in years of probable loss.

I'm a liar. I'm frightened to stop.
Afraid of a speech I might make,

corny over some stone with a name
that indicates Slavic descent—you there,
you must be first generation,
I'm third. The farm, I'm told, was hard
but it all means something. Think
of Jefferson, of the Constitution,
not of these children
beside me, bumming a smoke and laughing.

A View from Cortona

Land breaks yellow south below, pale squares
of green about to yellow. One long road
splits the summer on its way to Rome.
Twenty years ago today, the G.I.'s came.
Did bells ring then? Were the natives glad?
The liberators, loud and oddly young,
ignored this view, the lovely dome
of the cathedral halfway down the hill,
the yellow tile igniting summer
spreading to that wide south out of war.

Remember? No view? Long nights at home,
Nothing to do. Radio down so the old
could sleep. Staring at walls and trying
to write. Brown sugar on bread
and your life that might go on forever.
Only the garden dying each fall
or rain sudden on windows, breaking the void.
Nothing older than photos. Not one thing new
in the room. The 1880 valentine
kept flaking under the glass.

They think I'm German here. My passport
makes me friend. High in this hotel
I watch clouds play their shade across the miles

the G.I.'s came, loving wine so loud
Italians couldn't understand. Why stop here?
I was going to Perugia when this stark town
of medieval stone rode high above me,
at me out of sky. I turned up the hill
certain I'd vanish, someday, gone
in a moment, up a thousand-year-old street,
fat and silly from behind, curving out of sight
into a past weak as the future of stone.

Eighteen Days in a Tuscan Wood

for Mario Vannetti

Through those trees you traced a loud white roof
the tracers wove driving for that farm
where Germans hid. Not far, but years beyond
the guns, your home town towers medieval
(you can see it) up the sky. Long yellow days.
Patched farms where bird dogs train.
Twenty years: the wood's a pheasant grove.

Here with wife and son, no water, French guns
tracking thirsty down the slow hill
to the well, you must have heard the pigeons
circling the bells that celebrated wine
or dreamed the wine and prayed the baby
wouldn't scream. Day and day, the pounding.
One day, the pound retreating, Germans going north.

You came out timid to this gold dirt road.
To walk was lovely, fields and quiet air.
You walked away from war toward the towers
and the miles were clean. The bells rang out
the latest wine bigger than a bomb.

Viva La Resistènza

Cortona, July 5, 1964

The castle mad with decay, intimate streets,
flaring tile domes, faces that light
when I turn out not to be German—
whatever the charm, I think of the plaque,
of forty-three names torn from where they belong
and cut into stone, multisyllabic and stark.

It's never right. The band can't hit the notes.
The mayor forgot his speech. They place the wreath
awkward as food left at a destitute door
then march chaotically on to the graves,
another wreath ready, a cornet carving my ear.

After they've gone I mutter "Never again."
But what does that mean? Banner and flag and *viva*
our freedom? Better to fix on the pigeons
rising as one and changing sides of the square.
And better to pray no day finds me German,
rifle well oiled, my enemy spitting despair.

April in Cerignola

This is Puglia and cruel. The sun is mean
all summer and the *tramontana*
whips the feeble four months into March.
It was far too tense. Off the streets by five.
Flyers screaming begging children off
and flyers stabbed. The only beauty
is the iron grillwork, and neither that
nor spring was here when I was young.

•

It used to be my town. The closest one
for bomb-bomb boys to buy *spumanti* in.
It reeked like all the towns. Italian men
were gone. The women locked themselves in dark
behind the walls, the bullet holes patched now.
Dogs could sense the madness and went mute.
The streets were mute despite the cry
of children: give me cigarette. But always flat—
the land in all directions and the time.

I was desolate, too, and so survived.
I had a secret wish, to bring much food
and feed you through the war. I wished
you also dead. All roads lead to none.
You're too far from the Adriatic
to get good wind. Harsh heat and roaring cold
are built in like abandonment each year.
And every day, these mean streets open
knowing there's no money and no fun.

So why return? You tell me I'm the only one
came back, and you're amazed
I haven't seen Milan. I came in August
and went home in March, with no chance
to experience the miles of tall grain
jittering in wind, and olive trees
alive from recent rain. You're still my town.
The men returned. The women opened doors.
The hungry lived and grew, had children
they can feed. Most of all, the streets are wide,
lead nowhere, and dying in your weather
takes a lifetime of surviving last year's war.

Tretitoli, Where the Bomb Group Was

Windy hunks of light, not prop wash, bend
the green grain no one tried to grow
twenty years ago. Two nuns run a school
where flyers cursed the endless marmalade
and Spam, or choked their powdered eggs
down throats Ploesti tightened in their dreams.
Always phlegm before the engines warmed
and always the private gesture of luck—
touching a bomb, saying the name of a face
spun in without a sound at Odertol.

Hope to win a war gets thin when nuns
pour *strega* in a room where dirty songs
about the chaplain boomed. Recent land reform
gave dirt to the forlorn. That new farm
stands where I would stand in afternoon
alone and stare across those unfarmed miles
and plan to walk them to the yellow town
away from war, disguised in shepherd black.
That pumphouse hid three whores for weeks
until disease began to show.

Now, no roar. No one sweats the sky out
late in day. No trace of squadron huts
and stone block walls supporting tents.
Those grim jokes. The missions flown
counted on the plane in cartoon bombs.
Always wide awake toward the end
when the man came saying time to fly,
awake from dreams complete with mobs,
thick clubs and slamming syllables of hun
I couldn't understand, trapped behind
cracked glass somewhere deep in Munich
I had never seen, waiting for their teeth
to snip me from the drunken songs of men.

•

We drive off. Children wait for class.
Grain is pale where truck pools were,
parked planes leaked oil or bombs were piled.
The runway's just a guess. I'd say, there.
Beyond the pumphouse and restricted whores
where nuns and shepherds try to soar by running,
arms stuck out for wings against the air,
and wind is lit in squadrons by the grain.

Where We Crashed

I was calling airspeed
christ
one-thirty-five and
pancake bam
glass going first
breaking slow
slow dream
breaking
slow
sliding
gas and bombs
sliding
you end
now
here
explode
damn
damn
Steinberg
pilot
should
have found
more sky
you end
here

boom
now
boom
gone
no more
gone
good-bye
bye bye
boom
go boom
piled on
into panel
from behind
off
off
swinging
tire loose
strut caught
slow circle
turn
swinging
ripping
gas and bombs
aluminum
hole open
out
sweet
cheese-eating
jesus
out
clumsy
nothing
fuckass
nothing
shithead
nothing

moldy
cunteyed
bastard
nothing
stuck
shove
him
prick
jump
run
sweet
cheese-eating
jesus
run
gas
bombs
running
rain
faint rain
running
farmer
screaming
something
someone
.45
shoot
get back
shoot him back
gas and bombs
running
Stewart
R.O.
Klamath Falls
out
he's out
on the horizon

running
live
O'Brien
L.A.
broken foot
limping
away
all away
from gas
from bombs
Knapp
ball turret
joking
farmer
yelling
Steinberg
staring gray
and in this grass
I didn't die

Spinazzola: Quella Cantina Là

A field of wind gave license for defeat.
I can't explain. The grass bent. The wind
seemed full of men but without hate or fame.
I was farther than that farm where the road
slants off to nowhere, and the field I'm sure
is in this wine or that man's voice. The man
and this canteen were also here
twenty years ago and just as old.

Hate for me was dirt until I woke up
five miles over Villach in a smoke
that shook my tongue. Here, by accident,
the wrong truck, I came back to the world.

This canteen is home-old. A man can walk
the road outside without a song or gun.
I can't explain the wind. The field is east
toward the Adriatic from my wine.

I'd walked from cruel soil to a trout
for love but never from a bad sky
to a field of wind I can't explain.
The drone of bombers going home
made the weather warm. My uniform
turned foreign where the olive trees
throw silver to each other down the hill.

Olive leaves were silver I could spend.
Say wind I can't explain. That field is vital
and the Adriatic warm. Don't our real friends
tell us when we fail? Don't honest fields
reveal us in their winds? Planes and men
once tumbled but the war went on absurd.
I can't explain the wine. This crude bench
and rough table and that flaking plaster—
most of all the long nights make this home.

Home's always been a long way from a friend.
I mix up things, the town, the wind, the war.
I can't explain the drone. Bombers seemed
to scream toward the target, on the let-down
hum. My memory is weak from bombs.
Say I dropped them bad with shaking sight.
Call me German and my enemy the air.

Clouds are definite types. High ones, cirrus.
Cumulus, big fluffy kind, and if with rain,
also nimbus. Don't fly into them.
I can't explain. Somewhere in a gray ball
wind is killing. I forgot the stratus

high and thin. I forget my field
of wind, out there east between
the Adriatic and my second glass of wine.

I'll find the field. I'll go feeble down
the road strung gray like spoiled wine
in the sky. A sky too clear of cloud
is fatal. Trust the nimbus. Trust dark clouds
to rain. I can't explain the sun. The man
will serve me wine until a bomber fleet
lost twenty years comes droning home.

I can't explain. Outside, on the road
that leaves the town reluctantly,
way out the road's a field of wind.

Note from Capri to Richard Ryan
on the Adriatic Floor

Dick, I went back to those rocks today,
the ones we ate on nineteen years ago
a week before you ditched, a damn fool
being brave with land not far away.
I thought of steaks and quotes
from funny men. Two bottles of white wine.

The rocks have changed. Nineteen years
of wave and storm have given them
rough edges and the island rots with stores.
You should have tried for land not fame.
Four others ended with you and your bombardier
went babbling to Bari in restraint.

This is futile. Sharks don't carry notes.
What's your face like now with slow eels

sliding through your eyes? Bones can't glow
through barnacles and green piled dark as flak.
Your seatbelt rots too late. If wings
could bring you up and tricky currents
float you seas and seas to here, I'm not sure
I'd know you or would like your jokes.

Dick, I went back to those rocks today,
and sat there, glaring at the sea.

The Yards of Sarajevo

Time of day: a dim dream, probably
late afternoon. Children watch our train
pull into the yard. Other late dark
afternoons and porches seem remote.
These people, tracks and cars were what
we came to bomb nineteen years ago
and missed six miles through blinding clouds.

One war started here. The coal smoke
of our diry train compounds the gloom.
The past is always dim. A plot. A gun.
The Archduke falling. A world gone
back to mud. Our long day from Dubrovnik
grates to a stop. Air is getting black.
I was five miles up there sighting
on this spot. I can't speak Serb or read
Cyrillic listings of departure times.

Even long wars end. Dukes and Kings
tell peasants old jokes underground.
This was small and foreign five miles down.
Why am I at home? The tongue is odd,
the station loud. All rebuilt
and modern. Only the lighting bad.

Paestum

Life was Greek before Greeks came. The swamp
killed peasant babies, and the local dialect
had no word for hope. Today, old gods
are rooks, more Greek than ever
in and out of pillars that turn ancient pink
late each afternoon. Man always brought
his anguish to the sea. Sealight's best
for tears, and gods can hang offshore
staring you malarial or old.

In 1943 we turned these ruins
into first-aid stations, then gave first aid
to peasants we had shelled. A good wound
makes you cry "Stay with me" at the stars.
How much virgin blood is real
and how much spilled in some old play
on the amphitheater floor? In war
we take advantages to prove we are.

Word's gone back to the commercial world:
if you sail that region, stop there.
You will see our work and you can worship
when the sun is flat and shafts of cream
spray between our pillars from the sea.
Odd dark birds weave through black and pink
we planned. As for natives there,
they farm, die often from some fever
we have never seen, make love
more frequently than we, and when we sweat
erecting pillars, they laugh above their hoes.

Galleria Umberto I

Now it's clean. The whores seem healthy
and the bombed-out panes have been replaced.
This arcade's a monument to money,
in a city with a desperate need
for money, in a country with no need at all
for love. These shops will never sell
those gaudy chandeliers. The gaudy whores
display themselves forever with no takers.

I remember it a little more forlorn.
Not just roof glass gone, but harsh arrays
of junk on tables and pathetic faces
crying for ten lire. There were faces
broken by the war, and faces warped
by cruelty they'd learned, and faces gone.
I kept my face by turning it away.
It was here that John Horne Burns
saw war summed up, the cracked life
going on, taking what it would in gesture
and a beggar's bitter hand.

There's no metaphor for pain, despair.
It's just there. You live with it, if lucky
in a poem, or try to see it, how it was
under this dome roof with children dead,
the stench of death blown at you
off a sea we should have asked for wisdom
by wind we still should beg for tears.
In all our years, we come to only this:
capacity to harm, to starve, to claim
I'm not myself. I didn't do these things.

•

I did lots of things and I'm myself
to live with, bad as any German.
It's a place to start undoing. The whore
is certain in a storm that when it dies
new ships come in. How could this poem
with no tough man behind it, come to me
today, walking where I walked
twenty years ago amazed, when now
no one is hungry, the gold facade is polished
and they have no word in dialect for lonely?

MARATEA

Maratea Porto

In winter, Germans gone, the sea insane
explodes for miles and stutters, foam birds
down the stone. Back home, we prayed for this,
a cobbled street, the sand swept clean by storm,
always weather at us, lightning, sun,
and out there Sicily unseen, or rain
en route to where we stand, beside the ruin,
Saracen, where lookouts looked and waited
for the glint of a devoted mob.

The mongoloid cast out by family to beg,
the epileptic throwing seizures in the road,
church bells that won't let you think,
rats and fleas, the cats who scrounge for food—
all unforeseen. Back home we hide what's wrong.
The gong is soft except when rung for meals.
Here, far more than lovely lava caves
the sea gouged out, much more than crosses
on the mountain tops, the hands of women
cut by grass they pull and rope they weave
from grass, the hands and minds of man
gone stone from stone and sweat and little pay
are what we see and what we must believe.

And here we must believe the bombing spray,
the sea attenuated by the stone, squeezed in
until it screams relief and rockets to the moon

ahead of man. But also man, that Saracen
who stares forever in the boiling wind
beside his ruin, waiting for his day.

The Picnic in the Saracen Ruin

That rock shaped like a ship might scare us now
but we know stone is stone, the cross
is ornament, no mast. And danger
never comes by sea today. The tile
is not original. One must crawl on dirt
to watch the west through peepholes dark men cut
and one must sleep there snug in rumor
(there is no crusade) and wake when one oar creaks
because the sea is night. Our milk
and *mortadella* and the blue sea clear of shark
insist we nap against a parapet
of sun. To sailors this stone bulk
could never be just ruins in the moon.

Remember forts at home, thick logs and flints
and photos of the men? Here, the pines are thin.
A painter-spy tried hard but got it wrong.
The main room held an extra hundred
all with spears. The cries of first invaders
on the rock below were waves. The final clash
was sun tomorrow and the empty sea.
That cross is really recent and the stains
we thought were blood are flowers in the cracks.

Perhaps they wept and cursed the barren sea
and screamed at night: when will Christians come?
Let's take our orange peels home. Those glints
are gulls or rough spots on the sea.
Time has bombed the spears away
and men who can't be photoed must have turned

toward the mountain and the gleaming town,
memorizing nouns and starting up the stone.

Maratea Antica

On clear days here the sea is most clear.
Stones that died along the floor dance back
loud aqua in my peasant eyes. Ruins
left by Saracens stud north and south
this lava coast. When sun is cream,
late afternoon, I set my pulse for midnight.
By nine the dark will grind me into sleep.

Here I end old agonies of farms,
one farm burned, one wife in the asylum
forty years alone with angels saying:
stunted tribes will buy your ruined wheat.
Here I trade in sweat for stable spray.
And here I shake those families of farms,
who never spoke, the bitterness, the wrong
hacked out in rock with vicious hoes,
private rages at the edge of fields,
no one thinking next year's crop would come.

The sea is clearest on a clear day here.
Men are clear. The women never real—
ideal perhaps as they were painted
five, six centuries ago, too fat
in perfect places, much too strong
to dwell on men who climb their thighs.
The sea has thighs. Round rocks magnified
are glib with bottom invitations.
I dive from ruins and a Saracen
calls after me: go deep. That sea
is wheat, asylum, blue wine, all you need.
Go deep as cats in creamy afternoon.

One Son North to Naples

for Giovanni D'Alascio

Coming from a country where we never fail,
grow old or die, but simply move unnoticed
to the next cold town, it's hard to think
protective stone, warm people and warm sea
are not enough. Most hate ended here
when Saracens moved on. A shark off course
might stray in close or Sicily may send
a lightning storm, but only lovers use
the ruin where invaders went insane.

Rock is not enough. Rocks that try to kiss,
hug the sea to death and yet the sea
explodes and climbs away. One day
the *tramontana* rang the bells off key.
Priests went dissonant. It suddenly was clear
why girls dressed up for Sunday in the square.

The sea's so clear, no shark, no invaders
sneak past eyes that rake the sea each day
for food, and mountains drop the definite
firm gray they dropped for raiding eyes
nine centuries ago. Old friends, people
like the Vitolos, take all the passion
lightning storms or Saracens could give.
For an Italian, leaving home is easy.
You come back always knowing what to love.

Maratea Porto: The Bitter Man

He boots a cat, ass over claws, and laughs.
He lost the arm at Tobruk. His hatred
of *casa speranza*, home of the Count

imported from the north, is laughter too
nasty over the sea. The sea has been deserted
by the moon so long, tide is always out.
With sea this clear, even far offshore
underwater life is clearly bleak.

Late in day, he sits on the wall and waits
for sea to trap the sun. His memory
may blur at night. His dreams
are always clear—violent tides and a sun
locked high, two arms around
a one-armed moon, praying he'll enjoy
a muddy future and, deep in mud,
a creature, part lady and part home.

Non c'è speranza, I told him.
He laughed at my Italian. Others say
he lives alone and so is what he is.
Please understand. He has to kick cats
and hate Counts and laugh at Italian,
anyone's, really, Italian over the sea.

Cantina Iannini

Walls were painted blue so long ago, you think
of old sky you thought lovely turned as it did,
in your lifetime, dirty. Six crude wood tables
and the pregnant cat seem permanent
on the pockmarked concrete floor. The owner
gives too much away, too much free wine
and from his eyes too much grief. His facial lines
amplify in light the two small windows
and the opaque door glass flatten out.
To enter you should be poor by consent.

.

You and the world that hurts you should agree
you don't deserve a penny. Nor a clear tongue
to beg sympathy from wine dark as your life
and rich as your dream you still are nothing in.
And you should agree to cross your throat
and weep when the casket passes. You should kneel
when wind crosses the olive grove in waves
of stuttering coin. At nine the light goes down.
You weave home to homes you'll never own.

Only men in broken rags come back
to drink black wine under the painting
Moonlight on Sea a drunk thought lovely—
turned as it did, in his liftime, muddy.
You hear the wind outside turn white. Wasn't
some loud promise in another wine? Sea cliff
with a girl, her hair streamed out your lifetime
down the sky? Your wine is dead. Tomorrow
you'll return to this grim charm, not quite broken,
not quite ready to release your eyes.

Pizzeria S. Biagio

for Biagio Avigliano

When you hobble, tattered through the square
they say: Come in. We keep the maimed alive.
The specialty today: hare neapolitan
or *baccalà*. The price will be naive.
You go in old, remembering a war
hair half gone, your belly out of friends.
A saint is waiting with a cure-all wine.

The old saint rests above you, up that rock
the cloud hangs on. He pitied most the mute.

On clear days from that cliff, the port
throbs a day of scream straight down
and halfway down your final cry
this stony town, a fat man waving
"Lunch is ready" from the square in rain.

The war was bad. All those common bullets
going tricky in the wind, wounding you
years later when you paid down on a tomb.
Here, the cost of death is time: fifteen years
for daddy and your savings gone. Cost of life:
yourself, just going in defeated,
needing pasta and a wine to kill the storm.

While you were eating, tough Sicilian air
wiped the mountain clean. The latest saint,
a fat man, made you talk. Where you'd planned
to jump the next good day, a heavy cross
blew down, and rain runs off the square to farms
that shine below, lemon and bamboo,
vineyards, olive trees and teeth for plows.

Maratea Porto: The Dear Postmistress There

I run up the stairs too fast every morning
and panting for mail, I stagger inside
and there she sits wagging a negative finger.
Her frown is etched in and her mouth is sour.
Niente per voi, today.

This is Odysseus. I've come a long way.
I've beaten a giant, real mean with one eye.
Even the sea. I've defeated the water.
But now I'm home, pooped. Where's Penelope?
Niente per voi, today.

My name is Joseph and this, my wife Mary.
we've had a long journey and Mary is heavy.
The facts are odd. The child could be holy
and I wonder, have you a room in your inn?
Niente per voi, today.

I'm Genghis Khan and this is my army.
We've conquered your land. Now we want women.
Bring them today at high noon to the square.
After we've had them, we'll get out of here.
Niente per voi, today.

I'm Michelangelo, here to make statues.
I've lugged this damn marble all the way from the Alps.
I'll need a large scaffold and plenty of ropes,
a chisel, a mallet and oodles of wine.
Niente per voi, today.

Oh, heroes of time, you're never a hero
until you've endured ten days with no mail.
Slaughter the stars and come home in splendor.
She'll always be there at the end of the trail.
Niente per voi, today.

Maratea Porto: Saying Good-bye to the Vitolos

Should I say, my people? I turned to stone
against them long ago, the soupy pictures
of Christ, the crosses drugstores sell.
Cruelty that often goes with stone
makes men virginal or wrong. Outside
the sea has always beat against the rock,
the spray hung passionate, the local bell
sent word of worms to fat fish miles away.

I'm so American, embarrassed by their tears.
Don't they know the saint's bones, high
above us on the mountain, now mean nothing,
and good-bye is common now that love
is just a verb, active as the tide? Why
is Jesus bleeding in that photo on the wall
except to tell the world, when I'm gone
going will be fun? The bright day off the sea
dazzles the flies. Mad purple flies
around me, glint and sizzle and the shaking sea,
the mountain shaking and the saint's bones
raining through the spray, bells gone stale
and money low and this: last days in Italy.
I stand so still. My legs must be diseased.

I forgot my people long ago, reduced them
to some words and wrote their stones away.
Sea slants off their tears with light
no one should forget. I'm still American.
See, afraid to cry. How awkwardly I lean
to kiss them and how suddenly I say
good luck in cracked Italian as I turn my face.

Last Words from Maratea

THE PORT

Little has changed. Six dark mornings a week
women in black still trudge up the mountain
for grasses. And wherever the dawn comes from,
Africa, Greece, it still opens with cats
frantic for sanctuary, and pots of brown dye
for the fishnets boiling, with hogs discussing
who will bleed to death next in the street.
Later, the bells bang "up up, you need us"
over the sea that needs nothing, not even

boats that waited all night for tuna
the priest said he prayed for, whenever. Last year?
Real day begins with the clunk clunk of clubs
beating grass into cord, and the never meant,
bitterly said *buon' giorno*, and the knowing
black in their eyes: this is all we will have.
The boats return and no one asks how they did.
The bar, owned by the butcher, opens at nine
for no reason. The tiny store, pasta
and canned foods, opens. The tobacco shop opens.
The port is open. Total. But only to sun.

And you, *straniero*, why did you come?
It wasn't some cheap dream plus the luck
of a grant brought you here. You didn't pass by
on a ship and see this pink stone climbing
out of the sea that is bluer than all the lakes
of your life compounded by lies, and say
that's where I'll lie to myself forever and die.
And you're too bright to think there's love
deep in those sea caves, some long
brown girl the sea provided for you,
and who, up to now, has been kissed only by stars
desexed as they burned through the sea, or fingered
by anemones. You don't put faith in simplicities
either. The peasant with boredom and ax
doesn't have it made. You were going south on a train
and liked the sound of the name. And got off.

A map can make you dream. Do cartographers
still color China orange? And other things:
the way a barber's clipper and the old planes
you remember used to hum. And hum
was the sound of summer. On the barber's wall
was faded zodiac calendar—
were camels, pyramids and endless sand
part of the hum? The old man never explained.

He never talked. Just whistled awful to himself.
You walked beside him the dirt road home
silent too and warm. It wasn't always cruel.
It wasn't always soil and flat spade ringing
and hating a life that brought nothing,
hating rain and hating lack of rain. It
wasn't always threat: you won't have a home.
And it wasn't always the damn swamp you drank from
proudly, knowing it poison, proving
to the world you'd never die. It was always today.

You may never love violent under that sky
and wake up crawled on by stars. But this
is also today and the Mediterranean
has little tide. The grass is pounded tough
and women are weaving tough grass rope.
It's well past noon. You wait on the seawall
for the next storm. The bar and store
are closed. Cats are licking the blood
of the hog bled today in the road
and waves are eating one more cave
deep in the cliff under the Saracen ruin.
Let them ring bells or mount another
banal statue of Christ on the mountain.
Was he really that ugly, that vulnerable
to wind? This is all you will have.
The port is closed. Total. But only to stars.

FIUMICÈLLO

Bank, church, bar,
supermarket: new
at Piazza Gesù
owned by the Count
who's improving things
with government funds.
His textile plant

has been kind
employing men.
To date his plans
have weakened the wine.
The mongoloid sees
through Picasso eyes
everything's better.
Peasants with bread
walk straighter
home to their nothing.
Bank, church, bar,
supermarket, all,
all hopefully new
at Piazza Gesù.

THE OLD TOWN

Failure came built in. The town hung too high
in the sun for Saracens to miss. You walk
the ruins but you cannot guess the grief.
Bones of San'Biagio, patron saint of throats,
beached by storm (*miracolo*) eleven
centuries ago remain the prime attraction
for Germans in July. A monstrous
statue of Jesus blesses us all.

The mountain like the spread white arms
of Christ, blesses the town, the port,
the sea spread out to nowhere, the nowhere
of the lives below. Nowhere to go.
Even the sea seems recent. Misery
was always here. When weather's calm
wind must still come looking through the ruins
for a dog jaw to degrade. The Saracens
took everything except the priests.

•

It seems the right place for a town. Sun
all day and, not too far, flat stoneless patches
you can farm. And if your lover leaves you
you can dive straight down an audience
of stone, splattering the new town's main
piazza where they said they know your name.
You can send the children down for shark.
You can start a money: tuna on the tens,
men on twenties, and on fifties
women riding dolphins into caves.
And if families start scattering like stars
you can pass laws based on food, rejection
and the long drop justified to rock.

The Saracens were not impressed. They yelled
plunder loud enough for centuries to hear.
And here men said to hell with it and left.
Barring big rains now, accelerated erosion
or a sudden real estate deal,
this insufferable figure of Christ
will stand over us all God knows how long.
The town got smart and moved. You came back
to see it. You are the one who failed.

THE TOWN

The town is open. But only to cold.
You, *straniero*, why did you come? North
was the only direction open when that river
jammed with salmon. Where's the river here?
The train runs north. High fog eats the mountain
south to north and bangs of the church clock
wing north slow to fade. You can fake a home
in this failure. Good clothes worn on Sunday
never fooled you either. You can start a money
every day and food remains your only paramour.

•

It wasn't always cruel. Not always mean
and small though light was thin like this
from tiny windows and the bare overhead bulb.
You didn't always stare east where sky could be
over Chicago where someone might like you.
It was always today. An empty forest to play in.
A pond. The silence of fern. That great survivor
the alder living where giant firs
hogged all light and moisture. Remember
the first poem you heard: I go on forever.

After the poem, you found the start of a stream.
You traced it down, pool after sparkling pool,
the jittering miniature rapids, the silver gleam
of sand beds hit by sun. The noise of it.
The hum of water over and under
the fallen cedar. Dark spurt of trout.
Foam spun cloudy on cress. Foam
and cress so thick they hid whatever
those rich names meant: Cutthroat. Dolly Varden.
You wanted to be them. To wear their names.
To drive the whole length of the creek
with raw red women when the first rain fell.
To drive to the spring. I go on forever.

Whatever they color China it will burn bright
Chinese green. Green in your lifetime
you lost nothing but homes. Below, at Piazza Gesù,
there's faith in growth. Even the mongoloid saw
you're not a trout, you don't drive the length
of any creek. You don't claim, I go on forever.
But always *forestiero* and north is open.
North is blue, the bay where all streams die,
a sky not meant that pale on the zodiac calendar.

These are names to accept: *straniero*,
forestiero. You are you, the only man

in the station waiting the train from Sicily.
When summer comes and the Germans, you'll
be back with your river, liking the sound
of your name. Remember, long ago
the speech you'd plan to make in this cold?
Mention Huck Finn. Remember Italian.

Without friends: *senz'amici*.
Without love: *senz'amore*.
Without parents: *senza genitori*.

To hell with your speech. Just make sure
the name you like the sound of is packed.
Just hope to the high bones of a buried saint
no one cares when the train pulls out.

South Italy, Remote and Stone

The enemy's not poverty. It's wind.
Morning it beats you awake to the need
for hoeing and hoeing rock. The priest proclaims
it's not a futile wind. This air moves
with undercurrents of hope five stunted
olive trees pick up. You live all year
on the gallon of olives you sell
and hope the stone will be soil
enough to grow something in. Your hoe and wind
have fought this stone forever and lost.

Up north, the kind have issued your name:
paese abbandonato. It rings now
in this wind that clears my eyes. Your hands
are not abandoned, and the harsh length
of each day forces you to love whatever is—
a screaming wife, a child who has stared
from birth. The road I came on must be old
or some state accident. In heat, this place
is African. In cold, a second moon.

Even your tongue is hard. Syllables whip
and demons, always deposited cruel
in the prettiest unmarried girl,
must be whipped by the priest into air
where bells can drive them to rivers. Or she
will be sent out forever, alone on the roads
with her madness, no chance to be saved

by a prince or kind ox. And so on, a test
of your love. Only the ugly survive.

I'm still alive. My love was tested and passed
something like this. Much better soil.
A more favorable chance at the world.
I sent myself out forever on roads.
I'll never be home except here, dirt poor
in abandoned country. My enemy, wind,
helps me hack each morning again at the rock.

Storm in Acquafredda

You could see it way out crawling slow
across the sea, a line dividing gold and black
coming at you like yourself. Dark air
said it early in the olive leaves.
A silver flutter built ten minutes
into rage. Hours before the day went wild,
the sea went wild and rain began to carve,
shutters on the homes were fastened, streets
were cleared of children, and the reason
you like storms went vague when black arrived.

Thunder jars your teeth and something flashed
so sudden you assume from widely separated
olive trees split open it was lightning
but you're still half blind and certain only
it was light. What's electric is the sea
laddering white voltage up the cliff.
What's not electric is your life.
Nothing flashes past you anymore, not even
ugly women in convertibles. You'd settle
for the menial, say piecework packing vegetables
or peace, a passive marriage to the drainage,
giggling down ditches to the end.

•

Another gold-black line starts far out at you.
It is not you. Gold approaches slow
and it means nothing. Weather's no more
symbol than a broken heart. Bad storms come
and go, but lightning and the tons of rain
leave ruin sun can only make more clear.
You are lucky. Light cannot define you.
And the gold comes on. Gold water drips
off stone. Gold bakes the field dry gold.
Gold everywhere, more coming and it is not you.

The Park at Villammare

Some things you say how sweet to. A widowed aunt's
wax fruit. Painting: Indian Humble in Sunset.
The Lord's Prayer embroidered on a spread.
What you do is fake feeling, try to accept
faint tries at creation. Take this feeble fountain—
a gesture to Rome. And though flowers actually bloom
they don't seem to. Maybe petals are sparse
or light from the sea is too strong
and washes the color out. Anyway, it's wrong.
The trees are too lean, the children who run
through the trees too noisy, not charming.
Here, if you fall in love, it's love, or flight
from a desperate gray you didn't care
to suffer again brought on by this almost
protestant park. By the time those bells
stopped ringing your wedding, the swordfish
they sell in the park would be sold, the fruit stand
closed, children safe in their caves. You'd
wonder who this strange girl you married is,
holding your arm, and why when sun
was still noon you couldn't have stayed the man
you were, faintly created, finding your failures
warm to come home to and your fantasy clean.

Why Sapri Will Never Be Italian

Some days you're finished. Not even eels
squirming for sale in tubs, or the bay
naturally square, involve you. The first star
over the bay makes a star in your wine.
You don't drink Mediterranean sky, or
hear wind rubbing the moon. It must be the town,
the shops drab as Ohio, the streets laid out
nearly in grid forcing you back to your flag.

The gold name of your grammar school
high on brick might be Florence.
Here, you think how they beat the boy
in the schoolyard. His flesh was soft from
(later you learned) a glandular joke.
He screamed, defenseless and hurt. You
knew it was wrong. You didn't say don't.
Today, you give, even to organized beggars
fatter than you. Ten minutes from now
the movie will start down the street.

It was beg for a dime. Whining and whining.
Breaking the old man's dream. Run
through the woods to your beating.
Your rage dissolving in heat
in the dark. Never dissolved. You waited
deep in your throat for your moment.
Deep in your eyes a torment
no one wanted to see. You kept turning away,
your wisecracks wiser and your warm front
getting you by. One day, all suddenly over.
You were alone. Wind had already formed.

If these freaks, the malformed children,
twisted, purple women, the cracked men

were American, they'd be safe from taunts
of the normal. They'd be simply unusual,
in a comfortable, as we call it, home.
And if that star is really in my wine
my wine is usual. Great wines
have no relation with night, and great nights
little with the earth. Some days you're finished.
Eels squirming in tubs, and the bay
square from geographic joke, are bottled
for sale. You buy them and drink. Maybe
a star will stick in your throat, wind
and the moon play jazz, and your life
can crawl on itself in the form.

Beggar in Sapri

How much money would erase him in a dream,
his lids inflamed, his bare feet biblical
with sores? Why beg me, the strange,
but not the soldiers with their girls
two tables down? The bay across the street
is affluent with sun. Cars I can't afford
are tearing through the port. Yet he comes
to me in half a baseball uniform.
I won't compute the handout in American.

Disease that makes the lids that raw
must have a cure. At least a name.
Food is the affair of man and state
and after food, whatever life remains
angels can come down and peck.
I saw him feed his dog a scrap.

•

He waits somewhere on a stone thin street
without his eyes. He left them in my wine.
I drink the world's disease and shame,
two thousand years of love gone wrong
and here, a beggar's groan
is nothing when the church bells gang.

Sailing Dalmatia

I dreamed this coast before Croatia
was a word. Each tree stood alone.
Rocks were darker but the slant of light
across the bleak cliff was the same.
Birds were just that black, the silence
broken by the faint wash of our wake.
That's right, too. The only town was walled.
The girl was more familiar and more thrilled
with water, though her hair was blond
like this and blown across the blue dome
of a passing eastern church. In those dreams
churches were museums and the sky
roared a constant gray all night.

This may be home, black miles of water
and no men. No tongue I'd understand.
No loners either. Not one shack with smoke
warming my heroic hopes of being lost
Croatian on this coast. In that deserted castle
the locked-up king
is screaming for a grocery store or queen.
A girl from Illinois (she's not so blond)
would use the castle for a drunk. I'm
on her side but know the morning would be bad.

•

Best the ship go on, north toward the sun.
Here long enough, I'd tell those sharks—
attack the rocks. Other ships would come
and throw me scraps and laugh and leave me
staring after words I knew.

It really will be home. No place to live.
The sea not wild enough to break the sound
of churches with blue hair. Someday
that girl who sails on in my dream
will write me get-well letters from Nepal.

Remote Farm on the Dubrovnik-Sarajevo Run

Each afternoon the world goes by above it
on the train. Maybe I look down with envy
on the thin strip, the only flat spot
in this jagged land. The strip was cleared
of stone so long ago the stony hill that falls
long and steep toward it from the train, the gulch
that falls off on the other side, seem younger
than the farm. They plant their dead between
the house and where the brown men plow.

All so certain. Where you're born, you die.
That first of many terrifying days, a child
can stare his plot into a whale, or stare until
he knows exactly how his grave dug out
will look, a rich cut into soil
nothing grows in now. He must know he'll endure
the quakes, the shifting snow, the rain
that flashes down the boulders every spring
to sweep the farmland clean, to ready land
for planting. He must know other children
will respect his name because Cyrillic
settles like the weather into stone.

•

From tyranny the road out goes to states
more frightening than rage. If you run away
you cut your feet, your first scream comes back
doubled in the city, and one day old walls
seem like arms. I'll stay on the train
to Sarajevo, remembering a graveyard
in the country, a hot day and a woman
with a blue bouquet asking me directions
to a stone someone way back forgot to mark.

Spinning the Sava

for Joe Braycich

Popovich our guide is old and roads he knew
for forty years turn out wild or wrong.
Storks that nest in churches gutted wars ago
by guns, mock our plan for pike. Pig piss keeps
the tributaries high. Those white cranes
in the state-owned wood are stiff enough
to fill the state again with dreams of kings.

We spin the Sava near the peasant nets,
our spinners, flashing boys. The lone girl
on the bank and pike ignore our lures.
The Sava groans and lumbers like a stork.
In country ripped a hundred times
by tongues, field and town with nothing shading
brain and wheat from sun, a trace of Turk
in faces that ignore demands of grief
to look forlorn, we know that man is tough
and governments mean little, whip or chain.

Someday with luck our teeth will spin downstream.
The lone girl, wheat crop, crane and stork,
pike and peasant and forgotten king

spun out where rivers prove all borders
silly as a map. Fish get fat where pigs pollute
the spawning ground or memories of spawn.

Popovich and rivers never will grow old.
We spin our arms and wheat denies we try.
We cast our lives away and pike are storks
above us, flying slowly to avoid
colliding with the sun. We spin and no fish hit
and every cast, the excess nylon in the sky
becoming taut is peasant, deep and royal.

Christmas with Shepherds in Brefaro

No gifts today. Last night no monster star.
Cheese and wine start things. The teen-age daughter
looks too strong to rape, and listing all the animals
would be futile or insane. Their odors
can't be named that sting my eyes. In surrounding
mountains, rays of sun spot caves and yesterday
rumor of a new wolf reached the hut.

Nothing makes me nervous. Not the huge hawk
in and out of shadow casing geese, and not
the screaming lamb. My faith is in that photo
of some relative long gone. His black brows
fight the yellow fading of the print. I fight
too, but flabby enemies, just memories
of things I didn't like: the wrong hymn sung
on Christmas, tinsel on the cake, the awful style
of anything they bought. I don't fight much.
Style, I found out later, maybe here just now,
is doing things with strong hands right.

•

With no lights and no water and that ripe dung
odor through the door, why aren't they degraded?
Why not poor? Doesn't the blind grandmother
feel the flies that crawl her face?
Was life once so uncluttered I was happy
this unskilled? The father's strong hands mean
the wolf has no chance for the lamb, the hawk
had better go on flying till he starves in flight.

Italian Town Abandoned

No fish passed this way this century.
Town walls crack a little more when
big waves crack. The church seems tough,
too high for the sea and too far back
in rock for wind to eat. Of all things left,
the church will be preserved in ruin best.

Love, of course. From this high point
it's easy to pick out the secret routes.
Some girl, third house from the sun,
would run around the rock that screens
the church, run down the beach
where sunlight off the water
melts my look. She may be there yet.
He went back for mass and perished
with the town. Should I live here now
until my starving hands are beating
on what could have been the store?

Maybe madness is what builds a town
and storms are sane, the battering sea
that wrecks the town is playing.
On whose side is rain? A rapid plague
and dead phone could have plotted

all this crumble off the map.
What was the name? Decano? Veramer?
Gulls don't fly over here. If you
could see forever on that water
you would not sight land. No clouds pass
and no ship has this water on its chart.

Montesano Unvisited

With houses hung that slanted and remote
the road that goes there if you found it
would be dangerous and dirt. Dust would cake
the ox you drive by and you couldn't meet
the peasant stare that drills you black. Birds
might be at home but rain would feel rejected
in the rapid drain and wind would bank off
fast without a friend to stars. Inside
the convent they must really mean those prayers.

You never find the road. You pass the cemetery,
military, British, World War Two and huge.
Maybe your car will die and the garage
you go to will be out of parts. The hotel
you have to stay in may have postcard shots,
deep focus stuff, of graves close up
and far off, just as clear, the bright town
that is someone's grave. Towns are bad things happening,
a spear elected mayor, a whip ordained.
You know in that town there's a beautiful girl
you'd rescue if your horse could run.

When your car is fixed you head on north
sticking with the highway, telling yourself
if you'd gone it would have been no fun.
Mountain towns are lovely, hung way away
like that, throbbing in light. But stay in one

two hours. You pat your car and say
let's go, friend. You drive off never hearing
the bruised girl in the convent screaming
take me with you. I am not a nun.

With Anna at Camaldoli

Anna, that sea is tender but the land
below us flat hard yellow to the sea
is where we live. An ancient monk
is reading girlie magazines inside
the monastery wall, and unrecorded babies
are so crudely buried the amateur historian
who finds them will not be believed.

You're fifteen. Bells must ring magicians
home to stars, and crosses ward off meat.
No one is a monk. The world has only hermits
and though sea may welcome land
the land is men and seldom worse.
See those islands way out blue with bruises
and the cracked arms of peninsulas
that never mend. And watch the birds,
how once they leave the land their names
become obscure. You'll always call them seabirds
by the time they dot a cloud.

Days blow quick across that yellow flat,
raw from teeth of sharks and somedays
dazzling off the hides of dolphins
romping in a storm. Cloud and sun
and the remote gong calling monks to food
play your first grief out again
dark across your face. Whatever it was, Anna,
it could repeat. The sea repeats,
caressing rock into a tender sand.

Sailing from Naples

1

Once I said three gulls are often four.
Even the glint of my wake can't change
the bird count here. Naples climbs away,
committed red to cruelty, gold
to what endures. This year in Italy
succeeds that year of war. Streets are clear,
bullet holes in walls older than decay.

I was rigid loving what was worn,
land no one would farm, the brown
those buildings had become from threat,
a reek peculiar to defeat.
I was home in ruin, nothing,
and the acrid jokes we painted on the bombs.

When twelve I ran from love, afraid
she'd tease me to kiss, afraid of her hair
in her house, on the bus I took to the train
that took me to war, afraid of the air
and miles in air afraid for my tongue.
That was here. Italian Christmas
was cold, and we were cruel with food.

My hobby, staring east from home or from
the nose of a plane developed my teeth.
I bit the world in half, on the east half:
gold. On the west half: obscene fantasies
of east. Perhaps a mutual sun,
but in the west, every day a bomb
and every night red vengeance on three birds
remote as words—condor, rail and crake
bleeding in the dream. On the east half
never begging with a drum,

or tears or Naples in decay. Only
mansion, castle and the bright wide sky
Caravaggio ignored. For him, a man
from dim streets, what was lovely
lived in gloom. Down those streets today
I steal from the deformed. Naples climbs away
red for cruelty, gold for what is true.

2

I dwell on islands: Vashon, Bainbridge, Blake,
or Men-O-War, the dark slide of the boat
toward Seattle, gray in gray sky dying,
blind in light. Home is where
gulls reappear, repeat or multiply
in fog until your count has little hope
in salt air overtones of spooky horns.
Land must be somewhere, under offices
announced by bells. Of course, the river
yawning where you pass the flying horse
and Mobil red across the black
that wipes it out. It reappears
but where in shipyard lights the fog mutes?
Yards from where expected and a lone horn
blares you to cold terminals and beer.

I think I'll sob, insisting I'm committed.
Take me, Naples. Wait. My mandolin.
Good things come from dirt. My dirty arms
embrace you and you steal my watch.
Green for what endures: here, where Brueghel
caught a war, green blood twisted
in the tide, sail and cannon, crazy wakes
and two docks arms toward me. Wars have wars
and blond hair darkens after death.
Life lacks futility though futile in our pears,
a lot of stars in southern Italy.

•

But kelp whips twisted on the beach?
Forget it, man. If paint can dull a war
to art, if man can touch and not hurt—
I mean women—how the islands darken.
Tide is everywhere. The Chinese say
it's out, there, no whips left and torture now
is obsolete as smuggling or love.
Trust Montale and the *Libeccio*
to slam you home to dream. Trust
in peasants, Puget Sound and clams.

Take me, Naples. Wait. My dirty arms.

Dirty town of scream

committed hard to food.

3
Nothing is ignored but ruin,
far too common for the sea's concern.
One by one, the gulls, white
for life, gray for what must be,
unlock the bay. Indigenous sweet wops,
I see through your charm, your waving arms
and lies, warm voices, lovely cruelty,
clearly to your clean despair.

In my land only the ignored endure,
the wolverine, nameless streams the state
forgot to dam, ravines
with don't dump signs where citizens
of ghost towns dump their kissed debris,
sorry for the trash their eyes
will never own: all those photos lost,
the war we won, the oldest boy
who drank his way to prison in Tangier.

•

That rain in my face the night I ran
wasn't rain and her hair is vague,
wasn't night or my face, I say
to Naples climbing away,
red for cruelty, gold for what remains—
a definite number of gulls,
a land
where all doors open in.

The Lady in Kicking Horse Reservoir

[1973]

MONTANA WITH FRIENDS

A Map of Montana in Italy

for Marjorie Carrier

On this map white. A state thick as a fist
or blunt instrument. Long roads weave and cross
red veins full of rage. Big Canada, map maker's
pink, squats on our backs, planning bad winters
for years, and Glacier Park's green with my envy
of Grizzly Bears. On the right, antelope sail
between strands of barbed wire and never
get hurt, west, I think, of Plevna, say near
Sumatra, or more west, say Shawmut,
anyway, on the right, east on the plains.
The two biggest towns are dull deposits
of men getting along, making money, driving
to church every Sunday, censoring movies and books.
The two most interesting towns, Helena, Butte,
have the good sense to fail. There's too much
schoolboy in bars—I'm tougher than you—
and too much talk about money.
Jails and police are how you dream Poland—
odd charges, bad food and forms you must fill
stating your religion. In Poland say none.
With so few Negroes and Jews we've been reduced
to hating each other, dumping our crud
in our rivers, mistreating the Indians.
Each year, 4000 move, most to the west
where ocean currents keep winter in check.
This map is white, meaning winter, ice
where you are, helping children who may be
already frozen. It's white here too
but back of me, up in the mountains where

the most ferocious animals
are obsequious wolves. No one fights
in the bars filled with pastry. There's no
prison for miles. But last night the Italians
cheered the violence in one of our westerns.

The Milltown Union Bar

for Harold Herndon

(*Laundromat & Cafe*)
You could love here, not the lovely goat
in plexiglass nor the elk shot
in the middle of a joke, but honest drunks,
crossed swords above the bar, three men hung
in the bad painting, others riding off
on the phony green horizon. The owner,
fresh from orphan wars, loves too
but bad as you. He keeps improving things
but can't cut the bodies down.

You need never leave. Money or a story
brings you booze. The elk is grinning
and the goat says go so tenderly
you hear him through the glass. If you weep
deer heads weep. Sing and the orphange
announces plans for your release. A train
goes by and ditches jump. You were nothing
going in and now you kiss your hand.

When mills shut down, when the worst drunk
says finally I'm stone, three men still hang
painted badly from a leafless tree, you
one of them, brains tied behind your back,
swinging for your sin. Or you swing
with goats and elk. Doors of orphanages
finally swing out and here you open in.

Where Jennie Used to Swim

for Jennie Herndon

The Blackfoot bends, pools deep around
the cliff that bends it, and a brave man arcs down
yelling 'hey.' He splits the river clean. Foam
and his first wave die before they gain
the opposite sand. His cry and his exploded plunge
die in yellow tamarack high above her dream.
When she swam here, boys threw pine cones
at her bobbing hair. Tamarack was green
and promise, both in current and the summer,
hummed as warm as the plane she heard
but couldn't find hummed to glamorous lands.

Promise. Glamor. These thin out after
twenty-five hard winters. Jet engines make
no hum. Not one rattlesnake remains
for boys to nail on a weathered one-by-ten
for a parade through Bonner where
the girls applaud. Heavy August air
compounds the waste, the black smoke pouring
from the mill, the sunning girl reliving
the phone call from the hospital.

The swimmer climbs out chattering. This river
needs no calendar when tamarack turns gold
and someone, loved so much her final day
is rerun like a film each autumn
on the silver pool. The Blackfoot says: you lose
and rivers jump so honestly, even the rejected
cannot call them smug. A woman arcs
and arrows down the rock, her 'hey' gone ringing
up the canyon, her first wave fighting flow.

Where Mission Creek Runs Hard for Joy

for Joy Tweten

Rapids shake the low hung limbs like hair.
In your wine old fields of wheat replay
gold promises of what a kiss would be. In your face
a horse still flogs your face. Whatever is odd,
the Indian without a tribe who dresses mad
in kilts, the cloud that snaps at mountains,
means, to you, life at normal, no rest
from the weird. My obsessions too
ugly out in air and down the driving
water to the dam. We rest easy in these pines.
The run-off, lives or water, leaves us mute.

I fight the sudden cold diminished light
with flashbacks of a blonde, somewhere
outside Bremerton, her face my first sun
and I never knew her name. Was it you
across this table now, all centuries of what
all men find lovely, Mongolian and Serb,
invested in your face still pink from
the winds' slap and that sadistic wheat?
Money's in the creek. Gold stones magnify
to giant coins, and you poise gold alone
on rock above the wealthy water
and the sow swamp of some early bitter scene.

Kiss my wine and pour it down my tongue.
Pour it twisted down my hair. Protective armour
fragments in the creek's roar. You are right
to say the trees here grow too straight.
I am right to bring back all the harsh
bizarre beginning of the dirt, the long beat
of each sun across the cabbage, and the hate

that comes from nowhere, that's accounted for
in photos of ourselves we took and still sneak
looks at late at night. And we are right—
the coins are real, the low hung limbs are hair
and Mission Creek, this wild high run-off
in our mouths is clearly on its way.

Graves at Elkhorn

for Joe Ward

'Eighty-nine was bad. At least a hundred
children died, the ones with money planted
in this far spot from the town. The corn
etched in these stones was popular that year.
'Our dearest one is gone.' The poorer ones
used wood for markers. Their names
got weaker every winter. Now gray wood
offers a blank sacrifice to rot.

The yard and nearly every grave are fenced.
Something in this space must be defined—
where the lot you paid too much for ends
or where the body must not slide beyond.
The yard should have a limit like the town.
The last one buried here: 1938. The next
to last: 1911 from a long disease.

The fence around the yard is barbed, maintained
by men, around the graves, torn down
by pines. Some have pines for stones.
The yard is this far from the town because
when children die the mother should repeat
some form of labor, and a casual glance
would tell you there could be no silver here.

St. Ignatius Where the Salish Wail

for David and Annick Smith

It's a bad Good Friday, snow and mud
and mongrels in the road. Today's sky said
He'd weigh a ton tonight. A priest
unhooks the hands while Flatheads chant
ninety pounds of spices on the skin.
Another One, not the one they took down from
the cross, is lugged by six old Indians
around the room, five following with songs.

On a real Good Friday, warm and moon,
they'd pack Him outside where bright
fires burn. Here or there, the dialect
burns on their tongues. Elbow joints enflame
and still they crawl
nailed hours to the tomb. For men
who raced young April clouds and won, the pace
of reverence is grim. Their chanting
bangs the door of any man's first cave.

Mongrels have gone home. We slop
toward the car. Every year
a few less live who know the Salish hymns.
The mud is deeper. Snow has turned to rain.
We were renegade when God had gills.
We never change. Still, the raw sound
of their faces and the wailing unpretentious
color of their shawls——

Bad Eyes Spinning the Rock

for Warren Carrier

Spinning hymns downstream is fun. The worm spins
warm to German Brown, and warm to bad sight
Rock Creek splits the day in hunks a hawk can't count.
A fragment of a trout, half tree, half elk,
dissolves in light and could have been a cliff.
Current and a cross can blind a saint.

A good cast is loss of mills, of women
knocking five days following the burial,
words that never heal, silk organ droning while
the sermon crawls down empty pews, a plea
for money for electric bells. A cast is cold.
Nylon takes a life to reach the lunker caves.

Booze. The all night all day shack. Sneaking
home to rooms gone gray from piety
and calm. The Rock is ripping walls with horns
and down the cliff, jittering in blur
a hawk or hawks bomb scripture into pine.
A trick of wind: the deep flat run is clear.

All sermons warp with one slight knock.
Eyes are hands. Nylon sings and reassembles day
and day is cracked in silver jokes: whip and tug
and whipping rod, red ladder and white play,
a mottled monster ages down the net,
brighter than answer, big enough to see.

Dog Lake with Paula

for Paula Petrik

Snow air in the wind. It stings our lunch sacks,
arcs the nylon line. Being from the farm
you can take forever in your wild face
the boredom of wind across the boring glare.
On the farm, it's wheat. Here, water. Same.
Same blinding. Same remorseless drive
of yesterday and dream. A car starts
on the moon and suffocating caves
the mountain lion leaves are castle halls.

This wind is saying things it said at home.
Paula, go upwind to spawn, years across
the always slanted buffalo grass
and centuries past wheels that mill the water.
Deep in the Bear Tooth range the source of wind
is pulsing like your first man in the wheat.
It's not a source of wisdom. It's a wise mistake.
The wise result: pain of hungry horses,
howl of wild dogs in the blow. You swim upwind
so hard you have become the zany trees.

Look away when the lake glare hurts. Now,
look back. The float is diving. Deep down,
deeper than the lake, a trout is on the line.
We are, we always were, successful dogs.
Prehistoric beaches burn each dawn for loners.
Listen, Paula. Feel. This wind has traveled
all the way around the world, picked up heat
from the Sahara, a new Tasmanian
method of love, howl of the arctic whale.

To Die in Milltown

for Gene Jarvis

is to have an old but firmly painted name
and friends. The Blackfoot stops, funereal
and green, and eagles headed north
for sanctuary wait for our applause
to fly them home. At 6 A.M.
the fast train east divides the town,
one half, grocery store and mill,
the other, gin and bitter loss.

Even the famed drunk has begun to fail.
His face, fat yesterday and warm, went
slack thin color, one more eerie morning
off the river, bones of ugly women
in his bed. The timber train at noon
divides the town an hour into dying cars.
By four, all bears in the protective hills
hum the air alive. And should the girl
all drunks recall, the full one filled with sun
return, her teeth intact and after 40 years
her charm preserved in joke, the aging drunks
will claim they cheated death with mash.
Death, the Blackfoot says, but never snow.

To die in Milltown, die at 6 P.M.
The fast train west rattles your bourbon warm.
The latest joke is on the early drunk:
sing one more chorus and the nun you love
will dance here out of habit. To live
stay put. The Blackfoot, any river
has a million years to lend, and weather's
always wild to look at down the Hellgate—
solid gray forever trailing off white rain.
Our drinks are full of sun. These aging eagles
climb the river on their own.

Pishkun

for Jackie Smith

Looking at the model of a pishkun
in the Russell Memorial Museum
you have to think converging walls of rock
back and back ten miles across the plain.
The rest is clear: blind bison driven down
the cliff by Indians disguised as wolves,
and where the bison land, braves
with arrows finishing the twitch.

All for meat and hide. High priest crying
go down buffalo and break. The herd cracking
on the rock below. Scream and dust.
Five hundred tons of violence. Of silence.
A cry to women: bring the cleaning knives.

South of town, in a gulch of lovely
what I guess are aspens, frames of cars
are rusting and discarded shoes discolor
blue with mold. How many hundred tons
of lovers broke that mattress soaking
in the rain a bird shakes off the leaves?
How many, starved on barren claims,
could have used the glitter of those cans?
The world discards the world. Abandoned kilns
stunt the oldest pines. Thick brush
muffles the gurgle of a brook of runoff rain.

Charlie Russell, that fairly good, not really good,
sometimes good with yellow, often good with light,
never good with totals, total man, forgot
the world has garbage. He hangs
in a museum named for him, rare as bison
hung bewildered halfway down the stone.

Reclamation at Coloma

for Eric and Kari Johnson

This last estate of greed has been reclaimed
by drone. Slaves crawled down the mountain
to the cities, factories with unions
and a definite rate of pay. Without
indentured help, wells went dry and shafts
were left half dug. Exciting endings
of old True Detectives are obscured by worms
and no two shoes are mates. Only horseflies
prospered and they prosper still.
Bears will always leave tomorrow's meal.
For boredom there are only boring answers.

News thirty years ago remains mold-welded
to the walls. A lady, known to Butte police
as Al, has been arrested with a stolen truck
of beer in Boulder. Something about Hitler
faded where the rain leaked in. Housewives
faded from hard work and harder worry,
the baby sick, the gold slow coming
and the price of gold sung wrong
by men returning early drunk from town.

The drone is firm. Heat, a high prop plane
and insect hum reclaim five frames of cars
stripped clean of everything poverty could use.
Bedsprings are for singles. The broken sluice
could be the work of lightning or a final rage
and what's the difference now? Rats stay on.
The road out is the one the ghost took
years before his body quit and packed—
took off singing morning and did not come back.

Helena, Where Homes Go Mad

for Tom Madden

Cries of gold or men about to hang
trail off where the brewery failed
on West Main. Greedy fingernails
ripped the ground up inch by inch
down the gulch until the hope of gold
ran out and men began to pimp.
Gold is where you find it in the groin.

That hill is full of unknown bones.
What was their sin? Rape? A stolen claim?
Not being liked? When the preacher,
sick of fatal groans, cut the gallows down
the vicious rode the long plain north
for antelope, or bit their lips in church.

Years of hawks and nutty architects
and now the lines of some diluted rage
dice the sky for gawkers on the tour.
Also shacks. Also Catholic spires,
the Shriner mosque in answer,
Reeder's Alley selling earthenware.
Nowhere gold. Nowhere men strung up.
Another child delivered, peace,
the roaring bars and what was love
is cut away year after year
or played out vulgar like a game
the bored make up when laws are firm.

Not my country. The sun is too direct,
the air too thin, the dirt road packed
too hard. Someday a man
might walk away alone from violence
and gold, shrinking every step.

A small girl, doomed perhaps
to be a whore might read his early tears.
Let's read the hawks. She'll marry, he
go dry-eyed to the hot plain north
and strong, behind him—Helena
insane with babies and the lines of homes.

Silver Star

for Bill Kittredge

This is the final resting place of engines,
farm equipment and that rare, never more
than occasional man. Population:
17. Altitude: unknown. For no
good reason you can guess, the woman
in the local store is kind. Old steam trains
have been rusting here so long, you feel
the urge to oil them, to lay new track, to start
the west again. The Jefferson
drifts by in no great hurry on its way
to wed the Madison, to be a tributary
of the ultimately dirty brown Missouri.
This town supports your need to run alone.

What if you'd lived here young, gone full of fear
to that stark brick school, the cruel teacher
supported by your guardian? Think well
of the day you ran away to Whitehall.
Think evil of the cop who found you starving
and returned you, siren open, to the house
you cannot find today. You question
everyone you see. The answer comes back wrong.
There was no house. They never heard your name.

When you leave here, leave in a flashy car
and wave goodbye. You are a stranger
every day. Let the engines and the farm
equipment die, and know that rivers
end and never end, lose and never lose
their famous names. What if your first girl
ended certain she was animal, barking
at the aides and licking floors? You know
you have no answers. The empty school
burns red in heavy snow.

With Kathy in Wisdom

for Kathy McClelland

I only dreamed that high cliff we were on
overlooking Wisdom and the Big Hole drain.
I dreamed us high enough to not see men,
dreamed old land behind us better left
and we were vagabond.

We went twice to Wisdom, not in dream.
Once in day, odd couple after Brooks,
and then at night, dark derelicts
obsessed with fake
false fronts for tourists and the empty church.

I dream the cliff again. Evening. Deep
beneath, Wisdom turning lights on. Neon flakes
are planets when we touch.
I wake up shouting, Wisdom's not that much,
and sweating. Wisdom never will be bright.

Lord, we need sun. We need moon. Fern
and mercy. Form and dream destroyed.

Need the cliff torn down. To hold hands
and stare down the raw void of the day.
Be my contraband.

Three fat Eastern Brook a night, that's
my private limit. The cliff broke
and wind pours in on Wisdom
leaving false fronts really what they seem.
Morning Wisdom, Kathy. It is no dream.

Indian Graves at Jocko

for Victor Charlo

These dirt mounds make the dead seem fat.
Crude walls of rock that hold the dirt
when rain rides wild, were placed with skill
or luck. No crucifix can make
the drab boards of this chapel Catholic.
A mass across these stones becomes
whatever wail the wind decides is right.

They asked for, got the Black Robe
and the promised masses, well meant
promises, shabby third hand crosses.
This graveyard can expand, can crawl
in all directions to the mountains,
climb the mountains to the salmon
and a sun that toned the arrows
when animals were serious as meat.

The dead are really fat, the houses lean
from lack of loans. The river runs
a thin bed down the useless flat
where Flathead homes are spaced like friends.

The dead are strange
jammed this familial. A cheap fence
separates the chapel from the graves.

A forlorn lot like this, where snow
must crawl to find the tribal stones,
is more than just a grim result of cheat,
Garfield's forgery, some aimless trek
of horses from the stolen Bitter Root.
Dead are buried here because the dead
will always be obscure, wind
the one thing whites will always give a chance.

TOURING

Drums in Scotland

Trumpets. A valley opens and beyond
the valley, closed and open sea. This land
is tough north music. Green cannot hide
the rock it hides and if horizon softens
into roll, it is the terrible drums
you dream are rolling. It is a curved sword
carving gray. It is counter roll
to rolling sky. And you were never wanted.

Rain. Small windows muting light until
the living room was dull, a hunger
that would go on hunger for the girl.
No warmth in eyes, arms, anything
but words. No warmth in words. The cat
kept staring and the woman in the kitchen
banged about. What good words were you saying
that the small girl listened? You walked
two miles to visit every Sunday and she
always said come in. No invitation
needed in the country. You just went and lied.

That's a long sky there from Scotland.
Same gray. Same relentless drive
of sky and music. It is your dream,
that terrible rolling drum. You were never
wanted and she always said come in.

Chysauster

Only these stone hut walls record their lives.
We know: not Roman. We speculate them
pastoral and kind. We say the grass is modern
but this gross wind must have been here then
tearing their eyes like ours, blurring the enemy
that never comes. And without trees no love
was secret on this hill. Your hot glance
at a girl exposed you to the grunting god
they hid with cattle in the far hut you were not
allowed to see. Where did they suddenly go,
third century, before Penzance and the discovery
of tin? You have to shout your theory
in this wind and shouted it sounds silly.
Black plague comes back laughter and grass bends
obedient as ancient beets. The size of huts
implies big families or people so communal
they did not use names. No one's found a coin,
something that might indicate exchange.
You loved your sister and she mocked you
as you crawled the dirt toward her, your breathing
muffled by her cackle and the drumming sky.

Walking Praed Street

I've walked this street in far too many towns.
The weather, briefly: in Salerno, rain.
Same scraps of paper blown, same windows
full of girlie mags, the cheap gold lettering
on doors: suits altered. Come in and browse.
What happened to last winter? I am old.
What happened to the boiling oily girl?
The weather, briefly: in Chicago, bum.

•

I could sound cultured in the drab east end
or sweet in Soho, or in Barclays Limited
(so limited they don't cash Barclays checks)
gracious as I compliment the tube.
I'm learning manners. Thank you very much.
The money stops me. What is 8 and 6?
This is a town of jittering bitter hands.
The weather, briefly: Copenhagen, none.

Tonight I'll hear the jazz in Golders Green.
Tomorrow the Hampstead literary scene.
Next day, up river to the park at Kew
and next day, you. Ah, love, to feed the ravens
in St. James, and that frightfully stuffy,
hopelessly dignified, brazenly British,
somewhat mangy lion in the zoo.
The weather, briefly: in Palermo, snow.

The weather, oddly: in Sofia, luck
brought by an old storm to your window
and rattling off like first remembered hail.
Who's to know you fail and do not fail
and who's to know the banging storm within,
one wind returning empty to your soul
noon after afternoon. Love's possible in Bern.
The weather, always: desolate again.

You live this road forever and no love comes by.
The weather, fondly: in your home town, hurt.
The weather, happily: the same old dirt
you came from: in Seattle, you.
I've walked this street in lots of towns,
always foreign weather at my throat.
Same paper blown, same broken man
begging me for money and I overgive.

Somersby

Mercy Jesus Mercy
cries a stone
b 1586
d 1591
and Tennyson's brook
drones on

The Prado: Bosch: S. Antonio

Most men are rodents clothed. After fun
they mount pale fish and ride away, or lead cows
home to farms where every noon a wife explodes.
Saints do not erupt or disappear in vapor-trails
of life well burned. Saints sit bored alone
and play the old flood out again, complete,
completely sad, the river's flimsy green
buckling the home that might have stood a lifetime,
anchored by the woman's hostile face.
The daughter in the doorway, nude, expected nothing.
Crying love me to the swimmer was a gesture.

That huge face warped by failure, sun men or soil,
weighs on the saint, supports a second home
the river also ruins. Huge, yes and heaven
is white air. Hell is where you are, a table
bare but for the apple you don't want to eat.
A saint finds hunger holier than prayer
and life must be repeated empty, played back
every day, no variation. Sister must stay bitter
seated in high water, playing solitaire.
And rats must ride the winged translucent carp
into the ether, using their tails to whip
that little extra speed from fins before

oblivion's insured. The saint will live forever
replaying that watery hate day after day,
getting bigger until the picture
is a portrait. Even now his face outgrows
the woman, the explosion and the river.

The Prado: Number 2671, Anonimo Español

A little guts, self drama and it's done.
I understand you, two six seven one,
leaving the white fat town behind like that
safe in the moat, at every gate two cops
with spears insisting lovers on the drawbridge
chat within the rules. All bridges lead
to paths that lead to churches. The sea
and ship are so remote, to notice them
you violate the charm. Towers sparkle,
banners flutter clean. But in your last few dreams
rats nibbled at your arms. The king proclaimed
no peeking at the royal pornography bank.

The upper picture, granted not well painted,
hurt them. You, vertical spread eagle,
no perspective with your floggers
who admitted you were nice. You said
when men are dead, stars can talk to rivers,
glad clouds need never part. They said
what art. I say rivers run from towns
and torture out of paintings, why not man?

I'm plenty less than you. Call me forty-four.
Old enough to know what happened at the door.
They kept your things, said get out, die in weather.
Dogs will eat you where the only love's exposure
and there's dead rain between mother and your mouth.

We like it here. The drawbridge thundered down.
A cop said so long, friend—he wasn't one—
and you died quietly away behind a smile
you knew they'd find among your birds
and dogs, one dog crosseyed, ineffectual,
old, the other ferocious, black,
his teeth, the peacock and your hand
guarding your groin from the rook.

At Cronkhite

Light bangs empty barracks where
a corporal waits for orders
from the sea. The highest tide
since Caesar swept all wood away.
New huts are planned in China
and the urge to enmity
dries in wind that rips a banner into rag,
the wrong word from my mouth. Raw day
and cormorants are blazing over sand.

This debris is pure. The next girl
will come burning from the foam,
my name her checkpoint and my tongue
her navigational fix. It's official now:
the Army will return. This beach will roar
with cannon. Cormorants will dive
where sun began reflecting and the bones
of lovers shift with no help from the moon.

Kiss me wind and city white. The gate
is never golden and the green teeth
of a jumper rattle off the rock
each violent wave. My orders are:
find wood but don't invoke the tide.

I trust the hum, the next wave starting
from a continent of girls. I trust
I'll die but never Christmas day.

They'll say, he's gone. And someone:
good for him. The raw blaze of the void
might bring me wood tomorrow,
a hundred girls on whales all crying help.
I smile at China and memories of docks.
A dock here would be fatal. No rock wall
protecting piles from thrust and glare.
And what boat would stop here, sea whipped ladies
on the deck throwing me their eyes?

Upper Voight's, to All the Cutthroat There

You curve in dandelion wine and in
my dream of a receptive east. Windows
in my house are sanctuary and the four
hills east are fast with creeks
you live in. Why curve tornado from
the shade of cress or stone, why curve away
when I approach upwind, a bush toward
your home, that home of words in back
of any rock that pools the water dark?

I sneak fat and weightless on the log
you're under. I taste the chinese red
of thunder on your throat, jet spots
on your side that fade to spotless white
along your gut. What prayer brings you roaring
quick as words, unexpected, cruel
through gold? God is small. The wing
of eastbound liners six miles over us
is rigid as your fin when you don't move.

•

Such climb down. Logs left by the blaze
are hollow and I'm cut from crashing
through black crust. Vine maple, greasewood
and my past including last night
work against my search. And still I look,
certain you'll leave me, a bitter nun
starved for curve in my poem.

Taneum Creek

I don't come here after June when rattlesnakes
come out of caves and snore on stones
along the stream, though trout and trout remain
and I am keen to harm. Yellow bells have fangs
and jack pines rattle in the slightest wind.

The Gold Man on the Beckler

Let him pan. His sluice will rot and flake.
Here, the gold is river, coiling gold
around gold stones or bouncing gold down
flat runs where the riffles split the light.
With just that shack he built beside the stream
how could he get so fat? Where's the food from?
Why so cheerful with a flimsy roof,
no money and that crude hair in his ears?

What put him this far from the world?
Be out of your way in a minute. No cat
dies at home. Even as your spit lands
on my neck, I swear to you my bones
will not impose. Let the world have lovers.
Alders hide me and the crashing river
muffles any cry my other mouth might make.

•

If I could live like him, my skin stained gold
from this gold stream, I'd change my name.
I have to find a trout or something bright
but hidden by refraction, heavier than sin.
That's why today, my last day here,
while he is rinsing blankets in the river,
before I go that long east to my gold
I shout my best goodbye across the roar.

Cataldo Mission

for Jim and Lois Welch

We come here tourist on a bad sky day,
warm milk at 15,000 and the swamp across
the freeway blinding white. No theory
to explain the lack of saint, torn tapestry.
Pews seem built for pygmies, and a drunk
once damned mosquitoes from the pulpit,
raging red with Bible and imagined plague.
Their spirits buoyed, pioneers left running
for the nothing certain nowhere west.
Somewhere, say where Ritzville is, they would
remember these crass pillars lovely
and a moving sermon they had never heard.

More's bad here than just the sky. The valley
we came in on: Mullan. Wallace. Jokes
about the whores. Kellogg and, without salvation,
Smelterville. A stream so slate with crap
the name pollutes the world. Man will die again
to do this to his soul. And over the next hill
he never crosses, promises: love, grass,
a white cathedral, glandular revival
and a new trout, three tall dorsal fins.

We exit from the mission, blind. The haze
still hangs amplifying glare until
two centuries of immigrants in tears
seem natural as rain. The hex is on.

The freeway covers arrows, and the swamp
a spear with feathers meaning stop.
This dry pale day, cars below crawl thirsty,
500 miles to go before the nation quits.

Montgomery Hollow

for Stanley Kauffmann

Birds here should have names so hard to say
you name them over. They finally found
the farmer hanging near the stream.
Only insect hum today and the purple odor
of thyme. You'd bet your throat against
the way a mind goes bad. You conquer loss
by going to the place it happened
and replaying it, saying the name
of the face in the open casket right.

People die in cities. Unless it's war
you never see the bodies. They die in print,
over phones in paramouric flats.
Here, you find them staring down the sun,
flies crawling them like bacon. Wives
scream two days running and the pain is gone.
Here, you find them living.

To know a road you own it, every bend
and pebble and the weeds along it,
dust that itches when the August hayrake
rambles home. You own the home.
You own the death of every bird you name.
To live good, keep your life and the scene.
Cow, brook, hay: these are names of coins.

The End of Krim's Pad

for Seymour Krim

When they plan a freeway thru a city
they plan it deliberately thru places
you love most. They take out houses people
lived in years and people die in face
of the fear of loss. We call this progress.
We sweep their elderly bones out of sight
under the concrete carpet. If you have nothing
but a place to hide in, cage cave or kingdom,
a desperate paradise for the infirm, you lose.
You are the one the wreckers look for.

Fifteen years of Herman's various herds,
Cutty Sark and black whores curling on your floor
will not impress them. They will crowd around
and wonder why you're crying when the steel ball swings.
Some will offer advice: stay calm, attend
the church of your choice. You cannot tell them
wounded animals return to die in places
they found food when young. Good things happened here.
One black whore never ages in your dreams.

The building crashes. Plaster. Glass. The twisted
ends of toilet pipe. The repetitious phrases
of embarrassment: I'm sane now, sane and home.
No room you find to live in will be home. You drag
along the brute streets of this world, hunting
what we hunt, hurting when we can't. Stay homeless,
doomed to hound those human meanings we forget
every morning when gray light that might be
any time of day fights like a wounded dog
thru odors of used air, the whore beside you
purring in her dark expensive sleep.

Old Map of Uhlerstown
for Jackson and Marthiel Mathews

This map defines your home. The names
are coy bones now. The spillway's worn,
the floodgate stuck half-closed from age.
Under leaves that pile before the dam,
goldfish nose the surface for a meal.
This canal knows all, how style
must find a corner in the world
or die. You built that strong rock wall.

You commit forever to this charm—
bad luck in France—no money—fights.
If everyone you helped came here
you'd need a bigger map. From hills
behind you hawks fall suddenly as hate
to join you on the porch and chat
of cardinals and frozen waterwheels.

Lovers loved beneath that sycamore.
See them on the map, two dots on the lawn,
clawing as the sad canal goes by.
Wind is never cartographic line.
Real leaves fall. First blood of love is dry.
When wet it mapped a home that waited
sheltering the dead until you came.

A Night with Cindy at Heitman's
for Cynthia Keyworth

Outside: forecasts of humiliating storms.
We're both warm from Jim Beam and bad jokes

understood. One thing about hard wind—
no one fights in it. Loud air takes the place
of rage. You climbed a trembling chair
to see if you were lovely in the mirror.
Daddy's face was stuck there, blank and waiting
to be claimed. If you scream now as then
it will go unnoticed as the oaks crack off.

Storms are memories of old storms at the door.
Don't let them in. Just name them. I say shame,
the poverty, mundane and in the mind.
Hundreds of others with money next door happy.
You do not belong. When bells rang
your invitation to the wedding wild across
the lake, you had a boat and shabby clothes.

Hours of pool balls click. The liquor clicks.
The jukebox booms out fun I thought was dead.
My head is rolling full of ocean. You
are swimming countercurrent, your fin
resilient. You should have a weather
all your own. I've fantasized a thousand homes
to live in. You're in all of them and not in one.
Sweet derelict, your eyes spit
man's first bad weather back at it.

Point No Point

for John Duffy Mitchell

Even in July, from this point north
the sea is rough. Today the wind is treason
tearing at our flag and kicking that commercial
trawl around. We and salmon are beached
or driven down. A need to respond

to defeat—the need to go far—
A Cadillac blooming with girls—
is heritage the gulls who peel off now
across the strait to Double Bluff find fun.

Those cream cliffs miles across the sea
are latent friends. Seabirds are remote
enough to go unnamed, unnamed enough
to laugh a favorite harm away. Waves
go on buffooning and cheap stitching gives
and one bird is Old Betsy flapping north.

I know a flat and friendless north.
A poem can end there, or a man, but never
in a storm. The southbound tanker
cruises by unbudged by slamming waves.
Great bulk often wins and you and I
are fat and sipping beer and waiting
for this storm to rearrange the light,
for birds to come back named, with jokes
and for the sea to weaken, just enough
to kick back home on, never weak
as cream or flat as a summer lake.

Cornwall, Touring

for Marion Codd

We found the sea in pieces at Pendeen.
Sky was gray above our fun and loud
and rock split perfectly from rock to prove
the Continental Drift. Brazil fits tight
in Africa. We spoke one tongue before
we couldn't hear each other in that weather.
We found the sea in patches red from tin.

We found it white with fear along
the edges, black out deep with shags
racked croaking last year in the oil.
We saw bubble trails of nervous fish
twist through slabs of green, the alternating
gull and ghost of gull in sky
carved hot by lightning.

The dying young die slowly like a lawn.
That grass died wild, a suicidal dive
to pieces of Brazil. Water pounded rock
with favored odds and open tin shafts
played odd tunes we used to hear
at home when we were dying,
odds against the travel in our blood.

Farmers slide into wives the way
waves enter coves and bring us spectrums.
Our lives glint at us off those broken
bits of glass, stained windows
we broke out through, bottles of cheap wine.
We found the sea in pieces at Pendeen,
rock breaking off and rock homes far apart.

Shark Island

for Ann Jeffrey

Sun in our sails, our hooker wheels again
and again through the pollack school.
Our radio sends music through the village
you find sad, nine gray homes deserted
and no P.O. We toast our heavy catch
with stout. We lean back under a sky
wide as spread arms, sparkling with scales.

We are transported by our captain's hand
and breeze, are free and feel it under
those tortured rocks that tower and plunge
deep in green compounded by depth.
We are sailing an ocean and young.

The village nags. It dips and climbs, curves
by every pass we make through pollack
and it dies each time we see it. Where
are they? Were they happy? Did it hurt
to leave? We might grow old here, feed on
light from water and simple events—
the weekly boat with food from Bofin,
waving at hookers, pointing mute directions
on a noisy day. We might fake wisdom:
we have lived here long and understand
the urge to nothing, to a life inside.

Isn't it better, this wheeling, this sun
in our sails and the radio playing,
again and again through the school
with our greed. Monks get odd,
and without fans, hermits rage in caves.
Better to head for a loud port
where homes are loaded and the mail arrives.

The Tinker Camp

for Susan Lydiatt

Whatever they promise for money, luck,
a lifetime of love, they promise empty.
They beg us cruel ways, forlorn hand
stuck at us, pathetic face, or watch us
with dead eyes through rags they hung to dry.

They have cheated the last two centuries,
have lied and are hated, have stolen from
the unorganized poor. Even pans they sell
seem made of mean tin, and their wagons
gypsy as kisses you imagine when young.
Always the necessary, dreaded 'move on.'
They never park where we might picnic,
but camp on bare ground, just off roads
where dust from traffic cakes food,
police can eye and insult them, and access
to that long road out of scorn is near.
Our accent and our rental car are signals:
Steal. Beg. Don't feel anything. Don't dream.
They sleep well with our money. We
are the world that will not let them weep.

Cleggan

for Richard Murphy

The mackerel are in. Came on the in tide
inside the quay. Word went from boy to boy
and now they're trapped, a net between them
and the open sea, the out tide on the way.
A day of gift. The early out tide
left two sting ray on the flat. Two years ago today
lightning ruined the Martello tower.
The English ghost ran from Ireland free.

Boys throw rocks at mackerel and mackerel
go frantic up and down the draining trap.
Years of thick hands beating grief against
wild air that roared the hooker fleet to hell
and now a meal comes easy. We can wait,
drink stout and sing, certain
prayers unanswered all those years were heard.

•

Ireland is free. The young leave every year
for England and the bad jobs there. Pretty girls
stay virgin and the old men brag of nothing.
It's something to go on when life's as empty
as the sea of anything but life, swimming
way down aimless, most of it uncaught.
The mackerel are out. Went on the out tide
through a faint gap between net and quay.
It's an Irish day. A tinker boy, eyes far
on the Atlantic, asks why water angers
without warning and takes back unwanted meat.

Crinan Canal

for Arnold and Adele Tamarin

There was never danger in this black sad water.
Not one monster. Not one cruel event along
the bank. It was peaceful even when that carnage
raged up north. The plague passed by
without one victim, and if a barge
hauled contraband, the tedious rhythm
of its cruise always made the mean cop sleep.
The captain of the tug arrived from upstream country
angry: they still sing about the girl
who threw the lock gate open at the curve.

The danger is the world reflected off the black.
The peace of maple shade is doubled. Silence
is compounded until wrens are roaring
and the soft plunk of a frog goes off
beside us bang. Fields that never meant
a lover harm slant eerie, and the next town
promises no language or a stove.

We have followed and followed it down,
past farm and kiln, the seldom used repair shop,
the warm creak of rusted lock gate gears,
unattended locks and wild vines thick
as the quiet, and here's the end: the town
and stores sell candy. The final gate swings open.
The black canal turns generous and green
and issues gifts, barges, tugs and sailboats
to the open world. Never was a danger
and they float out, foam out, sail out, loud.

MONTANA

The Lady in Kicking Horse Reservoir

Not my hands but green across you now.
Green tons hold you down, and ten bass curve
teasing in your hair. Summer slime
will pile deep on your breast. Four months of ice
will keep you firm. I hope each spring
to find you tangled in those pads
pulled not quite loose by the spillway pour,
stars in dead reflection off your teeth.

Lie there lily still. The spillway's closed.
Two feet down most lakes are common gray.
This lake is dark from the black blue Mission range
climbing sky like music dying Indians once wailed.
On ocean beaches, mystery fish
are offered to the moon. Your jaws go blue.
Your hands start waving every wind.
Wave to the ocean where we crushed a mile of foam.

We still love there in thundering foam
and love. Whales fall in love with gulls
and tide reclaims the Dolly skeletons
gone with a blast of aching horns to China.
Landlocked in Montana here
the end is limited by light, the final note
will trail off at the farthest point we see,
already faded, lover, where you bloat.

All girls should be nicer. Arrows rain
above us in the Indian wind. My future

should be full of windy gems, my past
will stop this roaring in my dreams.
Sorry. Sorry. Sorry. But the arrows sing:
no way to float her up. The dead sink
from dead weight. The Mission range
turns this water black late afternoons.

One boy slapped the other. Hard.
The slapped boy talked until his dignity
dissolved, screamed a single 'stop'
and went down sobbing in the company pond.
I swam for him all night. My only suit
got wet and factory hands went home.
No one cared the coward disappeared.
Morning then: cold music I had never heard.

Loners like work best on second shift.
No one liked our product and the factory closed.
Off south, the bison multiply so fast
a slaughter's mandatory every spring
and every spring the creeks get fat
and Kicking Horse fills up. My hope is vague.
The far blur of your bones in May
may be nourished by the snow.

The spillway's open and you spill out
into weather, lover down the bright canal
and mother, irrigating crops
dead Indians forgot to plant.
I'm sailing west with arrows to dissolving foam
where waves strand naked Dollys.
Their eyes are white as oriental mountains
and their tongues are teasing oil from whales.

Ovando

Dust that clouded your last drunk dream
thickens in this degrading wind.
Sage uproots and rolls and ducks streak over
every day, reconnaissance, one inch
out of range. If you need meat, resort
to money, never charm. The weak ghost
of a horse demands false fronts, lean poles
to tie your wife to, automatic love
you and the town hate to make to clouds.

Not all dreams slide away. Not every river
travels south whatever maps might claim.
If you were mapped the color would be wrong,
no brown adequate for harm, no white
white enough for pain. The mountain
wise from battering ages of this wind
fakes a place among the hills. The wise bird
leaves each downwind chance for black holes
high in ice. You can plant yourself forever
and still wobble every storm.

Your life is sediment in your glass,
broken girls you never broke until
the world reissued storms. This is where you stop.
Even here, the women smell you out.
Wind this wild has always brought them freaks.
One smile a week will do. If dry air turns
what had been anger brittle, you
can fragment at pale leisure, one hair
at a time, one nose, one arm, all flaking
slowly until all of you is gone
except some silhouette, obese, passed out in dust.
Old women may have noticed but they say hello.

Driving Montana

The day is a woman who loves you. Open.
Deer drink close to the road and magpies
spray from your car. Miles from any town
your radio comes in strong, unlikely
Mozart from Belgrade, rock and roll
from Butte. Whatever the next number,
you want to hear it. Never has your Buick
found this forward a gear. Even
the tuna salad in Reedpoint is good.

Towns arrive ahead of imagined schedule.
Absorakee at one. Or arrive so late—
Silesia at nine—you recreate the day.
Where did you stop along the road
and have fun? Was there a runaway horse?
Did you park at that house, the one
alone in a void of grain, white with green
trim and red fence, where you know you lived
once? You remembered the ringing creek,
the soft brown forms of far off bison.
You must have stayed hours, then drove on.
In the motel you know you'd never seen it before.

Tomorrow will open again, the sky wide
as the mouth of a wild girl, friable
clouds you lose yourself to. You are lost
in miles of land without people, without
one fear of being found, in the dash
of rabbits, soar of antelope, swirl
merge and clatter of streams.

Montana Ranch Abandoned

Cracks in eight log buildings, counting sheds
and outhouse, widen and a ghost peeks out.
Nothing, tree or mountain, weakens wind
coming for the throat. Even wind must work
when land gets old. The rotting wagon tongue
makes fun of girls who begged to go to town.
Broken brakerods dangle in the dirt.

Alternatives were madness or a calloused moon.
Wood they carved the plowblade from
turned stone as nameless gray. Indifferent flies
left dung intact. One boy had to leave
when horses pounded night, and miles away
a neighbor's daughter puked. Mother's cry
to dinner changed to caw in later years.

Maybe raiding bears or eelworms made them quit,
or daddy died, or when they planted wheat
dead Flatheads killed the plant. That stove
without a grate can't warm the ghost.
Tools would still be good if cleaned, but mortar
flakes and log walls sag. Even if you shored,
cars would still boom by beyond the fence, no glance
from drivers as you till the lunar dust.

2433 Agnes, First Home, Last House in Missoula

It promises quiet here. A green Plymouth
has been a long time sitting across the street.
The lady in 2428 limps with a cane
and west of me fields open all the way

to the mountains, all the way I imagine
to the open sea. A three colored dog
doesn't bark, and between 2428
and 24 I see blocks away a chicken coop
in disrepair, what in the distance seems
moss on the roof and for certain
the windows out, for terribly certain
no chickens, and for beautifully sure
a gray pile of lumber in a vacant lot.

My first morning is cloudy. A rumpled
dirty sheet of clouds is crawling northeast,
not threatening rain, but obscuring
the Rattlesnake range. In 2430
a woman is moving, muted to ghost behind
dotted swiss curtains. She drives
a pale green Falcon. This neighborhood
seems a place where lives, like cars, go on
a long time. It has few children.

I'm somewhat torn. On one hand, I believe
no one should own land. You can't respect
what you own. Better we think of spirits
as owning the land, and use it wisely, giving
back at least as much as we take, repaying
land with Indian rituals of thanks.
And I think when we buy, just the crude fact
of money alone means we really pay out
some part of self we should have retained.
On the other hand, at least fifty buntings
are nervously pecking my lawn.

Ghosts at Garnet

Shacks are brown, big where things were sold,
wheat or girls, small where miners lived.
Some fell while we were crawling up the hill.
Standing shacks are pale. Old weeds believe
in Spring. The man with gun is good
on what the Chinese did. He'll go down
finding veins. A man who missed the vein
two feet was found by golden friends.

Pines are staking claims. Hard rock men
went harder hearing Chinese sticks explode.
The suicide, two feet from girls, believed
east eyes can see through rock. A hawk
was oriental, swinging far too silent
when the mail arrived. Five bars are gone
and recreation, violent and hot.

War drove them out. The latest envelope
is postmarked 'forty-two, the letter shot.
A pine impales the ore cart as if horses
left the cart, a target for the gunning sprouts.
What endures is what we have neglected:
tins that fed them, rusting now in piles.
For weeds all Mays are equal yellow.
Beneath our skin, gold veins
run wild to China. That false front on
the bar that stands is giving. Ghosts are drinking,
reading postcards, claiming stakes in men.

A Night at the Napi in Browning

These Indians explain away their hair
between despair and beer. Two pass out
unnoticed on the floor. One answers to a cop
for children left five hours in a car.
Whatever I came here for, engagement
with the real, tomorrow's trip to Babb,
the first words spoken 'white man'
split my tongue. I buy a round of beer
no phonier than my money is wrong.

Whatever story, I hear between the lines
the novel no one wants. A small aunt
whipped the brave who grovels now
in puke and odd hymns at my feet.
A squaw says no help from the mountains.
The Blood who stole her husband
breaks up all day in her beer. Children
drink us in through windows ten years thick.

It never ends, this brutal way we crack
our lives across our backs. With luck
we'll be soft derelicts. The next sun
is no softer, and I guess what good moons
must have said to them, some round white
ringing lie about the future—trout and kiss,
no ownership of sky and herds returning
fat from ritual songs. The moon outside
lights the alley to familiar hells.
And I, a Mercury outside, a credit card,
a job, a faded face—what should I do?
Go off shaggy to the mountains,
a spot remote enough to stay unloved
and die in flowers, stinking like a bear?

Camas Prairie School

The schoolbell rings and dies before
the first clang can reach the nearest farm.
With land this open, wind is blowing
when there is no wind. The gym's so ugly
victory leaves you empty as defeat,
and following whatever game
you will remember lost, you run fast
slow miles home through grain,
knowing you'll arrive too late
to eat or find the lights on.

Flat and vast. Each farm beyond
a gunshot of the next. A friend
is one you love to walk to, 28 below.
A full moon makes this prairie moon
and horses in a thick night
sound like bears. When your sister's raped
help is out of range. Father's far
from Mother and a far bell's
always ringing you can't hear.

The teacher either must be new each year
or renewed forever. Old photos
show her just as gray beside the class
of '35. Indians rehearse
the Flag Salute, and tourists
on their way to Hot Springs wave.
The road beside the school goes either way.
The last bell rings. You run again,
the only man going your direction.

Missoula Softball Tournament

This summer, most friends out of town
and no wind playing flash and dazzle
in the cottonwoods, music of the Clark Fork stale,
I've gone back to the old ways of defeat,
the softball field, familiar dust and thud,
pitcher winging drops and rises, and wives,
the beautiful wives in the stands, basic, used,
screeching runners home, infants unattended
in the dirt. A long triple sails into right center.
Two men on. Shouts from dugout: go, Ron, go.
Life is better run from. Distance to the fence,
both foul lines and dead center, is displayed.

I try to steal the tricky manager's signs.
Is hit-and-run the pulling of the ear?
The ump gives pitchers too much low inside.
Injustice? Fraud? Ancient problems focus
in the heat. Bad hop on routine grounder.
Close play missed by the team you want to win.
Players from the first game, high on beer,
ride players in the field. Their laughter
falls short of the wall. Under lights, the moths
are momentary stars, and wives, the beautiful wives
in the stands now take the interest they once feigned,
oh, long ago, their marriage just begun, years
of helping husbands feel important just begun,
the scrimping, the anger brought home evenings
from degrading jobs. This poem goes out to them.
Is steal-of-home the touching of the heart?
Last pitch. A soft fly. A can of corn
the players say. Routine, like mornings,
like the week. They shake hands on the mound.
Nice grab on that shot to left. Good game. Good game.

Dust rotates in their headlight beams.
The wives, the beautiful wives are with their men.

Phoning from Sweathouse Creek

I got three bulls and a native cutthroat, lover.
I'm phoning from the bar in Victor.
One drunk's fading fast. The other's fast
with information—worms don't work in August.
I found a virgin forest with a moss floor.
You and I can love there. Pack the food.
Sweathouse tumbles and where the bank
and cedar roots say this is where the shy cut
is, he is, and he comes lightning
out of nothing at your egg. Best of all,
the color. It could be the water, but the bulls
are damn near gold and their white dots
stark as tile. The orange spots flare
like far off fires. The body's tubular and hard.
Cuts are rose and peach, all markings definite
as evil, with a purple gill. The drunk
passed out just now. It's like a ritual.
They put him on a table where he snores.
They named it Sweathouse Creek because
somewhere way upstream from here
the Indians built houses over hot springs
where the sick could sweat bad spirits out.
That's the jukebox. The other drunk can't hear.
Screw him. This is August. I used worms.
But lover, the color, the markings on
the bulls and cuts, and that deep forest
and the moss—

The Only Bar in Dixon

Home. Home. I knew it entering.
Green cheap plaster and the stores
across the street toward the river
failed. One Indian depressed
on Thunderbird. Another buying
Thunderbird to go. This air
is fat with gangsters I imagine
on the run. If they ran here
they would be running from
imaginary cars. No one cares
about the wanted posters
in the brand new concrete block P.O.

This is home because some people
go to Perma and come back
from Perma saying Perma
is no fun. To revive, you take 382
to Hot Springs, your life savings
ready for a choice of bars, your hotel
glamorous with neon up the hill.
Is home because the Jocko
dies into the Flathead. Home because
the Flathead goes home north northwest.

I want home full of grim permission.
You can go as out of business here
as rivers or the railroad station.
I new it entering.
                    Five bourbons
and I'm in some other home.

Dixon

Light crawls timid over fields
from some vague source behind the hills,
too gray to be the sun. Any morning
brings the same, a test of stamina,
your capacity to live the long day out
paced by the hesitant river. No chance
you might discover someone dead.
Always you curse the limited goods
in the store and your limited money.
You learn to ignore the wind leak
in your shack. On bad days in the bar
you drink until you are mayor.

On neutral days you hope the school
is adequate though you're no father
and your wife left decades back
when the train still ran. You look
hours down the track. Perhaps a freight.
Only the arrogant wind. You think
the browns are running, hitting bait.
You have waited and waited for mail,
a wedding invitation, a postcard
from New York. You reread the book
about red lovers one more time,
pages torn and the cover gone.

On good days festive cars streak by.
You laugh and wave. Sun on blacktop
whirrs like ancient arrows in the sky.
Cattails flash alive the way they did
when lightning told them, die.
You catch the river in its flowing
never flowing frozen glide.

The small clear river jitters on
to join the giant green one lumbering
a definite west, a lake released.
Your heroes go home green. Bison
on the range are reproducing bears.

Hot Springs

You arrived arthritic for the cure,
therapeutic qualities of water
and the therapeutic air. Twenty-five
years later you limp out of bars
hoping rumors will revive, some doctor
will discover something curative
in natural steam. You have a choice
of abandoned homes to sleep in.
Motels constructed on the come
went broke before the final board
was nailed. Operative still:
your tainted fantasy and the delux hotel.

You have ached taking your aches up the hill.
Another battery of tests. Terrible probe
of word and needle. Always the fatal word—
when we get old we crumble. They wave
from the ward and you creak back down
to streets with wide lots between homes.
When that rare tourist comes, you tell him
you're not forlorn. There are advantages here—
easy pace of day, slow circle of sun.

If some day a cure's announced, for instance
the hot springs work, you will walk young
again in Spokane, find startling women,
you wonder why you feel empty and frown
and why goodbyes are hard. You go out healthy

on the gray thin road and when you look back
no one is waving. They kept no record
of your suffering, wouldn't know you
if you returned, without your cane, your grin.

Bear Paw

The wind is 95. It still pours from the east
like armies and it drains each day of hope.
From any point on the surrounding rim,
below, the teepees burn. The wind
is infantile and cruel. It cries 'give in' 'give in'
and Looking Glass is dying on the hill.
Pale grass shudders. Cattails beg and bow.
Down the draw, the dust of anxious horses
hides the horses. When it clears, a car
with Indiana plates is speeding to Chinook.

That bewildering autumn, the air howled
garbled information and the howl of coyotes
blurred the border. Then a lull in wind.
V after V of Canada geese. Silence
on the highline. Only the eternal nothing
of space. This is Canada and we are safe.
You can study the plaques, the unique names
of Indians and bland ones of the whites,
or study books, or recreate from any point
on the rim the action. Marked stakes tell you
where they fell. Learn what you can. The wind
takes all you learn away to reservation graves.

If close enough to struggle, to take blood
on your hands, you turn your weeping face
into the senile wind. Looking Glass is dead
and will not die. The hawk that circles overhead

is starved for carrion. One more historian
is on the way, his cloud on the horizon.
Five years from now the wind will be 100,
full of Joseph's words and dusting plaques.
Pray hard to weather, that lone surviving god,
that in some sudden wisdom we surrender.

Degrees of Gray in Philipsburg

You might come here Sunday on a whim.
Say your life broke down. The last good kiss
you had was years ago. You walk these streets
laid out by the insane, past hotels
that didn't last, bars that did, the tortured try
of local drivers to accelerate their lives.
Only churches are kept up. The jail
turned 70 this year. The only prisoner
is always in, not knowing what he's done.

The principal supporting business now
is rage. Hatred of the various grays
the mountain sends, hatred of the mill,
The Silver Bill repeal, the best liked girls
who leave each year for Butte. One good
restaurant and bars can't wipe the boredom out.
The 1907 boom, eight going silver mines,
a dance floor built on springs—
all memory resolves itself in gaze,
in panoramic green you know the cattle eat
or two stacks high above the town,
two dead kilns, the huge mill in collapse
for fifty years that won't fall finally down.

Isn't this your life? That ancient kiss
still burning out your eyes? Isn't this defeat

so accurate, the church bell simply seems
a pure announcement: ring and no one comes?
Don't empty houses ring? Are magnesium
and scorn sufficient to support a town,
not just Philipsburg, but towns
of towering blondes, good jazz and booze
the world will never let you have
until the town you came from dies inside?

Say no to yourself. The old man, twenty
when the jail was built, still laughs
although his lips collapse. Someday soon,
he says, I'll go to sleep and not wake up.
You tell him no. You're talking to yourself.
The car that brought you here still runs.
The money you buy lunch with,
no matter where it's mined, is silver
and the girl who serves your food
is slender and her red hair lights the wall.

What Thou
Lovest Well
Remains
American

[1975]

A SNAPSHOT OF THE AUXILIARY

A Snapshot of the Auxiliary

In this photo, circa 1934,
you see the women of the St. James Lutheran
Womens Auxiliary. It is easy
to see they are German, short, squat,
with big noses, the sadness of the Dakotas
in their sullen mouths. These are exceptions:
Mrs. Kyte, English, who hated me.
I hated her and her husband.
Mrs. Noraine, Russian, kind. She saved me once
from a certain whipping. Mrs. Hillborn,
Swedish I think. Cheerful. Her husband
was a cop. None of them seem young. Perhaps
the way the picture was taken. Thinking back
I never recall a young face, a pretty one.
My eyes were like this photo. Old.

This one is Grandmother. This my Aunt Sarah,
still living. That one—I forget her name—
the one with maladjusted sons. That gray
in the photo was actually their faces.
On gray days we reflected weather color.
Lutherans did that. It made us children of God.
That one sang so loud and bad, I blushed.
She believed she believed the words.
She turned me forever off hymns. Even
the good ones, the ones they founded jazz on.

Many of them have gone the way wind recommends
or, if you're religious, God. Mrs. Noraine,

thank the wind, is alive. The church
is brick now, not the drab board frame
you see in the background. Once I was alone
in there and the bells, the bells started to ring.
They terrified me home. This next one in the album
is our annual picnic. We are all having fun.

Saying Goodbye to Mrs. Noraine

And after forty years her flowers failed to sing.
Geraniums blanched. Her blue begonias lost
their battle to the dulling rain. The neighborhood
was dead and gone. Only lines of kindness
in her face remained and her remarkable
arbor, my thoughts of wine. I stood clumsy
on her porch and worried if she wondered
why I'd come. When I walked in her door
I knew more secrets than ever about time.

It turned out I remembered most things wrong.
Miss Holy Roller never had
an illegitimate son. The military father
had been good to animals and the Gunthers
were indifferent to Hitler when we stoned
their house. I remembered some things right.
A dog was scalded by hot paraffin.
Two children died and a strange man really lived
alone a block away, shades always drawn,
and when we sang our mocking song about
the unseen man, we really heard him beating walls.

The rest was detail I had missed. Her husband's
agonizing prolonged death. Her plan to live
her last years in another city south.

It was lucky you came, she said. Four days
and I'll be gone. Outside, on the road
the city'd never paved, gravel cracked like popcorn
and everywhere the dandelions adult years
had taught me to ignore told me what I knew
when I was ten. Their greens are excellent
in salad. Their yellow flowers
make good wine and play off like a tune
against salal I love remembering to hum.

A Good Day for Seeing Your Limitations

I wake, birds flashing on my lids. The dead
float off like sullen balloons and I climb
out of dreams where girls swim burgundy,
hair undulating like gills, and into the world
of real air, real firs bending only so far
in the rare morning wind. On page two
of the paper, the hour of sunrise and set.
The forecast is definite: no chance of rain.

The river that splits my town's inflated
near flood. Farms in the lowlands are fearful
and farmers resort to prayer, their cows oblivious
and grand in the pasture. The boy who loses
the fight will play the sneer of the girl
he fought for and lost, deep in his nightmare.
He will die daily in classrooms. He will find
coins in his blood. Obituary ages range
from 10 to 78. I lust over the knees
of the 4-H girls on page nine.

Maybe a coed I almost loved will return
today, to the school, abandoned by her husband,

nerves near storm, words searching my hand.
I have little to give. Just that durable gift
from Michigan, a century old, where a home
burned down and men from neighboring farms
pitched in to build a new one free.
They said, 'Don't worry,' and the dispossessed
stopped weeping and danced to ringing mauls.

The House on 15th S.W.

Cruelty and rain could be expected.
Any season. The talk was often German
and we cried at the death of strangers.
Potatoes mattered and neighbors who came
to marvel at our garden. I never helped
with the planting. I hid in woods these houses
built on either side replaced. Ponds
duplicated sky. I watched my face
play out dreams of going north with clouds.

North surely was soft. North was death
and women and the women soft. The tongue
there was American and kind. Acres of women
would applaud me as I danced, and acres
of graves would dance when sun announced
another cloud was dead. No grating scream
to meals or gratuitous beatings,
no crying, raging fists against closed doors,
twisted years I knew were coming at me,
hours alone in bars with honest mirrors,
being fun with strangers, being liked
so much the chance of jail was weak
from laughter, and my certainty of failure
mined by a tyrant for its pale perverted ore.

•

My pride in a few poems, my shame
of a wasted life, no wife, no children,
cancel out. I'm left neutral as this house,
not caring to go in. Light would be soft
and full, not harsh and dim remembered.
The children, if there are children inside,
would be normal, clean, not at all
the soiled freaks I had counted on.

A Snapshot of 15th S.W.

Burn this shot. That gray is what it is.
Gray gravel in the street and gray hearts
tired of trying love. Your house:
that ominous gray shake alone on the right,
pear tree bent in what must have been wind
and gray boy playing. The wind had a way
of saying The Lord Is My Shepherd high
in electric wires. That blur could be
a bitter wren or a girl named Mary Jane
running away from a prehistoric father.

The empty lot is where a home burned down.
Shriek of siren. Red on cloud. The suicide.
Every March, the orchard's vivid repair.
The good were quick getting out of here.
For others, the sea, a short mile on the map,
was a long way. Water was tattered
by the time they arrived, shiplanes out
clogged with kelp and debris.

The way out can be wild. Exotic poison
of rose thorn. Raw coyote for lunch.
The longer the gray heart took to teach

the heavier the thicket, the crazier
the plains and small towns. Lovers
forever foreign. Concrete walks replaced
crude cinder trails and cruel men
from another planet found a home.
When women crawled like dogs in the mean
beating sun, your gray blood warmed.
Bleached and tormented by steam,
a bird spiraled out of control.

Don't burn it. That gray is what it was.
Clouds are piling white above the sea
like phrases you believe. Echo of swallow.
Rings from a swallow tick widening
over the river and salmon refusing to mourn.
Deep back, out of camera range
the sun pulses on fields you still might run to,
wind a girl's hand on your ear.

December 24, Alone

Across the street my neighbor's colored lights
blink nervous as wrens. The street is treacherous
with ice, and on the radio between our all time
favorite carols, warnings to travelers.
The snow man in my yard leans headless west
and traffic is wisely sparse. A good night
to be in. Minus ten and wind. Black sky.
Ghosts in my fireplace attend me.

This is the night suicides go up. The Christmas
psychoses theory: Christ, the preferred son.
I remember a terrible man, cruel as weather
in Havre, and his timid children, even
today still cringing in their middle age.

And I remember my first bewildering urge,
a girl named Julia, huge, the form of her legs
when she twirled in a teasing wind, when
knowing I was turned on, she twirled home.
Across the street, children are opening gifts.

In this cold my snow man will lean forever.
He will never fall over. He will die at that angle,
his nervous system numb and his eyes
watery stones. The cruel man I remember
melted attended by dogs. His children are wealthy
and still repressed. They sleep with their money.
Julia twirls in the flames, in the carols
that leak in. Julia twirls in them.

Remember Graham

If we spend our life remembering what we love,
to be sure who we are, Graham endures like ivy.
Even if I were, and I wasn't, the poisoner,
nine dogs to my credit, I still might own by right
of blood the long poplar windbreak by the road.
If I were the bigot who ran the bar, September still
might die forever in the fern. Whatever's sad
about moving away is a replay in the throat
of some old deeper grief we'd rather forget.
Again, my car, not old this time, not burning oil,
dives down the hill I've hoarded twenty years
to Graham. All's improved. Fat dogs doze
in buttercups and the kind author of books
about peach trees waves from his porch.
And things are the same. Poplars sway like early girls
in dream and sun flushes the swallows
who ride thermals wisely into the world
of black dazzle and take their place with the stars.

A History of the Sketch

I learned this from the old: odor of lake
and crayola, odor of grave. Cycle completed
and locked. And that was another air, the one
with glittering kites, the one glittering music
from the dancehall rode across the lake.
Isn't it time again for the band to assemble,
trumpet to sparkle, drum to knock like a heart?
And isn't it time for dark women to jitter
through evening like bats, barely missing,
barely nicking the lake? Or should the first kiss
be the last, life from then on
lonely promise in the reeds where water tries
to lap but soft moss muffles the wash?
The blackbird offers no red wing of friendship
under the chilling cloud. Now, when I sketch
a perch and get the wrong green on his rib
no preacher hounds me to correct the color.
And empty days like these are full of time
to stare the color real until the perch
slips off the sketchpad into the lake
and darts for sedge. Bubbles of his going
bloom along the surface. They give off
definite odors hermits remember well.

Why I Think of Dumar Sadly

Forgive this nerve. I walked here up the long hill
from the river where success is unpretentious commerce,
tugs towing saleable logs and drab factories tooting
reliable workers home. Here, the stores are balanced
on the edge of failure and they never fail. Minimal
profits seem enough to go on one more day
and stores that failed were failures in the '30s.

The district failed from the beginning. The pioneer
who named it for himself died wondering what's wrong
with the location. Three blocks north the houses end.
Beyond them, gravel pits and Scotch broom.

The nerve I ask forgiveness for is in my gaze.
I see this district pale. When lovers pass me
on their way to love I know they'll end up hating
and fresh paint gleaming yellow on the meeting hall
peels before it dries. Whatever effort the grocer
makes to increase sales, he'll end up counting pennies
in a dim room, bewildered by volitant girls
who romp in clouds above his store. The family next door
is moving after thirty years to Phoenix. The well built
daughter of the druggist started sagging yesterday.

I think of Dumar sadly because a dancehall burned
and in it burned a hundred early degradations.
How I never knew the reason
for a girl's wide smile, a blue spot raying over dancers,
a drum gone silent and the clarinet alone. I hear
the sad last shuffling to Good Night Sweetheart. I take
the dark walk home. Now see the nerve you must forgive.
Others in pairs in cars to the moon flashing river.
Me on foot alone, asking what I do wrong.

Time to Remember Sangster

One of us would spot his horse, same white
as his mustache, and word traveled on warm air.
When he solicited orders at doors
we stole pears from his cart, that battered
gray board flatbed held together by luck.
He was obsolete as promise. His apples
felt firm green and his cherries were loaded
with black exploding sun. Those days

seemed ripe as women we expected to meet
under flowering trees when we grew up.

Summer and summer he came, he, the horse
and the cart beyond aging, all three
frozen ninety-two. To children
he was old as tears. We asked him what caused weather.
We asked him about future wars. He sat mute
as orchards abandoned to the heat.
Summer on summer our delighted thieving
went on until he died and summer went void.

They took me to his funeral. Open casket.
I exploded when I saw him, his mustache
touched up blue not looking like it looked,
his eyes shut tight as a canyon wall
of sand. They dragged me into the light.
Days I walked alone our street that empty summer
telling dogs, it's wrong. Thirty-five years later
in England, a place called Enfield, I saw
three white horses in a field so close to town
they seemed to not belong. I decided then
I liked the English. I never thought of him.

Again, Kapowsin

That goose died in opaque dream.
I was trolling in fog when the blurred
hunter stood to aim. The chill gray
that blurred him amplified the shot
and the bird scream. The bird was vague form
and he fell as a plane would fall on a town,
unreal. The frantic thrashing was real.
The hunter clubbed him dead with an oar—
crude *coup de grâce*. Today, bright sky
and the shimmering glint of cloud on black water.

I'm twenty years older and no longer row
for that elusive wisdom I was certain
would come from constant replay of harm.
Countless shades of green erupted up the hill.
I didn't see them. They erupt today, loud
banner and horn. Kingdoms come through for man
for the first time.

This is the end of wrong hunger. I no longer
troll for big trout or grab for that infantile pride
I knew was firm when my hand ran over
the violet slash on their flanks. My dreams include
wives and stoves. A perch that fries white in the pan
is more important than his green vermiculations,
his stark orange pelvic fin. And whatever
I wave goodbye to, a crane waves back
slow as twenty years of lifting fog. For the first time
the lake is clear of hemlock. From now on
bars will not be homes.

Again, Kapowsin. Now the magic is how
distances change as clouds constantly alter
the light. Lives that never altered here are done.
Whatever I said I did, I lied. I did not claw
each cloud that poured above me nude.
I didn't cast a plug so perfectly in pads
bass could not resist and mean faces of women
shattered in the splash. Again, Kapowsin.
The man who claimed he owned it is a stranger.
He died loud in fog and his name won't come.

Flying, Reflying, Farming

We are flying white air. The most pioneering
falcon of all is hopelessly beneath us.
Nothing above but sky bleached out

by the sun's remorseless hammering
through ozone. Our lives inch back below,
the farm gray because a cruel past, weather
or mother, turns the spirit gray. The oldest
daughter left one day for good. The first son
(how can I know this at this altitude)
is trapped for life. At best, he can only get rich.
What good reason could the pilot have
for suddenly pointing the plane at the sun
and cutting the power? I hear his
hysterical laughter all the air down
to rock. We implode into acres
of black we rehearsed every young rage.
Another farm, tiny as the attendant's voice
on the defective intercom slips back
beneath us, bright orange this time and home.
We are flying white air.

The aluminum creaks. The wing shudders.
We are flying rough air. Remember
the wing snapping back over Europe
(where was that?), the agonizing sheer
you saw in slow motion, the vomit
you held back with prayer, and your friend
spinning down fatal ether
man had no business in. Back at the base
you were sobbing fields away from the rest
and the shepherd in black offered you pears
and wouldn't take your money. You claimed
you paid him with tears but that made no sense.
The air is solid again. We eat our way north.
We are flying good air.

We have entered the pattern.
Power reduced. Flaps down. Seat belt sign on.
In a moment, no smoking. This is always

a major kind of return. Thirty years ago
we came down and laughed and shook hands
after a rough one. We congratulated ourselves
for being alive. Long before that
we were ignorant farmers. Remember the night
you came home cheated in town of the money
you'd saved to paint the farm green.
Your wife called you weak and you stammered
and wept. Late one morning years later,
drunk and alone, you remembered above us
air is white, and you knew your next wife
would forgive you, your crops come
fatter than clouds, old friends return.
We have landed on schedule. Reverse thrust.
We are safe. We are natural on earth.

Last Day There

All furniture's gone. It hits me in this light
I've always hated thinned the way it is
by tiny panes, when I leave now the door will slam
no matter how I close it and my groin will throb
hungry as these rooms. Someone left the snapshot
on the wall, two horses and a man, a barn
dark gray against gray light I think was sky
but could be eighty years of fading. Once I called
that unknown farmer friend. He stared back
ignorant and cold until I blushed.
What denies me love today helps me hold a job.

This narrow space I slept in twenty years,
a porch walled in, a room just barely added on.
I own this and I know it is not mine.
That day I found locked doors in Naples, streets
rocked in the sea. The sea rocked in the hands

of brutal sky and fish came raining from volcanoes.
I see the horses swirl into the barn. I hear
two shots, no groans. When I say I'm derelict
the horses will return to flank the farmer.
Again, the three die gray as April 7, 1892.

I'll leave believing we keep all we lose and love.
Dirt roads are hard to find. I need to walk one
shabby some glamorous way the movies like.
I'll rest at creeks. I can't help looking deep
for trout in opaque pools. I pass a farm:
it's home, eviction papers posted to the door,
inside a fat ghost packing wine to celebrate
his fear of quarantine, once outside, pleased the road
he has to take goes north without an exit ramp,
not one sign giving mileage to the end.

Places and Ways to Live

Note the stump, a peach tree. We had to cut it down.
It banged the window every wind. Our garden
swayed with corn each summer. Our crops were legend
and our kindness. Whatever stranger came, we said,
'Come in.' We ran excited. 'Someone's come to see us.'
By night we were exhausted. The dark came early
in that home, came early for the last time soon.

Some nights in motels, I wake bewildered by the room.
Then I remember where I am. I turn the light on
and the girl's still there, smiling from the calendar
whatever the year. When I'm traveling, I'm hurt.
I tune in certain radio stations by heart,
the ones that play old tunes like nothing worthwhile's
happened since that funeral in 1949.

•

When I'm in the house I've bought, I don't dwell on
the loss of trees, don't cry when neighbors move away
or dogs get killed by cars. I'm old enough to know
a small girl's tears are fated to return, years from now
in some Berlin hotel, though I seem to sit unfeeling
at the window watching it all like a patron.
I'm taking it in, deep where I hope it will bloom.

That is the crude self I've come to. The man who says
suffer, stay poor and I can create. Believe me, friends,
I offer you your homes and wish you well in them.
May kisses rain. May you find warm arms each morning.
May your favorite tree be blooming in December.
And may you never be dispossessed, forced to wander
a world the color of salt with no young music in it.

What Thou Lovest Well Remains American

You remember the name was Jensen. She seemed old
always alone inside, face pasted gray to the window,
and mail never came. Two blocks down, the Grubskis
went insane. George played rotten trombone
Easter when they flew the flag. Wild roses
remind you the roads were gravel and vacant lots
the rule. Poverty was real, wallet and spirit,
and each day slow as church. You remember threadbare
church groups on the corner, howling their faith
at stars, and the violent Holy Rollers
renting that barn for their annual violent sing
and the barn burned down when you came back from war.
Knowing the people you knew then are dead,
you try to believe these roads paved are improved,
the neighbors, moved in while you were away, good-looking,
their dogs well fed. You still have need
to remember lots empty and fern.

Lawns well trimmed remind you of the train
your wife took one day forever, some far empty town,
the odd name you never recall. The time: 6:23.
The day: October 9. The year remains a blur.
You blame this neighborhood for your failure.
In some vague way, the Grubskis degraded you
beyond repair. And you know you must play again
and again Mrs. Jensen pale at her window, must hear
the foul music over the good slide of traffic.
You loved them well and they remain, still with nothing
to do, no money and no will. Loved them, and the gray
that was their disease you carry for extra food
in case you're stranded in some odd empty town
and need hungry lovers for friends, and need feel
you are welcome in the secret club they have formed.

STRANGERS

Goodbye, Iowa

Once more you've degraded yourself on the road.
The freeway turned you back in on yourself
and you found nothing, not even a good false name.
The waitress mocked you and you paid your bill
sweating in her glare. You tried to tell her
how many lovers you've had. Only a croak came out.
Your hand shook when she put hot coins in it.
Your face was hot and you ran face down to the car.

Miles you hated her. Then you remembered what
the doctor said: really a hatred of self. Where
in flashes of past, the gravestone
you looked for years and never found, was there
a dignified time? Only when alone,
those solitary times with sky gray as a freeway.

And now you are alone. The waitress
will never see you again. You often pretend
you don't remember people you do. You joke back
spasms of shame from a night long ago.
Splintered glass. Bewildering blue swirl
of police. Light in your eyes. Hard questions.
Your car is cruising. You cross with ease
at 80 the state line and the state you are entering
always treated you well.

Farmer, Dying

for Hank and Nancy

Seven thousand acres of grass have faded yellow
from his cough. These limp days, his anger,
legend forty years from moon to Stevensville,
lives on, just barely, in a Great Falls whore.
Cruel times, he cries, cruel winds. His geese roam
unattended in the meadow. The gold last leaves
of cottonwoods ride Burnt Fork creek away.
His geese grow fat without him. Same old insult.
Same indifferent rise of mountains south,
hunters drunk around the fire ten feet from his fence.

What's killing us is something autumn. Call it
war or fever. You know it when you see it: flare.
Vine and fire and the morning deer come half
a century to sip his spring, there, at the far end
of his land, wrapped in cellophane by light.
What lives is what he left in air; definite,
unseen, hanging where he stood the day he roared.
A bear prowls closer to his barn each day.
Farmers come to watch him die. They bring crude offerings
of wine. Burnt Fork creek is caroling. He dies white
in final anger. The bear taps on his pane.

And we die silent, our last day loaded with the scream
of Burnt Fork creek, the last cry of that raging farmer.
We have aged ourselves to stone trying to summon
mercy for ungrateful daughters. Let's live him
in ourselves, stand deranged on the meadow rim
and curse the Baltic back, moon, bear and blast.
And let him shout from his grave for us.

Living Alone

I felt the empty cabin wasn't abandoned.
The axe, for one thing, blood still moist
on the blade. Then, warm coffee on the stove.
God, it blew outside. The owner, I said,
won't last long in this storm. By midnight
I was singing. I knew the cabin was mine.
Fifty years later, he still hadn't returned.

Moss covered the roof by then. I called
the deer by name. Alice, I liked best.
Winslow, next. Reporters came to write me up.
They called me 'animal man' in the feature
in the photogravure. The story said I led
a wonderful life out here. I said clouds
were giant toads but they quoted me wrong.

The coroner identified the bones as woman.
I denied I'd been married and the local
records backed me. Today, they are hunting all over
the world for the previous owner.
I claim the cabin by occupancy rights.
I pray each dawn. How my words climb cedars
like squirrels uttered by God.

Turtle Lake

for Sena

The wind at Dog Lake whispered 'stranger' 'stranger'
and we drove away. When we dove down that hill
and flared out on the empty prairie, home seemed
less ashamed of us. My Buick hit a note too high

for dogs at 85 and cattails bowed like subjects
where we flashed through swamp. The wind died
back of us in slipstream. The sky kept chanting
'move like you are moved by water.' When we rolled
into Polson we were clean as kings.

Turtle is a lake the odd can own. It spreads
mercurial around those pastoral knolls.
The water waits so still, we listen to grim planets
for advice. The beat of trout hearts amplifies
against the Mission Range and when that throb returns
our faces glow the color of the lake. This
is where we change our names. Five clouds cross
the sun: the lake has been six colors,
counting that dejected gray our lives brought in.

The old man fishing fills his limit and goes home.
The heron takes his limit: one. All five clouds
poured east to oblivion and from the west advice
is pouring in. This mute wind
deeds the lake to us. Our homes have burned down
back where wind turned hungry friends away.
Whatever color water wants, we grant it with a wave.
We believe this luxury of bondage, the warm way
mountains call us citizens in debt.

Late Summer, Drummond

for Ellen Skones

A long freight swims upwind. Each 4 P.M., the river
limps upwind on schedule. Angus doze beneath
the cottonwoods that flare and lean. The town beyond
the pasture, once a speedtrap noted for harsh fines,
now bypassed by I90, bakes the same dead gray
the arm bakes sheered by lightning from the tree.

The red caboose drags west sorry. The town drunk
staggers to the tracks and waves it gone.

With mean traps bypassed, no more fines to pay,
we're free to love the movement east, eastbound trees,
traffic on the freeway. Speed law: safe and sane.
Real speed: blinding. Real chance to make it: none.
Our best chance: love the leaf flash spreading white
above the napping cows. The town drunk knows
the world blurs, drunk or sober, and the world moves on
out of reach against the wind or with.

Boxcars full of cows go west for slaughter.
Underground, seepage from the river
ignites another green. The gray arm left by lightning
turns sheer silver in the rain. Real chance
to make it: none. Life becomes a hobby seen
like this from hills, the empty freight returned.
The town drunk waves goodbye to cars that flash east
safe as cattle when their dreams revive the grass.

Reading at the Old Federal Courts Building, St. Paul

The gavel hammered. The sentence tore my ear
and I went chained, degraded down these halls,
so terrified the letters jittered on the doors:
U.S. Marshal Detention Room; Court of Appeals.
What had I done wrong? The judge was marble.
The young girl witness laughed at all those years
I'd serve in isolation. The pillars smiled.
In my cell, I sobbed vengeance on their world.

That was years back, understand. The first fall
I had taken, the first hint girls might testify

against me all my life because I'm cowardly
and born infirm. And that was the first time
I began to understand my rage, the licensed anger
and resultant shame. Sentence after sentence
I went burning down these halls, flashbulbs
blinding as the prosecution evidence.

The renovation's clearly underway. Today
girls ask me how I started writing. I read
the poems I wrote in jail. Warm applause.
Autographs. Interviews. The judge died lingering
in pain from cancer. That girl who laughed,
first trial, is teaching high school and she
didn't know me when she said she loved my poems,
was using them in class to demonstrate how
worlds are put together, one fragment at a time.

Ode to the Trio Fruit Company
of Missoula

for Sarah Wilcox

See how the red name faded hard to sorry
on the yellow sign, and how the spur along
the loading platform's empty as a hand.
Most of all, listen to the silence, the nothing
that's behind those bolted doors, humming
like a note too old to hear. When Italians
move away, the air hangs silent as a pear.

Knock once. Then crack the frozen bolt with anger.
When plums dried in his dream, the office manager
brought all his energy to work. Inside, we find
the ledgers curled from sweat. The sickening odors

of some former fruit order us to cross the days off
on the calendar and wait, two life term prisoners.
The track stood barren just two days and crows flew north.

to Bigfork where the cherries flare. And if, here,
we must face the falling profit, the new way
apples are preserved, the failure of the railroad,
we should also know the vital way birds locate orchards,
we should also fly the stale air of our tiny cell,
poking the corners light ignores. The poor
feed well on those discarded planets they explore.

We are rich as tramps. Even in this gloom
a record shipment gleams and we cry *venga venga*
to a derailed train. In the supermarket
where the light is whole, we can finger lemons
for the right one and the price will ring.
Think how colors ring and how those loud pears climb
in tiers like choirs on display.

Old Scene

All the essentials were there, the river thin
from distance in the canyon below, the house above
the canyon and the old man pruning trees. Whatever
he felt left out appeared, the carnival band
in step on the dirt road, the road remote enough
to need a name, lovely girls asking directions.
The old man's house was the last one. After that,
the road forever in the sun. He looked down that road
every noon and nothing came—mail or flashing girl.
He needed a dog but that you couldn't provide.

In time you gave him wisdom. A way of knowing
how things are from photos. He stared long enough

to make the photoed live. A farmer told him
pears grew big in '97. Children danced at dawn
and horses, the horses ran and ran. You let him
ride one and you helped him learn which woman
in one picture loved him at the Baptist fair.

You joined him one day at the river. After hours
of trout you walked together up the long slope
where he pointed to his house. He said 'Come in'
and built a fire and you said 'I live here too.'
Some days, the road fills suddenly with clowns.
The carnival band plays every tune you love.
Lovely girls stream in. You are dazzled
by their sequins, and the odor of their cooking
makes you laugh. Other days, the road hangs
empty. Not even birds can raise the dust.

Landscapes

If I painted, I'd paint landscapes. In museums
I stop often at van Ruysdael, and the wind he painted
high in European oaks gives license to my style.
I move the barn two feet. I curve the hill down
more dramatic. I put a woman on the hill against
the light, calling me to dinner. The wind I paint
is low and runs the grass down dancing to the sea.

In no time I have aged the barn stark gray.
Obviously, my cows hate no one. My wife
across the field stays carved out solid on the sky.
My tossed kiss stings her through the waves of heat
plowed dirt gives off in August. My tossed worm
drifts beneath the cutbank where I know trout wait.
As long as wind is pouring, my paint keeps farming green.

•

When wind stops, men come smiling with the mortgage.
They send me the eviction notice, postage due.
My cows are thin and failing. My deaf wife snarls
and claws the chair. The creek turns putrid.
I said fifty years moss on the roof is lovely.
It rots the roof. Oaks ache but cannot stir.
I call van Ruysdael from my knees on the museum floor.

In uniforms like yours you'll never understand.
Why these questions? The bank was wrong. The farm
is really mine. Even now along these pale green halls
I hear van Ruysdael's wind. Please know I rearranged things
only slightly, barn and hill. This is real: the home
that warps in August and the man inside who sold it
long ago, forgot he made the deal and will not move.

Reconsidering the Madman

To him the window broken in the church
guaranteed oblivion. He ran out naked
in a record winter for Wyoming.
He said nothing's more heroic than a road
curving with the river warm away from farms
like horses curving into fog. He said a road
hardens like a man from weather.

We said good riddance to his crazy chatter.
One year later, we gave the day he left
a number not found on a calendar.
To celebrate the mayor composed a song
about a loving dog who killed ten snakes
to save the mining camp. We sang that loud
around the fire and we mocked the man.

•

Jokes turned into stories. Suddenly the lyrics
were about the fear of man, that man
most of all. Sweet Nick, we sang, Sweet Nick
(a name we'd given him), come home. The surface
of the river twitched from nerves. Swallows
strafed the trout in terror and when we screamed
old hymns our new church shook and broke.

Maybe he was right, the hope of roads goes on
and on. We found bones we think were him.
If not, why were they raving in the heat
and why would he head any way but south
where early every spring the roads suck blood
from rivers and the first chinook blows in,
blows in lemon and the yellow melts the snow.

The Cripples

Where were they headed, the one winged birds
tilted to compensate, dependent on thermals
to lift them over the mountains, and that annual blast
from the Gulf of Alaska to carry them far as Peru?
They seemed various ages, as much as 4,000 years
separating young from old, and they sang one song
with as many bold variations as throats. Their flight
was song and soaring. Through the county telescope
we saw they were various colors and shapes. Some
had belligerent beaks and others relied on the warmth
of their tints. Each seemed little alone. But when
we zoomed back and scanned, as a group they glowed
like glory children believe. We watched them
burn into dots, into nothing, and turned back
to our plowing as if they never had passed.

Invasion North

They looked soft floating down. White puffs that glowed
in sunlight like dandelion seed. And they landed
softly in the snow, discarded the billowing white silk,
formed squadrons based on types of weapon
and started marching at us, one drum rolling,
armor gleaming on their breasts. We tried to joke
inside the igloo fortress but we timed
the punchlines badly. Finally, the captain said
we'd better load. They were two miles off and closing.

They closed fast. The drum roared loud as cannon.
God, they were big. White uniforms and makeup.
Our mascot polar bear broke his titanium chain
and ran. The last order I remember from the captain
was retreat. I remember being alone. The wind against
my face. The walrus. Flashes on the horizon.
I knew without seeing it our fortress was destroyed.
And I knew somehow the enemy soldiers, those women
in military nylon had beaten us. I cried.

Of the entire garrison, I am the only survivor.
Lord, it's cold, wandering this ice alone. My radio
still works. The conquering women have offered me
the captain's skeleton, have promised amnesty
if I come in. They broadcast every day at noon
and again at nine on clear nights. They must think
I'm a fool. I've developed a terrible arsenal
in case I'm taken and I've stockpiled berries,
roots and dry meat, enough to last fifty years.

Cattails

It's what I planned. The barbershop alone
at the edge of Gray Girl swamp, the town beyond
drowsing that battering raw afternoon,
the radio in the patrol car playing westerns,
the only cop on duty dreaming girls.
When I walked in, first customer, the barber
muttered 'Murder' and put his paper down.
I hinted and hinted how sinister I am.
The barber said 'I'm sorry' when he cut my ear.

This is where I'd planned the end, in cattails
and cold water, my body riddled, face down
in the reeds, hound and siren howling red,
camera popping, the barber telling the reporter
what I'd said. And wind. Always wind that day,
bending the cattails over my body, bringing cloud
after cloud across the sun and in that shifting light
women whispering 'Who was he?,' and the cop
trying to place me, finding my credit cards,
each with a fictitious foreign name.

When my hair was cut, I walked along the bank
of Gray Girl swamp and watched the cattails rage.
When I drove out, my radio picked up the same lament
the cop had on. I tuned in on his dream.
They came to me, those flashing, amber girls,
came smiling in that wind, came teasing laughter
from my seed like I'd done nothing wrong.

The Hilltop

for Susan Zwinger

I like bars close to home and home run down,
a signal to the world, I'm weak. I like a bar
to be a home. Take this one. Same men every night.
Same jokes. Traffic going by
fifteen feet away and punchboards never paying off.
Churn of memory and ulcer. Most of all
the stale anticipation of the girl
sure to walk in someday fresh from '39,
not one day older, holding out her arms.

Soon, I say to no one late each night,
I'll be all right. I put five dollars
in the jukebox and never hear a tune.
I take pride drinking alone and being kind.
When I walk in, people say my name.
By ten, the loveliest girl in Vegas
swims about the room, curving in and counter
to the flow of smoke. Her evil sister
swings her legs and giggles in my drink.

When I'm at home, the kitchen light stays on.
Help me, friend. By dawn, a hundred dogs
are gnawing at my throat. My gnarled phlegm
chokes up yellow. My empty room
revolves tornado and my relatives
are still unnamed. A dozen practiced gestures
get me through the day. By five, I'm crawling
up the hill, certain I'll live, my Hilltop smile
perfected and my coin naïve.

Changes in Policy at Taholah

for S. J. Marks

They're denying whites the beach. The tribe says
no more casting for perch in the surf. No fires.
No walks under the moon. My instinct says we have done
much harm. The sea says nothing. The sea
has a violent way of cleaning the sand.

Be easy, wind and tide. The river's cringing this close
to the end. Ospreys dive to doom the salmon
or to doom. The undertow removes the bones
of preying fathers and in death the sea bass
pale out placid gray from black.

Even Indians pale. Spray flung wild as arteries
keeps draining human color.
The chief is white and dying.
Silhouettes of firs are black spears every dawn.
Bluebacks caught in tribal nets are sweating.

The ocean has the last word on possession.
The more threatening the day, the wilder
water's laughter. It leaves us sand to die on
and it leaves the bones it took twelve hours
every twenty-four before it takes them back.

Consider this a cry against the sea, S.J.
Grant the tribe its right to keep us out.
We'll get there anyway, even if we have to slant our route
like seabirds in, ranting on the downwind leg alive
on what the sea provides.

Indian Girl

for Bobbi

Days she looks at floors, a thick degrading cloud
crosses her face for minutes and I think of wheat.
And in what must have been slow days, I see a girl
packing dirt like makeup, preparing herself for years
of shacks and drunks, stale air filling morning
and the fire out, grease a soapy gray in pots.
You need a blind wild faith in crazy neighbors,
in rocket ships one plans to build for children,
the flight you will be taking in and out of stars.

Stars are not in reach. We touch each other
by forgetting stars in taverns, and we know
the next man when we overhear his grief. Call the heavens
cancerous for laughs and pterodactyls clown
deep in that fragmented blue. In that red heart
a world is beating counter to the world.
My sweet drum, be silent. War paint's running
down her face two centuries of salt. My skin
is bland. My pain can be explained away in bars.

Bad rains, I look for her. Look deep in reeds along
the stagnant ponds and deep in desperate ends
of boxcars. Someday, I'll find her huddled
fighting back the cold with tongues. My strong teal,
please know these words attend you always. Know years ago
long before you lived, I prayed for power of mind
to break these rigid patterns of the nerve.
And should it come, don't think I won't walk miles
of barren rails to touch you like a daughter.

The Swimmer at Lake Edward

He was crude as a loon on land. His tongue
drove girls away and he sat in taverns hours
and the fat piled up. Women and children
mocked him when he waddled home. Alone
in his rented room he made friends
with the wall and chair. He dialed Time
to hear a voice, and when the voice said 4 A.M.,
he said, no, that couldn't be the time.

He lost jobs fast. In interviews he blushed
and took the menial: watchman on the freights,
raking the ingot yard in the mill,
sweeping halls in the posh insurance firm.
He felt warm alone in his mind, no one
about and light cut in half by cloud
or a shortage of power. And he sang alone
in his mind, tunes he connected with rain.

The first warm day, he dove from the sky
into the lake we named for the king. We stood
on the shore and marveled at his wake.
When we applauded, he flashed away,
his dorsal fin the only point in the glare.
What was his name? We took home the salad
left over but forgot one blanket, a thermos
and the baby's favorite toy.

Ghost in a Field of Mint

for Sister Madeline DeFrees

The old man on the prison work release gang
hoeing asphalt followed us to Wilkeson

and those cyrillic graves, to Carbanado
and that one long empty street, Voight's Creek
and then Kapowsin and our picnic
in a field of mint. Wherever we went, old haunts
I wanted you to see, he hung there grim.
I ruined him with theory: sodomy, infanticide.
His bitter face kept saying we die broken.
Our crab patè seemed bitter and the sun.

In old poems I put evil things in Carbanado
where I'd never been because a word that soft
and lovely must be wrong, must hide what
really happened, the unreported murder
in the tavern, faithless wives. Clouds were birds
of prey. The cell door clangs before we know
we're doing wrong. The stern click of the calendar
damned us long ago to take pain on the tongue.

One day, alone in an asylum, I will find
a door left open and the open field beyond,
a wife beside that road the map forgot
waiting as prearranged.
She'll say, I'm crazy too. I understand.
From then on we will seek the harboring towns,
towns you never find, those flowers dying
certain the forlorn die wise. My sister,
we have been released for the entire day.

Iowa Déjà Vu

Did I come from this, a hardware store
in photos long ago? No customers.
No pleasures but the forced dream pike
are cruising hungry in the lake that glows
through oaks a small walk from the farm.
The church I must attend, hard dirt and plow,

sweating horse I swear at, all the hate
that makes today tomorrow.
Next farm down the daughters married Germans.
Girls don't like me in the town.

West of here love is opportune.
I get this from the soft cry of a train;
from magazines the barber lets me take.
West, it cools at night. Stars reproduce
like insects and wild horses sing.
Here it's planting time and never harvest,
nothing but the bitterest of picnics,
the camera just invented and in first prints
women faded and the children old.

Morning again. Morning forever. The heat
all night all day. The day of sweat
and heat forever and the train gone on.
It's where I began, first choking
on a promise to be nice, first dreaming pike
were hungry in the lake I didn't try.

The Freaks at Spurgin Road Field

The dim boy claps because the others clap.
The polite word, handicapped, is muttered in the stands.
Isn't it wrong, the way the mind moves back.

One whole day I sit, contrite, dirt, L.A.
Union Station, '46, sweating through last night.
The dim boy claps because the others clap.

Score, 5 to 3. Pitcher fading badly in the heat.
Isn't it wrong to be or not be spastic?
Isn't it wrong, the way the mind moves back.

I'm laughing at a neighbor girl beaten to scream
by a savage father and I'm ashamed to look.
The dim boy claps because the others clap.

The score is always close, the rally always short.
I've left more wreckage than a quake.
Isn't it wrong, the way the mind moves back.

The afflicted never cheer in unison.
Isn't it wrong, the way the mind moves back
to stammering pastures where the picnic should have worked.
The dim boy claps because the others clap.

LECTURES, SOLILOQUIES, PONTIFICATIONS

Plans for Altering the River

Those who favor our plan to alter the river
raise your hand. Thank you for your vote.
Last week, you'll recall, I spoke about how water
never complains. How it runs where you tell it,
seemingly at home, flooding grain or pinched
by geometric banks like those in this graphic
depiction of our plan. We ask for power:
a river boils or falls to turn our turbines.
The river approves our plans to alter the river.

Due to a shipwreck downstream, I'm sad to report
our project is not on schedule. The boat
was carrying cement for our concrete rip rap
balustrade that will force the river to run
east of the factory site through the state-owned
grove of cedar. Then, the uncooperative
carpenters union went on strike. When we get
that settled, and the concrete, given good weather
we can go ahead with our plan to alter the river.

We have the injunction. We silenced the opposition.
The workers are back. The materials arrived
and everything's humming. I thank you
for this award, this handsome plaque I'll keep
forever above my mantle, and I'll read
the inscription often aloud to remind me
how with your courageous backing I fought
our battle and won. I'll always remember
this banquet this day we started to alter the river.

Flowers on the bank? A park on Forgotten Island?
Return of cedar and salmon? Who are these men?
These Johnnys-come-lately with plans to alter the river?
What's this wild festival in May
celebrating the runoff, display floats on fire
at night and a forest dance under the stars?
Children sing through my locked door, 'Old stranger,
we're going to alter, to alter, alter the river.'
Just when the water was settled and at home.

Three Stops to Ten Sleep

Ho. The horses can water. We are miles
ahead of schedule thanks to cool weather
and a strong wind at our backs. Ahead
are the mountains where we plan to build
our city. Our bank will be solvent. Our church
will serve all faiths. We will pass tough laws
against fragmentation. Anyone threatening
unity will be sent to the plains to wander
forever. The plains have snakes and wolves
and much of the water is poison. Have the women
make dinner. We camp here. Tomorrow
we should be close to that forest, and the next day
we will find our place to live as destined.

Stop. It is farther than it seemed. No doubt
an illusion created by light off high snow.
Then, the wind changed and discouraged
the horses. They don't like wind full in their eyes
all day. I urge you to stop this bickering.
Remember, our city will be founded
on mutual respect. I urge you to accept
this necessary rationing of food.
Above all, remember, every time you frown

the children see it. Several already
have been crying and saying there will be no city.

Wait. The mountains are never closer. What
is this land? We lost too many last night
in the storm and those who remain
are the worst, the ones we hesitated to take
when we started back at the river. You
remember? That town where we first formed?
Those saloons and loose women? Let them grumble.
We are going on. Indians know
the right roots to eat and there's water in cactus.
Even if we fail, wasn't it worth the trip,
leaving that corrupting music behind
and that sin?

On Hearing a New Escalation

From time one I've been reading slaughter,
seeing the same bewildered face of a child
staring at nothing beside his dead mother
in Egypt, the pyramid blueprints approved,
the phrases of national purpose streaming
from the mouth of some automated sphynx.
Day on day, the same photographed suffering,
the bitterness, the opportune hate handed down
from Xerxes to Nixon, a line strong
as transatlantic cable and stale ideals.
Killing's still in though glory is out of style.
And what does it come to, this blood cold
in the streets and a history book printed
and bound with such cost-saving American
methods, the names and dates are soon bones?
Beware certain words: Enemy, Liberty. Freedom.
Believe those sounds and you're aiming a bomb.

Announcement

Tomorrow morning at four, the women will be herded
into the public square to hear their rights read aloud.
I'm pleased to sign this new law. No longer
will women be obliged to kneel and be flayed
by our southern farmers. This law says, farmers
must curb their mean instincts. From now on
women as well as men they use country water.

I'm sorry the farmers grumble. A way of life
is passing. But good things remain. The sun
still cares for the land. We still have our chant
that seduces rain in July. And women's tears
at the wonderment of tide will always be legal,
remainding us over and over of their depth of feeling.
Our laws have always respected women.

Let me remind you, by law we don't own the sea.
Only our Gods, the clouds, own salt water.
Our Bill of Rights simply assumes we may troll
Their blue property for pollack and mackerel.
When the clown-devil Nimbus plays dark tricks out
on the sea, claiming an occasional boat,
we pray to Cumulus, and He rumbles in thought.

In our wisdom we change what can be changed
and leave the other alone. We don't play around
with those inviolate structures of wind
that pile the souls of our ancestors high
on the evening horizon in luminous banks of gold
and the basic right we all have to die.
We grant stars what is theirs and fight misery.

For Jennifer, 6, on the Teton

These open years, the river
sings 'Jennifer Jennifer.'
Riverbeds are where we run to learn
laws of bounce and run.
You know moon. You know your name is silver.

The thought of water locked tight in a sieve
brings out the beaver's greed.
See how violent opaque runoff moves.
Jennifer, believe
by summer streams come clean for good.

Swirl, jump, dash and delirious veer
become the bright way home
for little girl and otter
far from the punishing sun,
games from organized games.

This river is a small part of a bigger.
That, another.
We get bigger and our naming song gets lost.
An awful ghost
sings at the river mouth, off key.

When you are old and nearing the sea,
if you say this poem
it will speak your name.
When rivers gray,
deep in the deepest one, tributaries burn.

Approaching the Castle

The riches we find inside will be in rich light
pulsing off walls of gold. For every man,
at least two girls, banquets featuring
Yugoslavian tuna in spiced tomato oil
and roasted Kashmir pig. A Sicilian liqueur
will leave us clear the morning after.
In the moat, five pound cutthroat trout,
no limit, no license required, a bait
that always works. In our excitement
we feel wind spurring our horses. The towers
ride high above us like orchestrated stars.

The drawbridge is down, the gate unguarded,
the coat of arms on the wall faded from rain.
Why is entry so easy? Why no sound?
We were told the court band plays heart thumping jazz
and clowns imported from France make laughter
a legend. Best we circle the castle
and think. Word was, the king would greet us
at the gate and roses shower from minarets.
We would ride in to trumpets and applause.

This winter, many have fallen. Supplies
are low. Those who came down with fever
headed back home. The governor sent word.
He advised us to go in, take notes and send back
a full report. We held several meetings
in the swamp and talked about entering.
Once, we decided to try it but stopped short,
intimidated somehow by the banner
saying 'Welcome,' one side
loose in wind and slapping stone.

Listen, Ripley

We quit that road of sad homes long ago.
Rain, too. That land lay better unmined
in our past. Pale gray fanatics died
like trout in mud. The cruel man on the corner
turned purpler than dawn. His wife became
a carving in the artifact museum. Recall, love,
how we set direction in our jaws and walked away
unafraid of roses. I still believe
the mother screaming 'Don't come back' was mine.

Wolverines we heard back home were mean
fell in beside us and we issued names for them
to use in the parade. There, in that land of banners
even obtuse statements of the local hermit
fluttered from the poles. Dawn came crawling
peach on high snow first, then lemon over wheat.
Hearts were checked for secrets at the door.
Those with none, you and I and some odd creature
from the prairie, sang noon free of charge.

We've been long in this country and we know the tongue.
As for sad homes, they were torn down.
Some nights, between two kisses I remember
some raw degradation in a gravel pit.
Remember sweat and blush and one old woman
in her shack alone, eyes
at her clouded pane converting shade of dead fern
on her weeds to lover. Remember how we shouted
when we passed her home 'Hang in there' going out.

Graves in Queens

The morning after a reading
at the YMHA Poetry Center

How long will these graves go on?
How long will my head ache from
that who's-for-loving booze?
Things went well until—but then
time's a damn sad thing—
time and the time it brings—
selection of a casket
in the mid-price range.

God knows I've curbed responses
in response to current trends
and practiced automatic ones.
Secretaries think I'm nice
except that one, but she—
This curve shows the cost of love
went up in late November
and where it intersects this line
representing the rate of pain
we call point kiss. A damn sad thing.
The stones go on and on.
Caskets must be touching underground.

Now we're welcome at the homes
of those who never spoke before.
Whee. Success. Money coming in.
Welcome at the homes of grovelers
I'm sure. Pigeons I have fed
found better pickings at the dump.
Molding apricots. The faded sign.
Big Lil. Dancer. On at nine.

Eleven. One. Last show. Last gala
strip-down strip-off strip-skin
show with count 'em twenty
gorgeous straight from Vegas and
above all clean cats on at three.
                    A damn sad thing.

From my room, a splendid view
of a statue of a stuffy man
who founded Uruguay, a land
I don't believe in although maps
still show it red below Brazil.
Should I say with noble waving
of my arms I'm free? Ah, liberty.
A gasper goo among nonentities.
A bone the dogs are tossing
to the dogs. Big Lil was a cat.
I believe in Paraguay, Peru.
It's the P that makes them real.
The U that starts out Uruguay
is not a P. UP. United Press.
                    A damn sad thing.

I never told you. Greenland floats.
Is often Africa when no one looks.
Has been Russia in its time and France.
Is never Italy because of snobbery.
I believe in Greenland. It's the G.
Gee. I'd give the world to see
that old gang of mine. A damn
sad bunch of damn sad things.
Lynn is less one eye in Singapore.
Winslow waits behind the door
that opens only at his feeding time,
a time time's sure to bring.

                    •

Last night what poem was it where
Joe Langland brought so many birds
down stone dead through the air?
And where did Claire McAllister
get such blond hair? And still
the graves go on. In Mukilteo,
Washington, the graveyard holds
twenty, maybe, all who died
as I recall by 1910.

I'll not die of course. My health
is perfect. I'll admit the jet
we're on our way to get
might crash in Iowa,
I smoke too much, and once
when thirteen at a seance
a spirit scared me half-to-death
forecasting I'd be killed
by rain. Such a damn sad thing.
And I'll select my casket
in the mid-price range.

The bus and graves go on. Millions—
and the lines of stone all point our way.
A damn sad thing. Let's go home to bed.
You didn't mean a thing when you were living
and you don't mean nothing now you're dead.

Starting Back

We were set once. When it rained, each man
got uniformly wet and our curses
rolled uniform over the plains.
Scarcely room for deviation or hope.
Each thing had one name. We aged unnoticed

by the day, exchanging only slightly
differing versions of our common fantasy.
Then, the mutant horses, sudden anger
of cow and glass, three-legged robins.
From that time on we put up houses.

That was (still is) when we started dying.
Windows got bigger. We made bigger curtains.
We stopped begging, took odd jobs
that paid well in vegetables and flesh.
One of us, whoever, invented the stove.
Another, love. Then our gradual discovery
of seasons, four names accounting
for the way trees looked, the relative warmth
of the wind. Copper in time. Tin. Gold.
After that, only some of us seemed right.

On beaches now we wonder what to do
about the vanishing dogfish. In hallways
we have learned to say hello, wear clothes
others approve of or cloth to irritate.
Some of us are starting back, tearing down
the factories, designing on purpose
flimsy tents. It will take long. Dragons
in the hills and sensual cousins wait
at the end. Someday, we will know for sure
we are alone. The world is flat
and the urge in the groin comes at 4 P.M.
Shoes are the last thing we will abandon.

Keokuk

Sky was glowering so thick that day in Keokuk
I knew none of us is loved. The town seemed
one long mill. The mill seemed old as mountains,

dark alps I remember in the war, dim air
full of bombers and the land beneath
a map of land from altitude.
The color made me cold. The homes that nothing
I was certain happened in stood mute so long
I imagined bad things happened in some mind.

I'm sure I saw a river there. I always am.
Even in desert where the parched town stands
abandoned to a spatial flow. If my
memory hoards decrepit boats it also still loves
clustered salmon climbing the Duwamish foggy dawn.
I hear the salmon roll the air and slip
back in. I hear the lost tug tooting 'help'
at Alki Point. When high tide creaks, the ray
of hope piles up like seawalls in the fog.

My Montana plates are signals. Yes, it's true
about the hunting. Better still, the mountains
wild with names. My favorite range: The Crazies.
Mad land opens where you run. Your gaze
must give the rescue team a chance to grow
on the horizon, framed in gold. How eagles
shift above me in the canyons. How Indians
remind me of the cattails I once fashioned
into arrows. I shot them at a friend and hid.

Listen, friends in war, dear salmon, dear old friends,
batter the factory down and live with famine,
your light heads cruising through the rubble,
Keokuk destroyed by bad prayers in the raid.
I've toured Seattle postwar days like this,
the districts indistinct, and aged girls giving way
to teen-age duplicates, my hair the color
I was frightened of in war. The ones who died
ride with me. They sing raw anthems you can't hear.

Topographical Map

Good morning. The horses are ready. The trail
will take us past the final alpine fir
to women so rare they are found only above
the snow line. Even high altitude trout,
the California Golden, find them exciting.
Flowers bloom so colorful there the colors
demand a new spectrum, and wolves turned yellow
in that arid atmosphere howl like angels
every dawn. You have a question? The region
was discovered by pioneers who floated
their findings on stars down to the flats.

If you stay a week in that dry dispassionate air
your thoughts go dreamy. Girls you like best
drift in the sky to music. When they hover
close enough to touch the music gets loud.
Young, you loved those tunes. Old, you will love
those odd breaks in time when memory sings
in your groin and girls in pairs are replayed
fighting like cats for your love, on clouds
in the valleys below. You'll ride those times
higher than song and magic arrow, and ride
the avalanche down to withering routine.

You were coward going in.
Nothing has changed. Alpine fir has all
but disappeared in our blinding progress.
The rest was infantile mouthing. I'm coward too.
The original settlers left no record but tears.
They wept on earth where it counts. They pointed
a vague hand west and we took it from there,
and here's where we are. If I were strong
I'd call those horses out again. The real
is born in rant and the actor's gesture.

Good morning. The horses are ready. The souls
of unique animals and girls above the moisture
wave hello when you come into view.

My Buddy

This then buddy is the blue routine.
You chased a fox one noon.
She hid in a golden rain.
You ran through the gold until
a rainy chill.
If that's it buddy it's a bleak routine.
What happened to you there
may never happen again.

So say buddy it is a bleak routine.
The word caves in your skull.
All eyes give you chill.
The fox shows up on the moon
on the horizon, laughing you blind
painting the routine orange.
What happens to you now
happens again.

Say you deserve it. That's a good routine.
I'm nothing, see,
to the storming worms.
The fox died warm in ground.
Now she's gone tell what a bitch she was
loud in a red routine
and say it never happened to you.
Don't show no pain.

Sweet dear buddy it's a gray routine.
A girl rode in off the prairie

a very snuggly cuddly
had a neat twitch coming in
ran off with another man.
Sorry buddy for the brute routine.
For you it can never happen
over and over again.

One rain more and glory afternoon
complete with gin
and trees gone nuts in the gale
that's always whipping even in heat
when you sweat like the dog you are
when you sweat and swear at me buddy
in my underwear
hoping I have your hair.

Boogie boogie buddy. Scarey boo.
Here's a foxy ghost for you.
One with a heart big as a smirk
and a hot toe in your ear.
You're still my buddy
aren't you?
Sorry. A bizarre machine.
Stay away from my gears.

Hell old buddy back to the routine.
I mean routine routine.
The time clock tied to your dong.
The same bitch punching your card
that very snuggly cuddly
off with another man.
Someday buddy you'll say the wrong thing.
We'll never be friends again.

What to do blue buddy now you're gone?
Sing a song? Sing of a lost routine?

Buddy on skins and me in my cups
crying play it, play it again.
No sense losing a tear to the floor
with a mug of beer in your hand
and the blind proprietor yelling
go on, buddy, go on.

The Art of Poetry

The man in the moon was better not a man.
Think, sad Raymond, how you glare across
the sea, hating the invisible near east
and your wife's hysteria. You'll always be here,
rain or gloom, painting a private Syria,
preferred dimensions of girls. Outside, gulls
scar across your fantasy. Rifled spray on glass
unfocuses the goats you stock on the horizon,
laddering blue like dolphins, looping over the sun.
Better the moon you need. Better not a man.
Sad Raymond, twice a day the tide comes in.

Envy your homemade heroes when the tide is low,
laughing their spades at clams, drinking a breezy beer
in breeze from Asia Minor, in those far far
principalities they've been, their tall wives elegant
in audience with kings. And envy that despairing man
you found one morning sobbing on a log,
babbling about a stuffed heart in Wyoming.
Don't think, Raymond, they'd respond to what's
inside you every minute, crawling slow as tide.
Better not tell them. Better the man you seem.
Sad Raymond, twice a night the tide comes in.

Think once how good you dreamed. The way you hummed
a melody from Norway when that summer storm

came battering the alders, turning the silver
underside of leaves toward the moon. And think,
sad Raymond, of the wrong way maturation came.
Wanting only those women you despised, imitating
the voice of every man you envied. The slow walk
home alone. Pause at door. The screaming kitchen.
And every day this window, loathing the real horizon.
That's what you are. Better the man you are.
Sad Raymond, twice a day the tide comes in.

All's in a name. What if you were Fred. Then none
of this need happen. What, sad Raymond, if
in your will you leave your tongue and tear ducts
to a transplant hospital. There's your motive
for trailing goats to Borneo, goats that suddenly
are real, outdistancing the quick shark
in the quarter mile and singing Home Sweet Home.
Motive, but no blood. Sad. Sad. The salty fusillade
obscures once more your raging playfield.
Better behind the glass. Better the man you were.
Sad Raymond, twice a night the tide comes in.

Sad Raymond, twice a lifetime the tyrant moon
loses control. Tides are run by starfish
and those charts you study mornings on your wall
are meaningless as tide. The near east isn't near
or east and Fred was an infant in your neighborhood
devoured by a dog. Those days you walk the beach
looking for that man who's pure in his despair.
He's never there. A real man walks the moon
and you can't see him. The moon is cavalier.
Better to search your sadness for the man.
Sad Raymond, twice a moment tides come in.

31 Letters and 13 Dreams

[1977]

Letter to Kizer from Seattle

Dear Condor: Much thanks for that telephonic support
from North Carolina when I suddenly went ape
in the Iowa tulips. Lord, but I'm ashamed.
I was afraid, it seemed, according to the doctor
of impending success, winning some poetry prizes
or getting a wet kiss. The more popular I got,
the softer the soft cry in my head: Don't believe them.
You were never good. Then I broke and proved it.
Ten successive days I alienated women
I liked best. I told a coed why her poems were bad
(they weren't) and didn't understand a word I said.
Really warped. The phrase "I'll be all right"
came out too many unsolicited times. I'm o.k. now.
I'm back at the primal source of poems: wind, sea
and rain, the market and the salmon. Speaking
of the market, they're having a vital election here.
Save the market? Tear it down? The forces of evil
maintain they're trying to save it too, obscuring,
of course, the issue. The forces of righteousness,
me and my friends, are praying for a storm, one
of those grim dark rolling southwest downpours
that will leave the electorate sane. I'm the last poet
to teach the Roethke chair under Heilman.
He's retiring after 23 years. Most of the old gang
is gone. Sol Katz is aging. Who isn't? It's close now
to the end of summer and would you believe it
I've ignored the Blue Moon. I did go to White Center,
you know, my home town, and the people there,

many are the same, but also aging, balding, remarkably
polite and calm. A man whose name escapes me
said he thinks he had known me, the boy who went alone
to Longfellow Creek and who laughed and cried
for no reason. The city is huge, maybe three quarters
of a million and lots of crime. They are indicting
the former chief of police. Sorry to be so rambling.
I eat lunch with J. Hillis Miller, brilliant and nice
as they come, in the faculty club, overlooking the lake,
much of it now filled in. And I tour old haunts,
been twice to Kapowsin. One trout. One perch. One poem.
Take care, oh wisest of condors. Love. Dick. Thanks again.

Letter to Bell from Missoula

Dear Marvin: Months since I left broke down and sobbing
in the parking lot, grateful for the depth
of your understanding and since then I've been treated
in Seattle and I'm in control like Genghis Khan.
That was a hairy one, the drive west, my nerves so strung
I couldn't sign a recognizable name on credit slips.
And those station attendants' looks. Until Sheridan
I took the most degenerate motels I saw because they seemed
to be where I belonged. I found my way by instinct
to bad restaurants and managed to degrade myself
in front of waitresses so dumb I damn near offered them
lessons in expression of disdain. Now, it's all a blur.
Iowa. South Dakota. Wyoming. Lots of troublesome déja vu
in towns I'd seen or never seen before. It's snowing
in Missoula, has been off and on for days but no fierce winds
and no regrets. I'm living alone in a house I bought,
last payment due 2001. Yesterday, a religious nut
came to the door and offered me unqualified salvation
if I took a year's subscription to Essential Sun Beam.
I told him I was Taoist and he went away. Today,
a funny dog, half dachshund, waddles through my yard.

A neighbor boy, Bud, poor, shovels my walk for a dollar
and on the radio a break is predicted. A voice is saying,
periods of sun tomorrow, a high front from the coast.
For no reason, I keep remembering my first woman
and how I said afterward happy, so that's what you do.
I think of you and Dorothy. Stay healthy. Love. Dick.

Letter to Sister Madeline from Iowa City

Dear Madeline: I'm getting strange when I drink. In Solon
I take a booth alone in the back and play old tunes
on the juke box, trying, I suppose, to feel some way
I felt when I was young. But things keep breaking in.
For instance, last night they had a live band and single
women from surrounding farms kept asking me to dance.
I wanted them to go away. I'm drunk, I said. I don't know
how to dance, and kept trying to remember every time
a woman did me wrong. I wanted to scream at the women,
leave me alone. Can't you see, I'm rotten. Go dance
with decent farm hands. I don't remember dancing
but I know I danced. Outside of these odd moments
I am doing well. Marvin Bell is fun to work with. The load
is light. No complaints except for weather. In the west
where we have mountains, we can always assume that hidden
from us but coming is something better. Here, no illusion.
The weather, seldom good, goes on forever. It covers
a dozen states. For instance, if it's lousy like usual
in Cincinnati, it is equally lousy here in Iowa City.
That's what's getting me down. At night in my trailer home
I drink alone into the early hours listening to Chicago
on the radio, a sentimental all night station. Last night
they featured Benny Goodman. And I think over and over
of a hundred rejections at the hands of merciless women.
And of women leaving. I think some days I should be like you
and embrace a religion, and hope to create for myself
a definite stance that keeps people away while I keep looking

for my real disposition, and not go to bed starving like I do,
bitter and plotting revenge. I have a plan, not serious,
for killing myself and leaving behind a beautiful note
in red paint on the ceiling, worded so the words would crawl
in the ears of women I have known like an ultrasonic hum.
And they would go mad, my life forever on their hands,
my words forever in their brains. The trouble with that plan—
they don't print the contents of suicide notes in the papers.
A conspiracy to discourage poets and drunks. And besides,
I happen to like Benny Goodman and booze, and maybe
tomorrow they'll play him again. A report says in Cincinnati
it's clearing. About time. Five A.M., and I'm wobbling off
to a dream of sea nymphs issued by the sea. Love always. Dick.

In Your Fugitive Dream

Though Tuesday, 11 A.M., the shops are locked.
You try the meat store. Only the muffled buzz
of a fly inside. You rattle the glass
of the drugstore, yelling "I have a prescription."
A 40-watt bulb burns over the soda fountain.
You think, when you find no one around, if really
the town is empty, wind should be blowing.
Sun presses the buildings down. Birds
on the street seem to be resting enroute.
You break into a dress shop and imagine women
you've had in clothes the manikins wear.
You rip a dress from a plaster figure and roar.
The way you yell "rape" it echoes about
the streets and comes back "hope" as it dies.
You find whiskey in the bar. You answer
your order with "Yes, sir. Coming right up."
When they find you the whole bar is laughing.
Men tell the police, "That guy's o.k.
Leave him alone," and the cop in charge grins.

You watch them search your luggage. Then
you remember what you carry and start to explain.

Letter to Simic from Boulder

Dear Charles: And so we meet once in San Francisco and I
learn I bombed you long ago in Belgrade when you were five.
I remember. We were after a bridge on the Danube
hoping to cut the German armies off as they fled north
from Greece. We missed. Not unusual, considering I
was one of the bombardiers. I couldn't hit my ass if
I sat on the Norden or ride a bomb down singing
The Star Spangled Banner. I remember Belgrade opened
like a rose when we came in. Not much flak. I didn't know
about the daily hangings, the 80,000 Slavs who dangled
from German ropes in the city, lessons to the rest.
I was interested mainly in staying alive, that moment
the plane jumped free from the weight of bombs and we went home.
What did you speak then? Serb, I suppose. And what did your mind
do with the terrible howl of bombs? What is Serb for "fear"?
It must be the same as in English, one long primitive wail
of dying children, one child fixed forever in dead stare.
I don't apologize for the war, or what I was. I was
willingly confused by the times. I think I even believed
in heroics (for others, not for me). I believed the necessity
of that suffering world, hoping it would learn not to do
it again. But I was young. The world never learns. History
has a way of making the past palatable, the dead
a dream. Dear Charles, I'm glad you avoided the bombs, that you
live with us now and write poems. I must tell you though,
I felt funny that day in San Francisco. I kept saying
to myself, he was one on the ground that day, the sky
eerie mustard and our engines roaring everything
out of the way. And the world comes clean in moments
like that for survivors. The world comes clean as clouds

in summer, the pure puffed white, soft birds careening
in and out, our lives with a chance to drift on slow
over the world, our bomb bays empty, the target forgotten,
the enemy ignored. Nice to meet you finally after
all that mindless hate. Next time, if you want to be sure
you survive, sit on the bridge I'm trying to hit and wave.
I'm coming in on course but nervous and my cross hairs flutter.
Wherever you are on earth, you are safe. I'm aiming but
my bombs are candy and I've lost the lead plane. Your friend, Dick.

Letter to Matthews from Barton Street Flats

Dear Bill: This is where the Nisei farmed, here where the blacktop
of a vast shopping complex covers the rich black bottom land.
Lettuce sparkled like a lake. Then, the war took everything,
farm, farmers and my faith that change (I really mean loss)
is paced slow enough for the blood to adjust. I believed
the detention of Tada, my friend, was temporary madness
like the war. Someday, I thought, it will all be over, this
tearing out everything, this shifting people away like
so many pigs to single thickness walled shacks in Wyoming
where winter rips like the insane self-righteous tongue
of the times. In Germany, Jews. In America, Japs.
They came back and their property was gone, some technicality
those guardians of society, lawyers found. Or their goods
had burned in unexplained fires. Tada came back wounded
from honest German guns and got insulted in White Center—
I was with him—oh, a dreadful scene. He moved justly bitter
to Milwaukee. Haven't seen him in years. Why do I think
of this today? Why, faced with this supermarket parking lot
filled with gleaming new cars, people shopping unaware
a creek runs under them, do I think back thirty some years
to that time all change began, never to stop, not even
to slow down one moment for us to study our loss, to recall
the Japanese farmers bent deep to the soil? Hell, Bill,

I don't know. You know the mind, how it comes on the scene again
and makes tiny histories of things. And the imagination
how it wants everything back one more time, how it detests
all progress but its own, all war but the one it fights over
and over, the one no one dares win. And we can deport those
others and feel safe for a time, but old dangers (and pleasures)
return. And we return to the field of first games where,
when we find it again, we look hard for the broken toy,
the rock we called home plate, evidence to support our claim
our lives really happened. You can say this all better.
Please do. Write it the way it should sound. The gain will be mine.
Use my Montana address. I'm going back home, not bent
under the load of old crops, still fat and erect, still with faith
we process what grows to the end, the poem. Your good friend, Dick.

In Your War Dream

You must fly your 35 missions again.
The old base is reopened. The food is still bad.
You are disturbed. The phlegm you choked up
mornings in fear returns. You strangle on the phlegm.
You ask, "Why must I do this again?" A man
replies, "Home." You fly over one country
after another. The nations are bright like a map.
You pass over the red one. The orange one ahead
looks cold. The purple one north of that is the one
you must bomb. A wild land. Austere. The city
below seems ancient. You are on the ground.
Lovers are inside a cabin. You ask to come in.
They say "No. Keep watch on Stark Yellow Lake."
You stand beside the odd water. A terrible wind
keeps knocking you down. "I'm keeping watch
on the lake," you yell at the cabin. The lovers
don't answer. You break into the cabin. Inside
old women bake bread. They yell, "Return to the base."
You must fly your 35 missions again.

Letter to Ammons from Maratea

Dear Archie: I hope the boat trip home wasn't long
but isn't any trip on the United States line? I'm trying
a bomber crash poem and I'm working in short lines.
I wish you were here to advise me on the timing.
You time them well. I'm lost without that harsh, often
too booming voice across the page. It snowed last night
in the mountains and I consider that un-Italian.
What a bust Italy was for you. Remember when someone
asked you what you'd do in Rome, you said, walk along
the Tiber and look at weeds. You should have come here.
Phyllis speaks Italian and you'd have gotten along.
The people here are honest and the setting—Lord, the rise
of stone mountains out of the sea and the sea clearer
than gin. When it storms, the sea is blue milk
and you can look at the little things, not just weeds
but the old sepia prints of dead men ringed with flowers
and the short silver fish they catch in the Mediterranean.
Like Corson's Inlet, it says, I say, come. I hope
Richard Howard accepts your invitation to spend time
with you and Phyllis on the ocean. What good company
he is, except he seldom is because he's always working.
The only bad thing here is, I'm lonely. For three months
I haven't spoken English to anyone, and my Italian
gets by only because the Italians are *simpatici*.
I'm wrapping up the book and going soon to London.
I've sent Richard the poems and the table of contents
and he says, that's it. What better guarantee?
I'll take the train, like the man in one of my poems.
I think I'll never see this again. But then I found it
like we find all things, by lucky accident, sometimes
not so lucky, and I'll carry it with me like a man
carries a dream of curved giant women who say, come
and beckon to us, come, and who are never there
and never go away. Your Neapolitan Buddy. Dick.

Letter to Hanson from Miami

Caro Mimo mio: My first trip south. It's not what
I'd expected. Flat all over, a dull placidity of sun, sky,
water, and a nagging feeling nothing is going on.
I went fishing in a barren ocean and I had some Vodka
in a bar with Donald Drummond, who is also wondering
what we're doing here. Fact is, I'm awfully frightened
and I don't know why. I keep feeling revolutionary
but I have no cause. I feel I am going to dynamite
the swimming pool. What have I got against the pool?
Or for that matter, the hotel? It must be the plane trip
down, my fear, still there, of flying, and the heavy drinking
I've been doing. The palm trees never stir. The air here
hovers in the air. I also feel the Cuban refugee waiter
hates me in the bar. Drummond, who is fine, gives me
a kind of strength. He's one of the last no bullshit men
left in the world. Don Justice is here but I haven't seen him.
I'm not sure I've seen anyone but Drummond. Though yesterday
I seem to remember I gave a reading, and on the fishing boat
this morning, was it yesterday, I had a civil conversation
with a good looking woman from Boston. I think I know
the reason I want to plant explosions. It's the same reason
I like an occasional mark of punctuation. A comma
between bears and a colon following alligator jaws.
Because I want a mark in time. I want to say: I was this,
then wham, do some awful thing and after say, now that
is what I am, and read the amazed looks on the faces
of friends. Would they line up and salute me on my way
to prison? The trouble with dramatic things, they die.
Charles A. Lindbergh. Wrong Way Corrigan. Sacco-Vanzetti.
So I do nothing. I become a passive part of the passive
Miami day, a long day, eternal maybe, and Drummond
is going back to Missouri, leaving me alone high over
the pool I'll never bomb, in the hotel I'll never bomb,
oblivious, happy. And it just struck me I'm as far from home

as I can get in the United States, a long diagonal line
across the country, and the wind that brings gray rainclouds
rolling home. Ci vediamo. L'altro Mimo. C'iao.

In Your Bad Dream

Morning at nine, seven ultra-masculine men
explain the bars of your cage are silver
in honor of our emperor. They finger the bars
and hum. Two animals, too far to name,
are fighting. One, you are certain, is destined
to win, the yellow one, the one who from here
seems shaped like a man. Your breakfast
is snake but the guard insists eel. You say hell
I've done nothing. Surely that's not a crime.
You say it and say it. When men leave, their hum
hangs thick in the air as scorn. Your car's
locked in reverse and running. The ignition
is frozen, accelerator stuck, brake shot.
You go faster and faster back. You wait for the crash.
On a bleak beach you find a piano the tide
has stranded. You hit it with a hatchet.
You crack it. You hit it again and music
rolls dissonant over the sand. You hit it
and hit it driving the weird music from it.
A dolphin is romping. He doesn't approve.
On a clean street you join the parade. Women
line the streets and applaud, but only the band.
You ask to borrow a horn and join in.
The bandmaster says we know you can't play.
You are embarrassed. You pound your chest
and yell meat. The women weave into the dark
that is forming, each to her home. You know
they don't hear your sobbing crawling the street
of this medieval town. You promise money
if they'll fire the king. You scream a last promise—
Anything. Anything. Ridicule my arm.

Letter to Annick from Boulder

Dear An: This will be your first widow Christmas. Such a young
death, Dave's. A rotten cheat. The thirty or forty years
he had coming torn way. I couldn't say at his grave where
we stood bowed, ignored by the freeway above us how
unlucky he was that he couldn't poke the corners of his life
and have fun. It was too grim, that's all. Too something damaged
to be anything but run from. To law. To literature. To film.
And he ran beautiful but not far enough. Forget that.
The beautiful never go far. They wait beside roads when we come back
from petty fresh triumph, holding our trophy, the head
of a lover high in a mock blood offering to the moon.
They remind us, like he did, word and not so often deed, of limits,
of the finite returned, clouds closed to end day at five P.M.,
sunset scheduled for six. I can't lose your pain, the sound
of your sobbing over the phone, the disbelief that this, this is done.
It is done, dear An. It is lousy and never over, but done
and you're in Spokane, making the movies he would have loved
about Indians, the tribes in decay and the tribes triumphant
in some vision that matters, some picture of waters and sand,
of lost sons returned bearing the scars of the green wind they sing
in that other country, the forbidden plain, the exact spot
dark blue rain ends and coyote goes free, no bounty from
this meridian on. But I get wilder than tribes and their tales.
This is the bad time, Christmas, and the myths are honed fine.
I don't believe in them but I do believe a part of us
passes above us, preoccupied on the freeway, the rest
below grieving at the grave. And that part passing oblivious west
was once the part in the cemetery, ignores and knows
what the heart is called on to absorb and reject and still pound
like an Indian drum or the ocean, to reach
by sound or in person the other, the greased final day
of the coyote, the curtain, the moment success and failure
make no matter. And it makes no matter whether we cringe
inside or roar defiance at stars. We touch each other

and ourselves no special day, no designated season,
just now and then, in a just poem under an unjust sky.
God, I get windy. This poem, any season, for you always. Dick.

Letter to Mantsch from Havre

Dear Mike: We didn't have a chance. Our starter had no change
and second base had not been plugged since early in July.
How this town turned out opening night of the tournament
to watch their Valley Furniture team wipe us, the No-
Name Tavern of Missoula, out. Remember Monty Holden,
ace Havre pitcher, barber, hero of the Highline, and his
tricky "catch-this" windup? First inning, when you hit that shot,
one on, the stands went stone. It still rockets the night.
I imagine it climbing today, somewhere in the universe,
lovelier than a girl climbs on a horse and lovelier than star.
We lost that game. No matter. Won another. Lost again
and went back talking fondly of your four home runs,
triple and single in three games, glowing in the record book.
I came back after poems. They ask me today, here in Havre,
who's that player you brought here years ago, the hitter?
So few of us are good at what we do, and what we do,
well done or not, seems futile. I'm trying to find Monty
Holden's barber shop. I want to tell him style in anything,
pitching, hitting, cutting hair, is worth our trying even
if we fail. And when that style, the graceful compact swing
leaves the home crowd hearing its blood and the ball roars off
in night like determined moon, it is our pleasure
to care about something well done. If he doesn't understand
more than the final score, if he says, "After all, we won,"
I'll know my hair will not look right after he's done,
what little hair I have, what little time. And I'll drive home
knowing his windup was all show, glad I was there years back,
that I was lucky enough to be there when with one swing
you said to all of us, this is how it's done. The ball jumps
from your bat over and over. I want my poems to jump

like that. All poems. I want to say once to a world that feels
with reason it has little chance, well done. That's the lie
I cannot shout loud as this local truth: Well done, Mike. Dick.

In Your Young Dream

You are traveling to play basketball. Your team's
a good one, boys you knew when you were young.
A game's in Wyoming, a small town, a gym
in a grammar school. You go in to practice.
No nets on the hoops. You say to the coach,
a small man, mean face, "We need nets on the rims."
He sneers as if you want luxury. You explain
how this way you can't see the shots go in.
You and another player, vaguely seen, go out
to buy nets. A neon sign on a local tavern
gives directions to the next town, a town
a woman you loved lives in. You go to your room
to phone her, to tell her you're here just
one town away to play ball. She's already
waiting in your room surrounded by children.
She says, "I'll come watch you play ball."
Though young in the dream you know you are old.
You are troubled. You know you need nets on the rims.

Letter to Reed from Lolo

Dear J.D.: One should think of Chief Joseph here, coming soft
out of the Lolo Canyon, turning right at the Don Tripp
Truck Stop and heading south for Wisdom where the white man
killed his wife. Instead, I think of that drunk afternoon,
still embarrassing, when you, Kittredge and I verbally
shot up the Lolo Tavern. I won't go to the P.O. here

for fear I'll see our photos on the wall. Even worse,
to find out what we're wanted for, to find a halfhearted
offer of a flimsy reward. The Lolo vigilantes
wouldn't recognize me now, not nearly so heavy,
sober as a sloth and given to civility. Still, I drive by
the tavern with my head down. I see you are teaching
with Tate, Cuomo and Fetler. Give Jim and George my best.
Don't know Fetler, but he's a fine writer. Went icefishing
saturday with Yates, Kittredge and our Indian poet friend.
No luck, as Welch says. Cold though. Jesus. The others lushed
it up in Perma. The Dixon Bar is off personal limits
since they misread our *New Yorker* poems and found them
derogating, not the acts of love we meant, not necessarily
for them, but all men and the degraded human condition
we knew long before we heard of Dixon. Why name a town
Wisdom? Why not because an Indian wept once over
the body of his wife, each tear a ton of resolve to make
the trek that will always fail, even if you cross the border
into Canada, and will always be worth while though it ends
a few miles short of your imagined goal, with you erect
in surrender, wind from the soar of ancient horses
blowing your hair, and your words, your words: "I
will fight no more forever" leaving the victorious bent
and forgotten, cheap in their success. Across this nation,
dying from faith in progress, I send you and Chris
and the baby a wordy kiss. I will write some more forever
though only poetry and therefore always failure. Dick.

Letter to Peterson from the Pike Place Market

Dear Bob: I'll be damned. The good, oh so utterly sweet
people of Seattle voted to keep the market as is.
I wish I could write tender lines. The way I feel
I could call to gulls in gull language, or name all fish
at a glance the way Wagoner can birds. I'm eating lunch

alone in the Athenian, staring across Puget Sound
to the islands, the blue white Olympics beyond
the islands and the sky beyond them, a sky I know
is reflecting the blue of the ocean. And commerce seems right,
the ships arriving from every nation, the cries of vendors
outside that leak in. Sol Aman the fish man looks good,
and Joe, the Calabrian. The taverns are as usual,
unpretentious, run down, human, and tiers of produce
gleam like Kid Ory's trombone. Today, I am certain,
for all my terrible mistakes I did the right thing
to love places and scenes in my innocent way and to spend
my life writing poems, to receive like a woman
the world in its enduring decay and to tell
that world like a man that I am not afraid to weep
at the sadness, the ongoing day that is draining our life
and is life. Sorry. Got carried away. But you know, Bob, how
in the smoky recess of bars all over the world, a man
will suddenly dance because music, a juke box, a Greek
taverna band, moves him and how when he dances we
applaud and cry go. That's nobility of blood, a recognition
by those who matter that in special moments
we are together facing the brute descent of the sun
and that cold brittle star we know already burned out.
Hell, that's enough. Wish you were here in the market
helping me track down the moment for some euphoric jolt.
The barbecued crab is excellent. Much love. Dick.

Letter to Stafford from Polson

Dear Bill: We don't know the new heavy kind of wolf
killing calves, but we've seen it and it's anything but gray.
We have formed a new heavy kind of posse
and we're fanning the Mission range for unique tracks.
The new wolf is full of tricks. For instance, yesterday
he sat all afternoon in a bar disguised as a trout

and none of us caught on. He's a wily one.
He even went home drunk and of course weaving slow,
passed two cars of cops and the Union '76
the usually sharp reliable and somewhat sly one runs.
I guess we're not observant. Aside from the wolf
things go well. This is where you may recall you stood
looking at Flathead Lake and uttered a Stafford line.
Impressed by the expanse you said something about going
on and on. And that's exactly what we've done.
We have a new club called the South Shore Inn,
fair food, good drinks and a panoramic view
of the mountains and lake. Also a couple of posh motels
have been added, a new supermarket and in progress
a mooring harbor for yachts. I personally think
the wolf wants to be one of us, to give up killing
and hiding, the blue cold of the mountains, the cave
where he must live alone. I think he wants to come down
and be a citizen, swim, troll all summer for Mackinaws
and in autumn snag salmon. I have to close now.
The head of the posse just called and two more calves
with throats cut were found this morning one mile south
of the garbage dump. Our chief said this time
we'll get him. This time we plan to follow his howl
all the way to the source, even if it means scaling cliffs
and beating our way through snow. Why does he do it?
He doesn't eat what he kills. I hope we find out. I hope
he breaks and spills all the secrets of his world.
By the way, it turns out he's green with red diagonal stripes
and jitters in wind like a flag. Take care, Bill. Dick.

In Your Small Dream

A small town slanted on a slight hill
in barren land. First building you see:
red brick with oriental trim. You say,
"A unique building," and the road forks

into three. Road left, brief with old men
leaning on brick walls. They frown the sun away.
Middle road, oblique and long. Same red brick
buildings but without the trim. Same drab
roasting buildings. Young men and cafes.
You call it Main Street. The third road
you never see. You walk up Main Street.
You are hungry. You take this opportunity
to eat. You have no money. They throw you out.
You return to the brief street. You ask old men
"Where's the unique building?" They frown
and turn away. You say, "I am a friend."
You know wind will level this town.
You say, "Get out. The wind is on its way."
The old men frown. The day darkens. You look
hard for the third road. You ask a giant, "Where?"
The giant glowers, "The third road is severe."
You run and run. You cannot leave the town.

Letter to Hill from St. Ignatius

Dear Bobbi: God, it's cold. Unpredicted, of course, by forecast,
snow and bitter air drove in from Canada while we, some
students and I, were planning a weekend fishing trip
to Rainbow Lake where, just last week, five of us in four
hours took 44 trout. For all I know that lake is frozen tight,
the trout dormant under the ice for the next five months.
We are shut down. This is a quiet town on the Flathead
Reservation, the staggering Mission Range just beyond,
the mission itself of local historical fame. A priest
some 80 years back designed a ceremony for Good
Friday, Indian-Catholic, complete with Flathead chants
in dialect. It's lovely. This early sudden cold I think
of it, how it reminds me of simple times that no doubt
never were, the unified view of man, all that. I wept
the first time I saw it, the beleaguered Indians wailing

the priest to Stations of the Cross. The pall bearers bearing Christ
outside around fires and crying the weird tongue stark
through the night. Bobbi, I don't mind those real old days broke down.
We had (still have) too many questions. You've known embittering winds
in Green Bay and you are not bitter for all the license
they gave. I resent you once told me how I'd never know
what being Indian was like. All poets do. Including
the blacks. It is knowing whatever bond we find we find
in strange tongues. You won't believe this but after my grim years
alone, a woman who loves me has come along. And she
chants when she talks in the strangest of tongues, the human.
I take her in my arms and don't feel strange. She is tall
and she curls in bed like a cat. And so, like Indians,
I chant the old days back to life and she chants me alive.
It's snowing, Bobbi. The flakes seem heavy and they fall hard
as hail. I claim they ring like bells. And sure enough the far
cathedral complements my claim. Chant to me in your poems
of our loss and let the poem itself be our gain. You're gaining
the hurt world worth having. Friend, let me be Indian. Dick.

Letter to Wagoner from Port Townsend

Dear Dave: Rain five days and I love it. A relief
from sandy arroyos, buzzards and buttes, and a growing season
consisting strictly of June. Here, the grass explodes and trees
rage black green deep as the distance they rage in. I suppose
all said, this is my soul, the salmon rolling in the strait
and salt air loaded with cream for our breathing.
And around the bend a way, Dungeness Spit. I don't need
any guide but the one I've got, the one you threw the world
like a kiss of wind ending hot summer, though of course
I am seldom called lover these days and in bad moments
when I walk the beach I claim the crabs complain. Aside
from those momentary failures I am soaring, looping the loop
over blackfish schools and millions of candlefish darting

in and out of glint. I think because the sea continually
divides the world into dark and gleam, the northwest sky
relieves us from the pressure of always choosing by being
usually gray, but of course that's only theory. No real
accounting for calm. The stable chunky ferry is leaving
for Keystone. Perch curve around the pilings oblivious in
their bulk to porgies and the starfish napping tight to barnacles.
They all remind me of Kenny, a boy I fished with from the pier
at Seola. When we got older I saw he was subnormal and I saw
the space between us grow, and finally we saw each other
in passing in White Center and didn't speak. We don't take
others by the hand and say: we are called people. The power
to make us better is limited even in the democratic sea.
Discovery of cancer, a broken back, our inability to pass
our final exam—I guess the rain is finally getting me down.
What matter? I plan to spend my life dependent on moon
and tide and the tide is coming, creeping over the rocks,
washing the remains of crippled fish back deep to the source,
renewing the driftwood supply and the promise of all night
fires on the beach, stars and dreams of girls, and that's
as rich as I'll ever get. We are called human. C'iao. Dick.

Letter to Bly from La Push

Dear Robert
　　　　　Lots of whales cavort and spout
three hundred yards offshore. The danger
of them there, high waves and cold winds mean
we cannot swim. I'm still not in my country
though fishnets dry and hostile eagles scan
our country's enemy, the empty gray.

It's green here, black green mostly, black
against dark sky—all pines are silhouettes.
Even the sun is solid, and red memories

of better runs, of bigger kings, of jacks
that tore the gill nets in their futile drive.
We have to lie or be dishonest to our tears.
Some days I almost know how tall brown wheat
goes gold against dark sky, the storms
that hate our wheat, the thunder
that will come for wheat, evangelistic anger.

My fish is trout. I hear the long jawed pike
can smile you dead when hooked. My symptoms
never die. I've been away ten years, and spray
has killed four houses I remember and the church.
Birds are still fanatic. The shore is raw.
That last rock fist: the void still makes it stick.
The whales are closer and in colder wind
I send warm regards as always,

Dick

In Your Blue Dream

You are fishing a lake but so far no fish.
The other men fishing are old. They nod approval
of your rod, limber and green. One yells advice
over the lake: develop the eyes of an osprey.
The sun goes down. You row to the shore.
A warden is there. He arrests you. He says
your bait is illegal, live meat. The old men
pay your bail. You sweat when the girl counts the money.
The sky fills with fish hawks each with a trout
in his beak. The streets fill with men enroute home.
You lose your sense of time. You ask the men,
all young, is this afternoon? They don't answer.
You run from man to man asking the time.
You forget your address. You knock on a door.
A luscious blonde tells you you have the wrong town.

You run through the swamp. The town ahead
glitters warm in the dark. You yell at the town,
where is my home? A mob of men with bloodhounds
is back of you somewhere. You hear them. You rush
for the lights. You are in the streets dirty in rags.
The people are elegant, dressed for the clubs.
You show them your key. They answer firmly,
you have the wrong country. Go north. You sob
in the streets. You say, this, this is my land.
The streetlamps dim. A cop says, go home.
When the posse of women find you in the desert
you are terribly ashamed. You babble on and on.
They point at you and laugh. One says, you look good
bleaching, good for a weathered skeleton.

Letter to Libbey from St. Regis

Dear Liz: Here's where I degraded myself for the last time
in front of a clerk, in the gift shop fingering copper
and begging one warped triggering response. Since then
I've been stable, lonely as this town, the solitary river
moving north. I never stop here on my way to Coeur d'Alene.
I pass through hoping 50 years of shame will ripen
into centuries and all men understand. A feeble hope.
Even now I see their grins. I look away at mountains
and I pray all distance widens and I grow old soon. You know,
reach that age where no one wonders why I can't get women.
The worst thing is, I burn alive each day. A letter comes
from some ex-lover and I burn. I tell others she
is coming back to town and they say good, then things may start
again, and I say yes, and inside I am screaming "save me"
and she never comes. I went back to the petty compensations,
writing poems to girls like this one, hoping to imply
a soul worth having, hoping old timidities returned
are temporary and the sun will win. On good days, this

is just a town and I am just a lonely man, no worse
than the others in the bar, watching their lives thin down
to moments they remember in the mirror and those half
dozen friends you make in life who matter, none of them
after you are young. I remember being laid three times
each morning by a tiger angel and that didn't solve
a thing. I went limp to work, feeling like a man, but hell.
I was the same one. And the demons, when they came,
wore the same demonic green they wear in Ireland.
Once, I stopped in Italy, the land no longer torn
by war and wholesale poverty, some village in the south
for coffee. I wowed them joking in bad Italian
and they yelled "ritorni" when I drove away. That's the day
I must remember as the distance widens and I grow old,
not too rapidly. I am dating a 19-year-old lovely
and things slip into place, days I find worth having,
stops I find worth making, flashing some of the old charm
at the waitress and murmuring "ritorno" as I drive away.
And you? How are you doing? Wherever in the world. Rain
has washed grass vivid where we threw up on the lawn, and bars
we hid in have improved the lighting. Next time through
to Coeur d'Alene, I'll stop here more than just to mail a letter.
I'll send you copper, a pendant or a ring. And I'll joke
the clerk to roaring. I plan more poems like this one, poems
to girls, to tiger angels better dawns provide. The dark
that matters is the last one. Autumn's spreading like the best joke
ever told. And I send this with my best laugh, as always. Dick.

Letter to Logan from Milltown

Dear John: This a Dear John letter from booze.
With you, liver. With me, bleeding ulcer. The results
are the horrific same: as drunks we're done. Christ,
John, what a loss to those underground political
movements that count, the Degradationists,
the Dipsomaniacists, and that force gaining momentum

all over the world, the Deteriorationists. I hope
you know how sad this is. Once I quit drinking it was clear
to others, including our chairman (who incidentally
also had to quit drinking), that less 40 pounds
I look resolute and strong and on the surface appear
efficient. Try this for obscene development: they made me
director of creative writing. Better I'd gone on bleeding
getting whiter and whiter and finally blending
into the snow to be found next spring, a tragedy
that surely would increase my poetic reputation.
POET FOUND IN THAW   SNOWS CLAIM MISSOULA BARD
I'm in Milltown. You remember that bar, that beautiful bar
run by Harold Herndon where I pissed five years away
but pleasantly. And now I can't go in for fear
I'll fall sobbing to the floor. God, the ghosts in there.
The poems. Those honest people from the woods and mill.
What a relief that was from school, from that smelly
student-teacher crap and those dreary committees
where people actually say "considering the lateness
of the hour." Bad times too. That depressing summer
of '66 and that woman going—I've talked too often
about that. Now no bourbon to dissolve the tension,
to find self-love in blurred fantasies, to find the charm
to ask a woman home. What happens to us, John?
We are older than our scars. We have outlasted and survived
our wars and it turns out we're not as bad as we thought.
And that's really sad. But as a funny painter said
at a bash in Portland, and I thought of you then,
give Mother Cabrini another Martini. But not ever again
you and me. Piss on sobriety, and take care. Dick.

In Your Hot Dream

You are alone on a desert. Hot blasting sand
peppers your face. Your horses are lost. Food
and water are low. You protest the construction

of a furnace. "My argument," you explain,
"is no living room." Speed boats race on a lake.
Other boats, old ones with sails, are burning.
You yell at horses: "Put out the fires." A horse yells
"This is my gear." You find a long stretch of beach,
cool wind and no people. You build a pyre
of driftwood and light it. The flame climbs miles
into the sky. You heap more wood. The flame licks
at stars. You dance the sand in hot glare
and sing an old song: Let The Rest Of The World Go By.
You cry and sweat. The ocean is flaming. The tide
is out of control. Old boats come to your rescue.
Their sails are full. Girls are blowing cold trumpets.

Letter to Gale from Ovando

Dear Vi: You were great at the Roethke festival this summer
in Portland. I love your phrase "and birds move on" because here
that's exactly what they do. It's far better to say
than "fly away" because that indicates they might have stayed
while "move on" says they're vagabond and starved. I'm hungry when
I'm here. It looks anytime like sunday with John Wayne in church,
leaving me helpless, waiting for the villains to ride in.
I only stop here on my way to fish, Brown's lake, or Cooper's,
to feel a part of the west, the brutal part we wave goodbye to
gladly and the honest part we hate to lose, those right days
when we helped each other and were uniformly poor.
How scattered we become. How wrong we end finally alone,
seeing each other seldom, hearing the wind in our teeth.
Roethke himself knew and hated to know the lonely roads
we take to poems. Miriam Patchen was right in her speech
in Portland: it's a one man route and sad. No help. No friend
along the way, standing beside the road with trillium.
And Dickey was right in *Playboy*, that part about the mind
becoming the monster and the monstrous ways we feed it

and it grows. My monster's desolate and kind. And in my
desolate home, the wind leaks in on sundays and finally
for all the gloom, I, not John Wayne, put the villains away
to rest, mark the headstones "no one" and start another poem.
Listen to yourself, Vi: "Lakes change, trees rot and birds move on."
And listen to ourselves move on, each on the road he built
one young summer while the world was having fun. Lakes change.
Trees rot. Roads harden. Whatever road, it was the blind one
and the only. Poems are birds we loved who moved on and remain.
Think of poems as arms and know from this town I am writing
whatever words might find a road across the mountains. Dick.

Letter to Welch from Browning

Dear Jim: This is as far as I ever chased a girl.
She's worth it, but she isn't here. Man, it's a grim pull
from Missoula in a car. Had a haircut in Augusta,
a drink in Choteau, Bynum and Depuyer. I wanted to arrive
well groomed and confident. I'm in a cheap motel,
the walls are beveled board and painted a faint green
that reminds me somehow of the '30s and a cabin
on Lake Meridian. I spent this night, the only white
in the Napi Tavern where the woman tending bar
told me she's your aunt. A scene of raw despair. Indians
sleeping on the filthy floor. Men with brains scrambled in wine.
A man who sobbed all night, who tried in strangled desperation
to articulate the reason. And the bitterest woman I've seen
since the Depression. Of course. The '30s never ended here.
They started. In the '80s. Some braves took turns apologizing
for a poor demented derelict who stole my beer
and bummed me twice for a quarter. One gave me fishing tips
for a lake on the reservation. What a sharp description.
I could see it as he talked. Grass banks that roll into the water.
No trees. Surrounding land as open as the lake. I thanked him
like I'd never thank a white. And I thank a lot of things

because tomorrow I'll be pulling out. When my car points south
I hope a waltz by Strauss is on the radio, the day is sunny
and the clouds so vivid in their forms I'll have the urge
to give them names. I'll never see you quite the same. Your words
will ring like always on the page, but when drunk you shrug
away the world, our petty, gnawing bugs, degrees and grades
and money, even sometimes love, I'll simply nod and pour.
I hope I find that girl. I plan to touch her in such ways,
tender and direct until she reaches for me every morning
out of instinct. She's up here, when she's here, doing social work.
I'll probably never find her. And while I'm at it, the food
in Browning is not good. Take care, Chief Boiling Whiskey. Dick.

In Your Racing Dream

You hitch a ride with a cyclist. You sit in back
and hold on. He's leading in a race. With you
on the cycle he slows down and others pass.
You say to him, "Faster. You'll lose." He says
"I'm thinking of food." You drift a sleepy canal
on a barge, warm horses on the bank, sweep
of grass to trees the wind and light bend
far off in warm air. The water barely moves.
It will take months to cruise home. You snarl
at a horse, "I'm running out of time."
The cyclist goes by. He yells, "I'm winning."
You try to yell "Wait" but choke. He goes on.
You are mayor of a town. The people bring
you their problems. You give advice from
your window. You cannot remember
the canal. You ask, "How did I get here?"
Someone calls you to dinner. You try
and try to remember the cylist's name.

Letter to Snyder from Montana

Dear Gary: As soon as you'd gone winter snapped shut again
on Missoula. Right now snow from the east and last night
cold enough to arrest the melting of ice. My favorite
bouncer, wind, stopped throwing clouds out of the joint for being
too gloomy. In short, you're gone and we've gone back to being
a small dreary city. Some of your grace hangs on. I still
have a date with that round pink girl. For her I have evil plans.
I am rubbing my hands like a monster. I am planning trips
to remote lakes in spring. I know it's not modern to think
of seduction as evil, but damn it that makes it more fun
and the more fun it is the more often I'll do it, I hope.
Students still buzz about your reading. Those who had turned you
into a god were happy to find you human. I should
have warned them. Should have warned all western Montana,
a warm force is coming. Snows will run off. The rivers
will scream and crack their banks. Winter will take a breather.
Speaking of love being fun, you never in your remarks
mentioned those two-minute male orgasms perfected
in India by, if I have it right, mystics. Why not?
Nor did you bring up those ancient Chinese techniques
of tortuous titillation. Remember, forests and land
(for me especially, fish) are not all that's worth saving.
There's also loving. Shit. Why tell you? You preserve that
every day without trying. But of course you're not here.
Last night, 20 below. A mass of tall arctic air
stands over us like a cruel father, though the weather now
is really a mother and this mother may go on forever.
What is needs, what we need, I, is another visit
from Snyder. For that, the glaciers are waiting, and bears
(for you especially, fish) and the green flaring pageant
of sky mating with hills. This letter was found wadded up
in a bum in the tundra who sends his warmest regards. Dick.

Letter to Scanlon from Whitehall

Dear Dennice: I'm this close but the pass is tough this year.
I'm stranded by this rotten winter. My car is ailing
and the local mechanic doesn't know what he's doing
or he does but never learned clear phrasing. It will take
four hours or a week. An odd town. A friendly waitress
says the main drag is the old road so I must have been here
but I don't remember. It looks like several towns
in Montana. Columbus, for one. Even, a little, like the edge
of Billings. You know. On one side, stores, cafes, a movie
theatre you feel certain no one attends. And across
the street, the railroad station. Most of all, that desolate
feeling you get, young hunger, on a gray sunday afternoon,
when you survive only because the desolation feeds
your dying, a dream of living alone on the edge
of a definite place, a desert or the final house in town
with no threat of expansion, or on the edge of a canyon,
coyotes prowling below and a wind that never dies. Girl,
you wouldn't believe the people who live alone, preparing
themselves daily for dying, planning their expenditures
to the penny so just when they die their money is gone
and the county must bury them, a final revenge on a world
that says work is good, plan for the future. They did. And dear
Dennice, bring their laughing bones no flowers. Pay them the honor
of ignoring their graves, the standard bird authorities
chip on stones, a magpie designed by the same man
you always see in towns like this, sitting in the station,
knowing the trains don't run. The soup in the cafe I was lucky
enough to pick of the available three, turned out thick
tomato macaroni, and the chicken salad sandwich, yum.
The mechanic says my car is done. He says, if I understand,
it's ready and no charge. He says, if I understand, he
just wants to be friendly and it wasn't anything really wrong.
Homestake grade is sanded. I may even beat this letter
to your home. It's saturday and I suppose there's a dance

somewhere in Butte tonight. Would you please consider?
Would you come? I hope it's one of those virtuoso bands,
you know, songs from all the generations, jazz, swing, rock.
And a big crowd. Girls in mini minis, tighter than skin
over their behinds, and a friendly bar, a table where
we can talk. Think about it. Say yes. Be nice. Love. Dick.

Letter to Wright from Gooseprairie

Dear Jim: The Bedfords are not to be found. Maybe
they've moved or I've seen them and didn't know it.
I remember most things different. The Bumping River
years ago seemed faster, seemed to play by lovers
on the bank with sumptuous singing, and the trout
seemed bigger too. The world seemed more in motion then.
Clouds pranced the way elk prance and jumped the way
native cutthroat do when hooked. And people seemed uglier,
more like the Bedfords were and probably aren't anymore
and more like people in war. I'm using too many r's.
Our wives are gone too. Mine's remarried. You're married
again, to an unclassified gem. Today, the clouds seem
to move over the meadows the way life seems in retrospect
to have drifted on a pre-set course, uninterrupted
by jolts, fights, sudden changes of direction. Naturally,
an illusion. But then, Jim, time comes to take a rest
the way it comes to take a piss, and to forget the uglies
and cruels, the damage a wrong cloud does. For example,
15 years ago if I had lost a four pound Dolly
after a long struggle I'd have slammed my rod
on the ground. Now, just minutes ago I stopped fishing
because the two trout in my bag are all I can eat.
I rented the same cabin we stayed in then, too big,
I agreed with the owner, for a single, but I have the money
and can pay for the past. I hope I always meet the cost
the way old clouds face doom. Meanwhile, sweet dreams. Dick.

In Your Wild Dream

You are fishing but have walked away from your rod.
Your rod bends and flies into the lake. You swim
to the rod and start reeling in. A huge fish in on.
A gray fish. Bloated. Dull. You finally land him.
On shore he snarls, a vicious mustard dog.
He wants to kill you. He rages with hate and glares.
A man you don't know is holding him back.
The dog strains at the rope. The man says "a Girl fish,
that's what he's called." You are riding a camel
in Athens. The citizens yell, "We are not Arab. This
is not sand." The camel is a yacht. You cruise
a weird purple river. Girls doze on the bank. One
stands up and waves. You yell, "Where is the town?"
You are alone. Fishing again. You catch nothing.
You dream you are dreaming all this. Around you
beautiful flowers are blooming. You know now
you need nothing to live, food, love or water.
Youg giggle and giggle because you are free.
Birds above you keep flying away.

Letter to Haislip from Hot Springs

Dear John: Great to see your long-coming, well-crafted book
getting good reviews. I'm in a town that for no reason
I can understand, reminds me how time has passed since we
studied under Roethke, Arnold Stein, Jack Mathews and
Jim Hall at Washington. Two of them are gone already.
I think of that this morning and I get sad. This motel
I took for the night, hoping to catch the morning fishing
at Rainbow Lake, is one that survived after most others
went broke when they discovered the hot springs simply didn't
work. No therapeutic value. None of that. The old climbed
up out the steaming water still old. The cripples still limped

after three weeks of soaking. I'm a little lame myself
these days. Bad hip from a childhood accident. Skeletal
problems show up as we enter middle age. Our bones
settle in and start to complain about some damn thing that
happened years ago and we barely noticed it then.
Who thought 25 years ago we'd both be directors
of Creative Writing, you at Oregon, me here at
Montana, fishing alone in the Flathead wind, in lakes
turned silver by sky, my memories so firm, my notion
of what time does to men so secure I wish I'd learned to
write novels. Now I can understand the mind that lets Sam
wander off to Peru on page 29 and come back
twenty years later in the final chapter, a nazi.
I know why I always feel sad when I finish a novel.
Sometimes cry at just the idea that so much has happened.
But then, I'm simply a slob. This is no town for young men.
It sets back off the highway two miles and the streets stand bare.
When I drive in, I feel I'm an intrusion. When I leave,
I feel I'm deserting my past. I feel the same sadness
I feel at the end of a novel. A terrible lot has happened
and is done. Do you see it happening to students?
I do and say nothing, and want to say when some young poet
comes angry to my office: you too will grow calm. You too
will see your rage suffer from skeletal weakness you picked
up when young, will come to know the hot springs don't work, and love
empty roads, love being the only man casting into
a lake turned silver by sky. But then, maybe he won't,
no matter. The morning is clear. I plan to grab breakfast
at the empty cafe, then head to the lake, my Buick
purring under the hood as Stafford would say. And I plan
to enjoy life going by despite my slight limp. Best. Dick.

Letter to Mayo from Missoula

Dear Ed: I get the sad news from Des Moines no doubt not sad
for you, that you're hanging it up. That's our loss, everyone

in this game who's teaching poems and ways to write them. You bailed
me out of a classroom jam several times in Portland
at Lewis and Clark that spring, phrasing what I should have said,
clear as Indian sky. But then you have an advantage
over me: you know poetry. I never could read Milton
even in school when I had to. I could recognize Donne
was good but never quite understood him. I suppose I've always
depended on men like you to set it all straight after
I've taught some poet wrong. Ed, I have two retirement
fantasies. One, I walk out of the building the last time
alone, no one saying goodbye. The lights are off. The hall
is dim with winter afternoon. Somehow the retirement
plan got fouled up in the computer and I have no
money to live on (Social Security was voted out
two years before by the new progressive Republican
party). I walk alone in the raw gray air that stings me
cold, to my shack on the river where I sit and wait
to die. No one comes to see me. Finally, I go mad
and am taken away to a home. Two, the speeches ring
in the sunlight. All my students, twenty-five years of them
cheer me as I rise to accept their acclaim. Some of them
are famous poets and they stand up and say, "It's all because
of him," pointing to me. I sob like Mr. Chips and their
applause booms through my tears. I walk alone down the campus,
their voices yelling my name behind me. I am crying
in the car (new Lincoln) and my wife (28, lovely)
comforts me as we speed to our vine and moss covered home
on the lake where I plan to write an even more brilliant
book than my last one, "Me and John Keats" which won the NBA,
Pulitzer, APR, Shelley, Bollingen and numerous
other awards and made me a solid contender for
the Nobel. I fear, Ed, neither will do for you, mainly
because you don't take a bullshit kindly. O.K. then this,
I want to retire kind and hardheaded as you, to know
not once did I leave the art, not once did I fail to accept
the new, not once did I forget that seminal coursing

of sound in poems and that lines are really the veins of men
whether men know it or not. And if the saying of it
is, at Stafford says, a lonely thing, it is also
the gritty. Take the hard road home. That is the road you came on
long ago, without drum or banners, without some poet
trying and failing to praise you from the brush in some damn
fool poem like this one. I guess you get what I mean. I mean
take care now. Leave labor to slaves. Give my best to
Myra and show this letter only to trustworthy friends. Luck. Dick.

Letter to Levertov from Butte

Dear Denise: Long way from, long time since Boulder. I hope
you and Mitch are doing OK. I get rumors. You're in Moscow,
Montreal. Whatever place I hear, it's always one of glamor.
I'm not anywhere glamorous. I'm in a town where children
get hurt early. Degraded by drab homes. Beaten by drunken
parents, by other children. Mitch might understand. It's kind
of a microscopic Brooklyn, if you can imagine Brooklyn
with open pit mines, and more Irish than Jewish. I've heard
from many of the students we had that summer. Even seen
a dozen or so since then. They remember the conference fondly.
So do I. Heard from Herb Gold twice and read now and then
about Isaac Bashevis Singer who seems an enduring diamond.
The mines here are not diamond. Nothing is. What endures
is sadness and long memories of labor wars in the early
part of the century. This is the town where you choose sides
to die on, company or man, and both are losers. Because
so many people died in mines and fights, early in history
man said screw it and the fun began. More bars and whores
per capita than any town in America. You live only
for today. Let me go symbolic for a minute: great birds
cross over you anyplace, here they grin and dive. Dashiell
Hammett based *Red Harvest* here though he called it Personville
and "person" he made sure to tell us was "poison" in the slang.

I have ambiguous feelings coming from a place like this
and having clawed my way away, thanks to a few weak gifts
and psychiatry and the luck of living in a country
where enough money floats to the top for the shipwrecked
to hang on. On one hand, no matter what my salary is
or title, I remain a common laborer, stained by the perpetual
dust from loading flour or coal. I stay humble, inadequate
inside. And my way of knowing how people get hurt, make
my (damn this next word) heart go out through the stinking air
into the shacks of Walkerville, to the wife who has turned
forever to the wall, the husband sobbing at the kitchen
table and the unwashed children taking it in and in and in
until they are the wall, the table, even the dog the parents
kill each month when the money's gone. On the other hand,
I know the cruelty of poverty, the embittering ways
love is denied, and food, the mean near-insanity of being
and being deprived, the trivial compensations of each day,
recapturing old years in broadcast tunes you try to recall
in bars, hunched over the beer you can't afford, or bending
to the bad job you're lucky enough to have. How, finally,
hate takes over, hippie, nigger, Indian, anyone you can lump
like garbage in a pit, including women. And I don't want
to be part of it. I want to be what I am, a writer good enough
to teach with you and Gold and Singer, even if only in
some conference leader's imagination. And I want my life
inside to go on long as I do, though I only populate bare
landscape with surrogate suffering, with lame men
crippled by more than disease, and create finally
a simple grief I can deal with, a pain the indigent can find
acceptable. I do go on. Forgive this raving. Give my best
to Mitch and keep plenty for yourself. Your rich friend, Dick.

In Your Dream on the Eve of Success

You are talking to a man named Buss. You knew Buss
when you were a child. In life he tends bar. In your dream

he sells greeting cards but not from back of a counter,
in a famous department store. In life
he was your hero, the star softball pitcher
in your grammar school. Your university president
comes to the door. He is elegantly dressed.
Buss holds open the door for the president.
The president can't get through. You help Buss
hold the door open. The president barely gets by.
He seems weak. He limps. He checks some papers
with some men in the next room. You and Buss
watch him through glass. You tell Buss you are a poet.
You ask Buss about his father. Buss says his dad
lived like a gambler. The president tries to cross
the room. His legs are weak and spastic. He falls
helpless on the floor. Two women rush to his side.
He is calm. He tries to show them the papers.
He starts to choke. A woman puts a tomato
in his mouth to stop his choking. You know
he is dying. You cannot understand his calm.

Letter to Kathy from Wisdom

My dearest Kathy: When I heard your tears and those of your
mother over the phone from Moore, from the farm
I've never seen and see again and again under the most
uncaring of skies, I thought of this town I'm writing from,
where we came lovers years ago to fish. How odd
we seemed to them here, a lovely young girl and a fat
middle 40's man they mistook for father and daughter
before the sucker lights in their eyes flashed on. That was
when we kissed their petty scorn to dust. Now, I eat alone
in the cafe we ate in then, thinking of your demons, the sad
days you've seen, the hospitals, doctors, the agonizing
breakdowns that left you ashamed. All my other letter
poems I've sent to poets. But you, your soft round form
beside me in our bed at Jackson, you were a poet then,

curving lines I love against my groin. Oh, my tenderest
racoon, odd animal from nowhere scratching for a home,
please believe I want to plant whatever poem will grow
inside you like a decent life. And when the wheat you've known
forever sours in the wrong wind and you smell it
dying in those acres where you played, please know
old towns we loved in matter, lovers matter, playmates, toys,
and we take from our lives those days when everything moved,
tree, cloud, water, sun, blue between two clouds, and moon,
days that danced, vibrating days, chance poem. I want one
who's wondrous and kind to you. I want him sensitive
to wheat and how wheat bends in cloud shade without wind.
Kathy, this is the worst time of day, nearing five, gloom
ubiquitous as harm, work shifts changing. And our lives
are on the line. Until we die our lives are on the mend.
I'll drive home when I finish this, over the pass that's closed
to all but a few, that to us was always open, good days
years ago when our bodies were in motion and the road rolled out
below us like our days. Call me again when the tears build
big inside you, because you were my lover and you matter,
because I send this letter with my hope, my warm love. Dick.

Letter to Goldbarth from Big Fork

Dear Albert. This is a wholesome town. Really. Cherries grow
big here and all summer a charming theatre puts on
worthy productions. It is Montana at its best, lake
next to town, lovely mountains close by, and independent
people, friendly, generous, always a discernible touch
of the amateur I like. Nothing slick. Montana is
the rest of America 50 years back. Old barber shops
you walk into and don't have to wait. Barbers who take
a long time cutting your hair to make sure they get in all
the latest gossip. Bars where the owner buys every fifth round,
and you buy one for him now and then. Albert, I love it

despite what some think here reading my poems. The forlorn towns
just hanging on take me back to the 30's where most poems
come from, the warm meaningful gestures we make, the warm ways
we search each other for help in a bewildering world,
a world so terrifyingly big we settle for small
ones here we can control. There's a bitter side, too, a mean
suspicion of anything new, of anyone different
or bright. I hate that. I hate feeling as I become well
known that I'm marked: poet, beware. He has insight.
I don't like being tagged negative because I write hurt
as if my inner life on the page is some outer truth,
when it is only my view, not the last word. When it is
not the world photoed and analyzed, only one felt.
I like best of all in Montana how people who've had
nothing from the beginning, never expected a thing,
accept cruelty, weather and man, as normal and who have felt
the bitter strokes of life's gratuitous lash (oh, poets
catch that one), are cheerful, receptive and kind to the end.
So for all their suspicion and distrust of me, they are
my women, my men. And I, who came from the seacoast,
who love the salmon, the damp air of Seattle, finally
have come to call this home. That means, when I say it, I lived
here forever and I knew it first time I saw it nine
years ago. Albert, Big Fork brings out the mountain in me.
And trout help, too. Just now, a stranger drove by and waved.
And I waved back my best wave, Albert. I shouted at him
"hello," and it came back doubled by hills. At you too. Dick.

In Your Big Dream

Though alone, you know just over the hill
the army is ready. You decide, if they come,
you'll say you support their cause. You dwell
in the ruins of a church. A bird you know's
ferocious circles the church. You see him

through the huge gaps in the roof. You pull
the bellrope thinking clang will drive him away.
But will it attract the army? You are free
from gravity. You lift five feet off the ground
and glide. You decide to follow a river
all the way to the sea. People along the way
warn you, a monster's downstream. You walk
the streets of a deserted city. You know
it was deserted recently because the lights
still burn and markets display fresh meat.
If anyone comes, you'll say you're chief of police.
Enemy subs pop up on the sea. They shell
the coast. You wave your hair in surrender.
Only one man comes ashore, a small man.
He refuses your terms. He says it's not your land.
You whine. You beg him to take you prisoner.
Bison stampede the plain. You climb a mountain
leading seven men who look like you. They depend
on you for their safety. You climb higher
and higher until you are alone under a sun
gone pale in altitude. You climb above birds
and clouds. You are home in this atmosphere.

Letter to Birch from Deer Lodge

Dear Michele: Once, according to a native, this town
had a choice: state prison or university, and chose
the former. They didn't want whatever radical
was called in those days students and professors with ideas
messing up their town. Now guards in towers, nothing to do,
keep tabs on the streets, the teens cruising the streets in cars,
and report to parents or police anything amiss.
So the town became the pen. They even built a drive-in
across the street from the wall. Burger D and fries within
the shadow of penance. I think, when I'm here, how silly

prisons are, how, if we tore down the grotesque wall and let
all but a handful out, life would be no different, and how
we imprison people not for crimes but simply because
we don't like them, they are unrefined. Crime is our excuse.
Some poets equate themselves with criminals. That may be
because we share the same desolate loves, the same railroad
spur along the swamp ignites some old feeling of self
inside and when the sky comes gray late afternoon across
the world on sunday, we know we're friendless and the hounds bay
in the distance sniffing for our trail. We are equally cowed
by the official, by men who never clown or smile.
And we, poet and felon, know how certain times are right
for others, wrong for us. We die 4 P.M. on friday
when the fun begins for others. And we are like the teens
of Deer Lodge, always under the censorial eye
of the tower. We find secret ways to play. No one
except poets know what gains we make in isolation.
We create our prison and we earn parole each poem.
Michele, our cell door's open like the dawn. Let's run and run.
The day is windy and alive with fields. Your friend. Dick.

Letter to Oberg from Pony

Dear Arthur: In a country where a wealthy handful
of people tear down anything you could possibly love,
break your affectionate connections with yourself by whim
for profit, would move, if they could make money moving it,
the national capital to Dubuque, have already
torn down Walt Whitman's home, tried, damn their souls,
to wreck the Pike Place Market, and in their slimy leisure
plot to dismantle Miss Liberty and move her one piece
at a time to Las Vegas where, reassembled, she
will be a giant slot machine (pull the right arm please,
the one with the torch), you'd love to pack your things and move here.
This is lovely. This is too great for a poem. The only

way here is by dream. Call it Xanadu or Shangri-La
or Oz. Lovely old homes stand empty because somewhere
in this floundering world, the owners toil and plan to come
back here to die. I hope I die here. I want to spend my
last years on the porch of the blue house next to the charming
park the town built and no one uses, picnic tables ringed
by willows and the soft creek ringing in the grass. I hope
to sit there drinking my past alive and watching seasons
take over the park. This is only to assure you, Art,
that in a nation that is no longer one but only an
amorphous collection of failed dreams, where we have been told
too often by contractors, corporations and prudes that
our lives don't matter, there still is a place where the soul
doesn't recognize laws like gravity, where boys catch trout
and that's important, where girls come laughing down the dirt road
to the forlorn store for candy. I love Pony like I love
maybe fifty poems, the ones I return to again
and again knowing my attention can't destroy what's there.
Give my best to Barbara and take care. Dick.

Letter to Blessing from Missoula

Dear Dick: You know all that pissing and moaning around I've
been doing, feeling unloved, certain I was washed up with
romance for good. That has come to an orgiastic halt.
From nowhere came this great woman. I wasn't looking
even when she was suddenly bang in my life. I mean
bang in all the best ways. Bang. Bang. Richard Blessing. And years
of loneliness faded into some silly past where I
stared moodily out my windows at the grammar school girls
passing each morning and fantasized being young again
but with circumstances better than the first time and with
an even newer than new morality current. To
say nothing of saying to myself over and over
"I am retired from romance. I am a failure at love.
Women don't like me. Lecherous, treacherous, kindless klutz.

Oh, that this too too flabby flesh should grow solid. Do not
go gentle into that defeat. Let us go then, you and I
into the deserts of vast eternity." As you can no doubt
see, things became warped, including my memory of how
certain lines go, and all for the wisest of causes:
self-pity. Do not depend on others for sympathy.
When you need sympathy, you'll find it only in yourself.
Now, I need none but I still defend self-pity. I still
say, if this woman hurts me I'll crawl back to my cave.
The snow doesn't get me down. The solid gray overcast
doesn't make me moody. I don't get irritated by
cold clerks in the markets, or barbers who take too long
trimming my hair. This woman is statuesque and soft
and she loves me, meaning she is at my mercy. Have you
noticed when women love us how vulnerable they are?
How they almost challenge us to test them, to be bastards,
to see how much outrageous shit we can fling their way?
Maybe, that's why we've been ripping them off for centuries,
I don't blame them for bitching, turning to movements, fem lib
or whatever they call it. This time, I'm not saying, prove it,
prove your love by not objecting as I steal your money,
set fire to your hair and break your toes with the boots
I took off a dead German soldier at Tobruk. I am
simply going to prove I'm worthy of her love and I feel
I am, which must mean I love her. Boy, am I becoming
tender, and am I ever certain she will not hurt me.
I'll give her no cause. I accept maybe for the first time
love and I luxuriate in it, a glutton, a trout
who had a hard time finding the spawning ground, who swam time
after time the wrong river and turned back discouraged
to the sea, though at moments the sea was fun. Those sex-crazed
sharks and those undulating anemones, can't beat them
when you've had a few drinks though you wake up diseased and raw,
your gills aching and your fins stiff with remorse. That's enough
metaphor. This morning I feel as masculine as you,
and I regard you as the C. C. Rider of poetry,
criticism and trout. This woman will curve from now on

lovely in poems and streams. Look for her in the quarterlies
and pools. I mean real pools, the ones you come to
with Lisa when you take her on picnics. And take Lisa
on picnics. Give her and her cooking my love. Your friend, Dick.

In Your Dream after Falling in Love

Two cops who are really famous actors
playing cops are arrested and must go
to jail. "Not there," one cries. "We'll be killed."
They enter jail with fear. The other prisoners
gloat and yell, "Look who's here. Let's scrub them
good." They give the cops a bath. The cops protest
but seem to enjoy it. You are relieved. You know
things are all right. You are on a tall building
counting the cars way down in the street.
A man whispers, "They seem to be crawling."
"No. No," you say, "they are bright." A worm
turns on you, a giant, big teeth. He means
to eat you alive. You think quick. You
tell him a joke. He laughs himself sick.
He becomes a gull. He climbs up out
of the world of stale air. He is soaring,
a monster glider, and singing, "I am me."
The cell door opens. Fred Astaire dances
his way past the warden into the country.
The warden applauds. A headline says
prisons are abolished. You feel hurt.
You think you'd like your old cell back.
"No way," the grass murmurs, "no way."
You know you have lots of time to catch
the luxurious ship parked at the pier.

Letter to Gildner from Wallace

Dear Gary: The houses in Wallace are closed after 94 years.
Apparently because those forces of Christian morality,
the Republicans, accused the Governor of coddling sin.
One thing about politicians, they can never be whores,
they're not honest enough. They screw men in ways that only
satisfy themselves. I sit in this last bastion
of honesty left in the land, this town Lana Turner
came from (I'll always love you, Lan) with the five best reasons
to be shut down: Oasis, Sahara, U. and I., Lux
and Luxette. Gary, I'd like to tie the self-proclaimed forces
of morality in chairs and bring in swinging professors
and good librarians to lecture on real civilization
for at least ten years, and those who cater to plebiscitic
prudes would have to pass an exam before they could eat.
They wonder why no one believes in the system. What system?
The cynical lean with the wind, whatever one's blowing,
if you'll pardon the vulgar expression. No, Gary, I'll
issue a curse out of my half-Irish past on the hyper
respectable everywhere. May the bluebird of happiness
give you a venereal disease so rare the only known cure
is life in the tundra five hundred miles from a voter,
the only known doctor, a mean polar bear. May the eyes of starved
whores burn through your TV screens as you watch Lawrence Welk.
I'm getting far from my purpose. I wanted to tell you
I still love your poems, then got hung up on people
who won't leave people alone. The most beautiful building
in Wallace is the unused railroad station. The lovely
thing is the way the citizens know in the undergrounds
of their hearts that this isn't right, this sudden shutdown
of what men came to expect long ago when they came down
from Lookout Pass and the cold, and the first lights they saw
in the distance warmed them to push on into the waiting
warm arms of release. That's one thing poets best never forget.
May the bluebird of happiness help us remember. Best. Dick.

Note to R. H. from Strongsville

Long day on the road, R. H., and three trips now
I've ended here, in one or another
plastic motel, always the same face at the desk,
polite and pale, and I register
remembering my license number,
leaving what I don't know blank, who I represent.

You're young when you start writing poems, never
dreaming a career that leaves you vodka
and Fresca and some take-out Chinese food,
not good, alone with a grainy TV
watching a Perry Mason replay.
You saw it before but forget the murderer.

I know you're from these parts, some vague wealth
in Cleveland, a manufacturing (clothing I think you said)
fortune, and faced for a long time mournfully,
always in my mind manfully,
close odds on battles for your blood.
Mother at seven to five, a TKO by the eighth.

Mason is trapping the killer. His thundering questions
are closing the trap. An old hack actor is sweating.
Now his big moment: confession.
Now a political program and the other channels
are weak. When I'm alone, no sound, the vodka
and the room begin a roaring of their own.

Call me Weaksville. I'm an R. H. too.
That's not a common bloodtype, just
a way of saying silent roar is where we meet,
usually in print. Better to dream of markets
filled with people, noise, all foods you love to eat
far from Strongsville. They exist.

In Your Good Dream

From this hill they are clear, the people
in pairs emerging from churches, arm
in soft arm. And limb on green limb
the shade oaks lining the streets form
rainproof arches. All day festive tunes
explain your problems are over. You picnic
alone on clean lawn with your legend.
Girls won't make fun of you here.

Storms are spotted far off enough
to plan going home and home has fire.

It's been here forever. Two leisurely grocers
who never compete. At least ten elms
between houses and rapid grass refilling
the wild field for horses. The same mayor
year after year—no one votes anymore—
stocks bass in the ponds and monster trout
in the brook. Anger is outlawed.
The unpleasant get out. Two old policemen
stop children picking too many flowers
in May and give strangers directions.

You know they are happy. Best to stay
on the hill, drowsy witness, hearing
the music, seeing their faces beam
and knowing they marry forever, die late
and are honored in death. A local process,
no patent applied for, cuts name, born date
and died too deep in the headstone to blur.

White Center

[1980]

Museum of Cruel Days

It's not you, this dead long moan from the past,
the whip coiled, not just for display but to fit tight
in the case. No guard. No guide. You want to feel
a shudder down your neck but the mural is bad,
Serbs tearing Turk horsemen down, Turk swords
flashing, faces screaming louder than any face screams
and softer than April outside in Belgrade where
for all the good good weather and government bring
seasons must go on and someone rule.

These momentos seem ancient. Seem recent.
The woman who brought the key babbled in Serb
though her face was dark Turk and her eyes flashed
a far different smile than her teeth. And you,
alone inside where few tourists come,
you guess the anguish where mace and chain seem
nothing more than old metal. You might have found them
yourself, some afternoon in those pits where you played.
You killed the villain. The girl didn't care.

You hear of anguish. One village nearby, the Germans
shot every male dead in front of mothers and wives.
The count: 7,000. The reason: one captain sniped.
Doesn't that go back further, gratuitous blows
and always the radio on, the indifferent tune?
You scanned the dial days and found no comedian.
You will feel nothing in time. And you can listen
like a hungry dog and not hear the women who cry
'come back' every day at the meadow.

Sweet grim people, some days it hurts, this way
we ought to feel and cannot, this volume of grief
that crawls down the ages dissonant in its demand.
A Turk whip is no grain of sand.
That cry for help in the night fell short
of the seawall where you danced and lectured the tide.
You'll remember dull brown this museum's dominant color
and maybe the skin of that woman who waits in the house
next door to lock up after you leave.

Don't come back. Peasants are free and still peasants.
The soil's too rocky to farm. You gather
from some skirmish now going on, the Turks
are ferocious as ever. And if inside you
a fist waits to beat back the bad man you are
that hand opens in hunger. The market opens
and peasants start eating. Not well. Just staying alive.
You're armed with local coin. Buy whatever hunger
looks good on the stand.

After a Train Trip, One Town Remains

If you stopped there it was only to refuel.
Chances are you went by fast and the town curved
by you in the tricky lens the window
of a fast train is. The style: American,
last century farm. The state: someplace high plains.
Much as you like wind on the scene, the vane
didn't move on the water tower. You don't remember
one woman outlined lovingly on sky
or a dog bent hoping someone would want him.

It makes no sense, that town hanging wherever
you are, whatever you do. It reminds you
of nothing, the religion, if anything, grim.

The highest point was the steeple, protestant you think,
for certain not lax. It hovered like a mean bird
over the six homes you counted and you know
if you lived there you'd go to church or be stoned
in the dirt streets Monday, saying hello.

Years later you take the same train. You find
the same town. This time, a tavern, neon
"Grain Belt on tap" in the window and neon cross
on the church. You count nine houses. The market
that must have been there before has macadamed
the parking lot. When you pull out you look back
long as you can. Not very long.

Doing the House

for Philip Levine

This will be the last time. Clearly
they will tear it down, one slate shingle
at a time and the man here now, last
occupant, face the color of old snow
will leave for the cold he is certain of,
sweating more than last night's bad wine.
He is the man I would have become.
When he leaves he wires the door
and padlocks the wire. When he comes home
he knows his is the one unkept yard
on the block. The weeds, he believes,
are the weeds that will cover his grave.
The style's so old the house does not belong,
not even alone, the way it stood '14
to '44, brush on three sides
not much better, scrub hawthorne
and salal and the dogwood threatening

to die, huge now in some neighbor's
backyard and blooming a white
I don't remember like the walls
yellow as sick eyes inside where I move
room to room, one wall gone, another
for no good reason put up blocking
the kitchen from the room where we ate.
We called it the eating room
and my claim on this has run out.

It's nice of the last man here
to let me come in. I want to tell him
he's me, menial job at the door plant,
table set just barely for one. I want
to tell him I've been writing poems
the long time I've been away and need
to compare them with poems
I left here, never to be written, never
to be found in the attic where hornets
starve and there's no flooring.
Are they wild? Do they ring sad and real
as the years here would have become,
as real and unseen as women
would have been dreamed, curled
in the corner where light still
has a hard time? And later, Lord,
later I would have prayed
and begged to be forgiven for the blood.

This will be the last time. The road
outside's been paved twenty years,
the road no one ever came down
long as I waited, except for a bum
who whistled, "I'll Paint the Clouds
with Your Sunshine." Now the bus
downtown's routed by, every ten minutes

fresh diesel fumes. Across the street
only three of the old homes remain,
one where a sad man lived,
a man who drank himself to the grave
and drank his way into my poems
at least twice. He was the first sad man
I remember. I preferred sadness
to anger and I preferred him
for too long a time. My last gesture
will be at the door, facing east.
It will be a look at the hill
two blocks away, that delayed dawn
every morning and stood between me
and a nation. I live east of that hill.
Thanks to the man with a face the color
of wet salt, the second true sad man
on this block, it is not madness
for the first time I have gone home.

Scene

One day at a time. And one barn.
Lovers inside and horses ignoring the lovers.
And the creek nearby. The willows.
That was the scene. I forget the sky.
The sky, let's say, was green
and dotted with silly clouds
that looked like dimes.

Then the horses were lovers.
The lovers had gone to the creek
to celebrate their bones
under the willows and green
under the drifting dimes.
Let's say the lovers were green
and this dream is about them.

And let's say let's say woman and man!
One barn at a time. One moon.
The dimes are dark monsters
ignoring the lovers, the horses
who are also lovers and asleep.
Deep inside deep that is the scene
and I never wake up.

Second Chances

I can't let it go, the picture I keep of myself
in ruin, living alone, some wretched town
where friendship is based on just being around.
And I drink there a lot, stare at the walls until
the buzzing of flies becomes the silence I drown in.
Outside, children bad mouth my life with songs
their parents told them to sing. One showers
my roof with stones knowing I'm afraid
to step out and tell him to stop. Another yells,
"You can't get a woman, old man. You don't get a thing."

My wife, a beautiful woman, is fixing lunch.
She doesn't know I dream these things. She thinks
I'm fine. People respect me. Oh, she knows all right
I've seen grim times. But these days my poems
appear everywhere. Fan mail comes. I fly east
on a profitable reading tour. Once in a while
a young girl offers herself. My wife knows that, too.
And she knows my happiness with her is far more
than I ever expected. Three years ago, I wouldn't
have given a dime for my chances at life.

What she doesn't know is now and then
a vagabond knocks on the door. I go answer
and he says, "Come back, baby. You'll find

a million poems deep in your destitute soul."
And I say, "Go away. Don't ever come back."
But I watch him walk, always downhill toward
the schoolyard where children are playing 'ghost,'
a game where, according to the rules, you take
another child's name in your mind but pretend
you're still you while others guess your new name.

With Ripley at the Grave of Albert Parenteau

He is twice blessed, the old one buried here
beneath two names and a plastic bouquet from Choteau.
He lived his grief out full. From this hill
where Crees bury their dead to give them a view,
he can study the meadow, the mountains
back of mountains, the Teton canyon winding into stone.
I want to say something wrong,
say, this afternoon they are together again,
he and the wife he killed by mistake in the dark
and she forgives him. I don't want to admit
it's cold alone in the ground and a cold run
from Canada with a dog and two bottles of rye.

Say he counted stones along the bottom of the Teton
and the stones counted him one of them.
He scrubbed and scrubbed and never could
rid his floor of her stain.
He smashed his radio and the outside world
that came from it, and something like a radio hum
went on in him the slow rest of his life.
This is the first time I knew his white name.

•

We won't bring him real flowers this afternoon
jammed with the glitter of lupin and harebells.
This is the west and depth is horizontal.
We climb for a good view of canyons and we are never
higher than others, never a chief like him.
His grave is modern. His anguish goes back—
the first tone from struck rock. You and I,
we're civilized. We can't weep when it's needed or counts.
If you die first, I'll die slow as Big Bear,
my pale days thin with age,
night after night, the stars callow as children.

With Melissa on the Shore

My sudden daughter, grays are latent in that sea.
This moment we turn gull. We ride white spray
over a water sky two freighters ago ignited.
This is where we started, gill and fin and slow scan
of the ocean floor. Waves wiped out all traces
of our birth. No sign of a home, no proof
we ever lived are two insistent grays.

What if the horizon's laughter arrives
over and over, and this thin afternoon it seems
we're little on this beach? What other creature claims
his arms are wings and buzzes the crabs taking cover?
That's one game the dolphin wouldn't dare play.
We fall to the sand tough with laughter. The surf howls
dry disapproval and reads the Bible alone.

Other games matter. Listen. The pound. Here
we face our failure, words we should have said,
anger that spilled over last Tuesday (you don't
remember), the beggar we should have asked in.
The sea is fond of saying that's nothing.

Waves caving on sand say Melissa. The world makes demands
at impossible times and goes on burning with thirst.

And we go on burning. Like water. This is where we
and sky touch each other and tingle. Out there
real gulls clown high over what makes us sad,
that debris we try to forget. Gray is where we start.
What follows the first gray is luck. Look,
that blue's bigger than any sky in Montana.
Foam glows in the dark, white with bones of dead sole.

The Ballpark at Moiese

for Matthew

1

Score tied in the 8th, the only fans, bison
high above the park, turn back to their food.
A home run now, two on, would break the game
wide open. You're anxious in the box.
You pull the trigger on the fifth pitch
and it's over. Over the center fielder's head.
Over the trees in center field. Over moon
and inland gulls, it settles like a dead cloud
on the sleepwalking river
enroute to Japan.
The longest home run ever seen.
Did you see that, bison?

2

These tracks are dead.
Put your ear to them.
You hear no hum of train,
the Polson run that died.
You think of wrong blood
and the anonymous donor.

The Flathead river
moves like luck in sleep.

Men we couldn't find today
even in photos
took that train to Polson
where the lake
laughed blue as girls
and music improved
with each drink.
What that trip meant after
the week's grim labor
and the grimy way they felt
awkward down the track
waving their pay at bison
and the Mission Range.

Money. Fun.
The road takes off to Polson
like a vein.
The train
is on display in Kalispell.

3
Listen. In this dream I am
the only one watching a softball game.
I decide to play one more season.
I go to the home of Ed Schmidt
our first baseman.
His wife, Margaret,
a beautiful woman, greets me at the door.
Ed is out but Ed, she tells me,
will be glad to play again.
I wake up happy,
too old for the game.

4

You were born with wrong blood, saved
by miraculous transfusion. What I'm saying
is accept that blood. After 14 years
it's yours by right of artery and heart.
I should be wise and I'm not. Fifty years
of mistakes and I marry your mother
thinking this time I'll be right. Accept
that blood and dream the anonymous donor.
His hair failed brown. His eyes
beg love in catacombs. His life comes back
event after event in out of way places like Moiese
where he struck out often and made errors.
I should be wise and give blood that others
may dwell on their lives, immediate tingle
of women, the joke that cracked everyone up
that summer in Polson. How did it go?
Know I was right to marry your mother.
Know your blood gains momentum and size
like the river.

5

Crow Creek Reservoir to Dixon.
You can find a thousand spots to picnic.
Even the best ones, grass and shade tree,
ring with something lost. Not tribal ways
of feeling about space. Not some better way
things never were before the white man came.
Red or white, the orphan from Ronan
lives among strange animals
who turn away and graze.

6

What we want to save grinds down finally
to the place it happened, dim charm
of four worn spots we used for bases.
A small boy runs the home run out again

alone in snow. Did you see that, bison?
It comes back often that the river doesn't care
the last game died on the scoreboard.
It comes back once a lifetime
we heard someone cheer.

And what you did that day, score tied,
ignored by bison, the drive
you sent beyond retrieve, you take home
because it cannot mean. Because
it is ignored and lost. Circle the bases again
and claim they speak of it today in Dixon,
the old men in the bar
who were not there,
who every afternoon
takes the train that does not run
to Polson anymore.

Wheel of Fortune

One way of going is to bang the door your last time
out of the house, your rage hanging like dangerous gas
on the sun porch where your wife and children are crying.
You send them a postcard from Sweden saying you're sorry
you took all the money out of the bank and you hope
they're not going hungry. You meet a blonde someone
you saw once in a movie and boy is she lovey.
You've taken up painting and already have a dealer
in New York, another in London. Five of your oils
are in European collections and a new museum
in Amsterdam has signed you to a five-year contract.
If it wasn't for one reviewer, a man whose name
sounds a little like the name of your favorite river,
who calls your best shots amateur and once in the *Times*
said you paint like some retarded spastic, you'd really

be happy. You keep his reviews in a scrapbook
and each night sit there reading them over and over
planning his murder. Naturally, you no longer paint.
The museum is suing you. The blonde is having an affair
with Burt Lancaster. Tired and broke you go back home,
the one you slammed out of when this poem began.
You sit there contrite in your rocker and watch TV.
Your wife is cooking your favorite: clam *fettucine*.
The children say you watch too many crime shows,
you ought to take more walks.

Open Country

for George

It is much like ocean the way it opens
and rolls. Cows dot the slow climb of a field
like salmon trawls dot swells, and here or there
ducks climb on no definite heading.
Like water it is open to suggestion,
electric heron, and every moon
tricky currents of grass.

               Let me guess;
when you repair the damaged brain
of a beaten child or bring to a patient
news that will never improve, you need
a window not a wall to turn to.
And you come back here
where land has ways of going on
and the shadow of a cloud
crawls like a freighter, no port in mind,
no captain, and the charts dead wrong.

The Other Beaverbank

for Mildred

The river seems to sour and we can't recall
who's buried under the mound. We might guess
a name like Poor Bear. We might remember
the sequence: first, the crack of ice,
then tons of drowned bison pouring north,
and finally, for it was spring surely by then,
the crackpot preacher blew his trumpet
loud over the water and swans flew off.
With so much gone, it was natural to sell.

And it's natural to want it back, not just
Beaverbank but the whole wide scene,
the far bank of sand, the three islands
named for Spanish ships and the evening sweep
of falcon counter current. The Missouri
releases and fills like a heart. Some new tenant
we hope will chase some old ghost away
and all swans come home. Surely it's spring:
the cottonwood leaves turn over silver
and flash. We could dig and dig
and find no human remains. The mound?
That was an early joke of settlers.
They knew when they heaped the dirt and stomped it
round like the dome of some early tribe
we'd create the rest years later,
handsome bones and beads,
the sad tale of one who lost it all.

At the Cabin

We ripple aspen the way we move out
in the morning meadow wind. Stay close

through the buffalo willow's manic perfume
across the field of lupin where the fresh track
of a cougar gives us the direction not to go.
We climb high lichen and below us
farther than our first dream of the void
the north fork of the Teton cannot move.
We are frozen deep in hunger.
If we tumble coupled down the rock side
bouncing from the last ledge out in sky
in final isolation like the eagle, like the bones
of Crees, we'll shatter on the valley floor
separate as stars. Love's the best way
to feel safe. Love on moss. Love on springy bed
of juniper. And there must be definite ways
of telling how the mate remaining, widower Mallard
or warrior Cree who killed his wife by mistake
doubles his grief every storm.

Pale letter from home: "We hope you return
someday. We love you still." The pages
ride thermols like white spastic birds
across the canyon to Uninhabited Mountain.
More than letter disappears. More than past.
The red hawk stumbles, catches himself and climbs.
The cougar, spurred by rumor of a spacious cave,
turns south to Ear Mountain and a hoped for role:
I am good enough to own a home.

We come back tired. Ways of hating the past
sour inside us. We bore ourselves remembering
children in ruin, too many tears at the pass.
If the Teton falters, move the rocks.
No matter how water jitters, water
has no nerves. Rivers flow because the first law
of all land is slant. The second, desire to ride.
We ripple aspen the way we move back
to the cabin baking in motionless noon.

And the aspen ring. The river loosens at its pools
and takes off shooting wildly at the sky
like some drunk cowboy, his first night back in town
after centuries of good work done.

Birthday

for Paul Levitt
with equal shares in December 21

Wind deserted the pond this morning. The day
aged badly under a single cloud, and birds
abandoned this air where lilies stop waving
and microscum moors to the base of reeds.
Cattails doze under the light's warm weight.
Remember salmon, how they once climbed
over each other frantic to die? Even rivers fade.
Under wings, sudden, out of a birdless north
cars are out of gear and my life runs
empty roads like a sick hand on a map.

Regions beyond worn needs to clown, a man
waits by the road for out-of-date wagons.
The wagons won't come. His children grew weary
calling clouds candy, frying mud on a rock.
They ran from the calendar south. He grows
the same sick corn every year. He tries reading
the girls better ways. Miss August is best,
the least stained by wine he throws at the wall.

If the wind would return, south to north, some
old comforting motion, opening, closing the skies,
letting man peek at the stars and his grave,
I could face those years I lived ashamed
of the demented grocer and his run-down store,

dust on jars, meat dark in the case, the tab
he ran for the poor. I could use the wind
like others use religion, to tell myself
it's ok to be out of rivers and weak.

With wind high, bewildering, I can't imagine
the poor being robbed, an arrest being made.
That fanatic who screamed in the street
about Christ and found cancer her savior—
she's part of my life. On this short day
when air rides green, let's welcome back
with early eyes the shifts of giant bird flocks.
The relentless pour of bruised fish up creeks
that barely trickle and spark, named after miners
the world photoed and lost, who stare at our faces,
their dead eyes hoping for a strike.

Repairing the House, the Church, Restoring the Music

for Aunt Sara

In early hymns cries came faint
from far off. Someone needed blood.
Money, I said, will make it right.
What I knew seemed echo. The hymns went out
with little hope and came back white as Christ
from tired stars. I admit I faked tears.
Every wrong note hit.
I hated the not meant different shades
of plaster on the walls and the half meant light
in the vestibule. I take on faith
Christ paled from less than loss of blood.

•

Part of us remains alone. That's good.
All these years I never told a soul about
the thirteenth wren, the first twelve dead.
Take the destitute choir. Isn't it right
given what happened in the interim,
tremoring itself seems firm and walls
whatever color hold out cold.
When tears are real, bad music's not that bad.

I promised myself I'd come back one day
serious about a chapel that cracks
and patches itself with sky
and locate for the first time what we are,
the warm center that has always been,
fireweed that overnight covers the raw dirt
of a meadow cleared by machine.
I kept that promise this morning and, Jesus
or none, stars found their second wind.
These weeds we walk were garden lost
one year to no special music,
music all the same.

Leaving the Dream

Every day became a slow July. Sweat, it was clear,
was what he would do forever. He learned early
women weren't waiting in barns when the workday ended.
It would be wife and children, not much love and no money,
no sun but the one he must labor under,
That's how I saw him, bitter far back in himself.

What did he dream? I dreamed him drunk and alone.
And I dreamed another man younger than him
and strong poking fun when the old one fell in the dirt.
I dreamed he dreamed a hundred bluegill day at a lake

and a cooling wind low in the oak. When my dream grew firm
wild dogs pulled him from my sleep.

You think you've got it? Forget it. That young strong man
I dreamed was not me. The old man had more than one day
of fun. Some good weather repeats. He was more proud
    than my dream credits him and he was less sad
than whiskey might make him seem. Besides, when old
no matter how sharp you may limp in some child's crippled eye.

Lake and slow rivers were home for women with fins.
I've gone back to white creeks with Indian names,
the first promise life makes: it's all downhill and dance.
This time I know better. I can center on the song.
I never dance. Just listen to the band.
The old man sits home caked with day labor and worn.

Last night the young man called the old man a failure.
The old man seemed phoney. He spoke ignorantly
of what the young man knew well, and his weeping seemed fake.
I begged, 'Leave him alone. I still love him. He's poor.'
The day moves loud in the leaves like a tremoring past,
some form in the dust, a blinding sky on the way.

Beaverbank

for Ripley

Light from the river brightens your old room.
The heron you called Pete returns still young
to sweep the river like a cloud. This bend's
the one the river loves to make, moving easy
to the bank and curving easy as the moon.
Your eyes ride water and your eyes climb trees.
Nights were filled with horses and each morning

all that final summer twenty years before
beaver crossed in wild herds to the island.
You saved your brother from the undertow.

Call it home when the house you lived in
fades slow as carp swim. The empty house
stands detonative in the sun, tick, tick
of the bomb you left there deafening the ghost.
And it's a sad girl sees that one house lost
to weather and the strange tune starting far back
in the sky and growing as the jobs you held
pile up on your clearance form. The day
your clearance comes declaring now you're eligible
to dream return, a corporation
buys the property and lies about its plans.

Love, I lost that one house too. Long ago.
And I feel nothing now except the faint dream
time to time that had I stayed there
in my makeshift room my poems would still be
personal as doom, ring wild with fear
until some troubled reader pounded on the door.
I will not answer. I will not go outside
to walk the river. And the beaver when they reach
the island and are safe will not come back
to mind. The deer will not go home.

Go back like you go away, not afraid of loss
and fearful loss will not be there to celebrate
some far off winter when you stumble on
the ruins, your eyes downriver gray.
Your fear means you lose nothing. Your brother
has four children, and the current rides
in such firm ways no map gets out of date.

The Towns We Know and Leave Behind, the Rivers We Carry with Us

for James Wright

I forget the names of towns without rivers.
A town needs a river to forgive the town.
Whatever river, whatever town—
it is much the same.
The cruel things I did I took to the river.
I begged the current: make me better.

Your town, your river, or mine—
it is much the same.
A murdering man lives on the land
in a shack the river birds hate.
He rubs the red shriek of night from his eyes.
He prays to water: don't let me do that again.

Let's name your river: Ohio.
Let's name all rivers one in the blood,
red steam and debris in the blood.
Say George Doty had a wrong head.
Say the Ohio forgives what George did
and river birds loved his shack.
Let's name the birds: heron and sweat.
Let's get away from the mud.

The river is there to forgive the town
and without a river a town abuses the sky.
The river is there to forgive what I did.
Let's name my river: Duwamish.
And let's admit
the river birds don't hate my home.
That's a recent development, really
like mercury in the cod.

•

Without a river a town abuses the air.
The river is there to forgive what I did.
The river birds hate what I did
until I name them.
Your river or mine—
it is much the same.
A murdering man lived on the bank.

Here's the trick;
We had to stay drunk
to welcome the river
to live in a shack
to die on the bank
beneath the bigoted sky
under the river birds
day after day
to murder away
all water that might die.

A murdering man is dead on the bank
of your new river, The East,
on mine, The Clark Fork.
It is much the same.
Your river has gulls and tugs.
Mine has eagles and sky.
I rub last night from my eyes.
I ask bright water what's happened.

The river, I am not sure which one,
says water has no special power.
What should I do?
Or you?
Now water has no need to forgive
what shall become of murder?
How shall we live
when we killed, when we died by the word?

•

Whatever the name of the river,
we both had two women to love,
One to love us enough we left behind
a town that abuses the day.
The other to love the river we brought with us,
the shack we lived and still live in,
the birds, the towns that return to us for names
and we give them names knowing the river
murders them away.

Fort Benton

for Jan

This was the last name west on charts.
West of here the world turned that indefinite white
of blank paper and settlers faded one at a time alone.
What had been promised in Saint Louis proved
little more than battering weather and resolve.
Hungry for women and mail, this town
turned out to watch the Mandan dock.

Church was a desperate gesture, prayer
something muttered bitter. One we called friend
the long Missouri here followed his babble
into the breaks and no one looked for his bones.
We still don't look for friends who turn into air.
Given the right seed and seasonal luck
a love of land becomes a need for each other.

The river slides into the breaks. Nothing comes back,
man, Mandan, the latest word on sin.
Trains killed boats and died in their turn.
Where we look deep the river smirks.
Let's recognize 'hello there' and 'nice day'

spare us those improvements that give way
beneath us like the bank someday for sure.

The best towns, no matter how solvent, seem
to barely hang on. This is the town to leave
for the void and come back to needing a home.
It may be the aged river or the brick hotel
on the bank, heavy as water, or the ritual
that shouldn't be hard to start: the whole town out
shouting 'come back' at the breaks one day a year.

High Grass Prairie

Say something warm. Hello. The world
was full of harm until this wind
placated grass and put the fish to rest.
And wave hello. Someone may be out there
riding undulating light our way.
Wherever we live, we sleep here
where cattle sleep beside the full canal.
We slept here young in poems.
The canal runs on without us east
a long flow into Fairfield. The grass flows
ever to us, ever away, the way it did
that war we dreamed this land alive.
The man we hoped was out there
saw our signal and is on the way.
Say something warm. Hello. You can sleep
forever in this grass and not be cold.

Brief History

Dust was too thick every summer. Every winter
at least one animal died, a good friend,

and we forgot the burial ritual after our Bible
washed away in the flood. We mumbled anything
that occurred to us over the grave. Finally
ouly our wives were left to hate, our children
who ran off to Detroit and never came back.
How we raged at change, the year the ground
went fallow, the time our wheat grew purple
and the government couldn't explain. Less fish
in the lake every year, grain prices falling
and falling through dark air, the suicide bird
who showed us the good way out. The century
turned without celebration. We tried to find fun
in the calendar, the strange new number, nineteen.
It was women held us together. They cautioned
us calm the day we shouted we knew
where millions in diamonds were buried
and ran at cattle swinging the ax.
We forget that now. We are planning hard
for the century ahead.

Medicine Bow

This is the way the road bent then, wide and sullen
across baked earth and I was with two bums
I'd picked up outside Meeteesee. That was a day
I thought being kind was important because the world
that summer was dust and rejection, and banners
of welcome in Red Lodge hung limp. I was drunk.
Heat soured the sky. The day would come I vowed
when I would fight. I bought a room for the bums.
The next day I gave them both money in Loveland
and waved goodbye and drove off smug as the rich.

How many years ago was that? What songs played out
miles of what should have been, on whatever station

the radio found leaking through acres of cactus?
What happened that day in Medicine Bow? Sudden snarl
of the woman running the motel. The knife I kept
under my pillow that night, convinced that here
at last I'd found the source of all evil, the final
disgrace, world ending a way no poet predicted.

My Buick was yellow then. This one is green and zips
to Laramie easy. The whole business that day
in Medicine Bow and Medicine Bow seem silly.
It may not have been here at all. The brown block
hotel seems familiar, but it may be the road, the way
it bends into town is wrong. Denver stations
are coming in clear and that time I got nothing.
When you drive fast, hay seems to fly.

Overlooking Yale

for Hillis Miller

Top Of The Park, Hillis. Top of the World.
Long Island Sound bounces a gold ball
of dawn off a reflective glass building
(the firm inside bankrupt) and it lands on The Green.
The Green lies white in ice
and out of sermons. I am out of wisdom,
eating French toast cooked the year
Yale was founded, too timid to complain,
too far from home to trust my manners.
I'm sure I'm being observed
and my act is not clean. Western paranoia.
John Wayne. Three centuries short
of history. One of stability. Way ahead
in weather and rustic charm you can't trust.
With Yale below in gold light, I feel
I should have read Milton, ought to be

in the know about something, some key remark
Dryden made about Donne. Not concerned
with the way we talk to old cars,
pat their hoods and murmur "sweet hero."
Two hundred thousand miles and only
five changes of oil and one valve grind.
I should try for salvation but below
the three chapels lock tight as a witchburner's heart.
Out west, survival is enough. Here,
the lone gull that hides in the sun
like a World War II fighter plane
and dives on the small shop below, the one
with a sign I can read, "Living Things,"
has no stature after the raid, perched
puffy and proud on the grotesque K of C building
awaiting a drum roll and the DFC.
And you'd best not trust either the warm way
light looks filling the streets, nor warm looks
on student faces when you make a major point.
They'll remember you wrong in time,
your point will be perverted to their purpose
and all purpose is impure. I remember
what I do for nothing and no reason fondly,
staring New Haven away and in its place
a garden from way back and the sweat
of those who could barely read and write,
bent to immediate weeds, first sprout
of carrot, promise of lettuce and bean,
all the way across this nation,
and inside the house, four books counting
The Bible and all but The Bible long
out of print. And I don't feel I have come
so very far from that. Top Of The Park.
Top of the World. The limousine leaves soon
for New York and the plane, the plane for points west.
For sure we die at either end of the run.
For the first time the east is not the east

dreamed from a hill on the edge of Seattle.
Give that gull his medal.
When you see a ghost, try to be nice.

Imagining Delaware

When I imagine Delaware
I see a lonely canal,
a lock gate stuck half open,
water crawling out slow foam.
I see a man
also lonely, and grieving.
I am not sure why.
If it's Monday
the sky's a promissory green.
Later in the week
the sky's grim white.

I'm speaking our time,
the time I imagine.

The man keeps his face turned.
It's hard to tell he's grieving,
to see his tears for sure.
Once in a great while, a woman,
not invited, not from Delaware
(I imagine no Delaware women)
passes between me and him.
I want to imagine more,
not let the scene end there,
the shadowy woman gone,
the man still turned,
the sky by now heavy
with threat of night.
Dog or dinosaur,
I want something more.

•

I've never been in Delaware.
It must be something like that,
however it's put,
soft 'pass away,' hard 'die.'

A Good View from Flagstaff

Let's take it as it is: acres flowing
yellow north and people so small in the distance
we believe them happy working fields.
Despite the heat, the sun is less than cruel.
Soil is wet black and the wheat rolls far enough
to be a lemon sea. Silos waver
and are silver salmon two wines into lunch.

This view is what one needs to love the world
when things go bad. Take Naples, '67, me alone
in Vomero, no sleep for nights, endless sweat,
my system out of chemical whack from weeks
of suicidal drinking and the sad scenes of my life
locked with me in the hotel room like bats.
Far off, through my window, a white apartment
building gleamed each morning and I knew
out there beyond me somewhere was a world
worth having because it caught the sun
and sent the light back to the sea confirmed.
Because it sat there quiet far away.

A good view here. We ignore the mean acts
in the houses though we can't forget they go on
daily with the soul's attrition. We are certain
why the plowhorse limps. Spread the way it is
by wind, the world in cultivated patchwork
claims we travel on the right freight one day
and the years are gone. At worst
they're more than nothing. The best friends
we remember took us home the way we are.

Port Townsend, 1974

On this dishonored, this perverted globe
we go back to the sea and the sea opens for us.
It spreads a comforting green we knew when children—
celery—Wesson Oil can—through islands. It flares
fresh immediate blue beyond the world's edge
where dreams turn back defeated and the child weeps
replaying some initial loss. Whatever it does for us
it is resolute, even when it imitates sad grasses
on the inland plains and gulls are vultures overhead
hidden in the bewildering glare.
Aches of what we wanted to be and reluctantly are
play out in the wash, wash up the sand and die
and slip back placid to the crashing source.
The sea releases our rage. Logs fly over
the seawall and crush the homes of mean neighbors.
Our home, too. The sea makes fun of what we are
and we laugh beside our fire, seeing our worst selves
amplified in space and wave. We are absurd.
And sea comes knocking again in six hours. The sea
comes knocking again. Out there, salmon batter
candlefish senseless for dinner. The troller flashes
his dodger through the salmon school. The sky widens
in answer to claustrophobic prayer. The sea believes us
when we sing: we knew no wrong high back in the mountains
where lost men shred their clothes the last days
of delirium and die from white exposure. We found one
sitting erect, his back against the stars, and even dead
he begged us to take him west to the shore of the sea.

Getty

Today, I remembered Getty, the old man
at Price's lake who rented boats and coughed

and told me he was gone. Moss caked his lungs
and a sky I'd forgotten drifted in his eyes.
The brooks I caught were dazzling and wild.
I shouted 'Lord love Getty' at the trees.
Nothing came back. The young sheen of willows
hung over cedars dark and grumpy with age.

I came back early next spring but Getty
prophetically blue, had gone, that winter
I stayed home in Seattle and wrote hard
to make 'alive' and 'violent' do for the sky.

Some days the fish don't bite. You know that.
And we die at wrong times, like Friday.
Whatever day Getty died, it could not be special
or wrong, an old man like him, alone
with a lake, no urge to go after trout
and no particular feeling when nylon
arcs out over the water, hangs that one moment
all moments pulse, first kiss, first soft light
in the eyes of the girl who seemed nothing last week,
and settles soft as a far teal
and waits.

Let's see. What happened today: a mild fight
in the tenure meeting. We voted nine to one 'no.'
A disturbed student raged in my office
about elk roaming some desert for water.
A swim—I felt my arms harden
and knew I was building more wind.
On the way home, night ignited the town
and I thought of a speech: In conclusion,
let me say Getty let me say—
I remembered his eyes and the sky in them,
his easy prediction coughed out
like we had plenty in common.

The Small Oil Left in the House
We Rented in Boulder

That's a place I've been. The town
small across the river and compact. Two women
gather salad cress. Two men chat on the far bank.
No doubt May—flowers flaring, quiet river high
and no doubt nothing more than the tree in bloom
goes on. I didn't want to live there then.
I want to live there now and not go mad.
I still believe there was a time I could.

It must have been enough to see the buildings
double in the river, to know that roadless world
where you go nowhere ever and the old
pass wisdom down, time of day for pike, time
of moon for planting, time to die and float away.
And since the world stops where the river bends
from sight, the body must pass on to some place
warm in the minds of children though they have
no word for heaven and the hot wind reeks.

Orofino, Idaho, is close, but wrong.
For one thing, there's a bridge, and one day
moments after a child had drowned, I drove by
on my way to Portland, past the frantic divers
and the wailing mother, and I kept going,
concentrating on the radio, the tune playing,
"Adios," oh lovely, from the local station.
That was May and God the river roared.

At Our Best

Face the moon. Ask: is it less, now that man
has been there? That's what some claim. They say

we've dirtied that gleam and lovers must look
elsewhere for support, Venus or the stars
burned out, burning with illusion like all love.
We kill our wives to have the other woman.
When wives die they fix us in their final stare.
Their eyes ask why. We turn away ashamed.
We move to the country where the nearest law
and telephone are miles beyond the humorless rim
of the mountains and we beat our dogs at dawn.
Their howls can't reach even the next farm.
Their eyes ask why. We move back to the city.
Our lives are sodden on our backs. We shuffle
alley to alley alone, mumbling thanks
for a dime we know's devalued like the moon.
Once, beached by storm, we found a shark jaw
polished by tide, light from China, sand.
We shouted, "We are wealthy," at the moon.
No confirming word came back. Only the level wind
slanting our fire east and we leaned west
against direction and sang. We didn't care
our words lived less than a moment in sky.

Graves

The flat year, when summer never arrived
grass lived green to August and we buried love
under the grass and marked the grave with a stick.
Wherever we went that fall, Mexico City,
Istanbul, we vowed to go back next year
and dig love up, resurrect love, make love
something for the ages. We planned disciples
and a book big as the Bible. It was all set,
even the witnesses historians believe.

Years later, we found the stick knocked down
by rain, but the spot was certain, there

twelve paces from the apple tree, on a line
with the bay and the anchored freighter
we knew would never move. We dug
and dug. Two moons went by. No love.
We rechecked memory and map and still
only brown dirt and the earthworms twisting away.

We should never have named what we buried.
We know now it wasn't love. Nor a tin can
packed with diamonds. Whatever it was,
dead cat, dead salmon, it flourished
only when skies are odd, when the summer
we expect fails and those abnormal rains
keep the world green longer than the eye takes
to imagine "nothing certain" instead of "love"
on the headstone, rivers fat and trout spawning
year round as if September will not end.

Dwelling

They won't go away, the sea perch
circling piles, the searun cutthroat
hammering home upriver in rain.
I try to ignore them, to focus on women,
on the news. They swim between the lines.
They live in puddles too muddy to see them.
And I see them. They live in dry caves.
They migrate cloud to cloud across
a sky that's always flowing. Bass and catfish,
carp, pompano and cod. What if one day
they were gone? What if all creatures, animal
and man, arrived in some sane ratio?
Would air still stream, light still battle
down tidepools to spot the twenty-ray star?
And would I still feel you cannot die badly
though you scream for mercy and pray
the sky stopped at your door made a mistake?

Changes at Meridian

It's a problem, why I'm here with amplified rock
from the resort hammering the shoreline straight
and driving the planted trout deep where catfish lived
before they were poisoned away. Coves I remember
aren't coves anymore and perch are not welcome
since Fish and Game labeled them scrap. Where I row
the lilies seem decor. No trace of Robert's cabin caving
under the weight of moss. No sunfish nest under the dock.
No old man, set hard in himself, rowing me home.

It's not that no one knows me after forty years
or that at 5 P.M. the surface reflects a world
hopelessly changed for the worse. What nags is
loss of loss, the desperate way I brought farms back
because I wanted the pastures always slanted gently
into the lake, warm reflection of willow and cow,
the old man cautioning patience days the crappie went dormant.
These don't come anymore as if I don't need them
and this rehabilitated water, these clustered dull homes are ok.

One poet said it is enough to live perpetually in change.
He didn't believe it. I say we want everything static
including farms we lose and rebuild. That way,
when the fish start feeding and the first chill of day
reminds us we haven't come far, home is a mild row back,
we love the old man repeating over and over,
"Keep your line in the water." Change or no change,
with the right bait this world has twenty-three moons.

Guns at Fort Flagler

Some foreign freighter crawls a blue path north
to Juan de Fuca and we let it go.

We didn't used to. All who entered here,
this passage between Marrowstone and Whidbey,
were invaders and we made them pay.
We pointed these black cannons at them
and we shouted 'boom'
and they came coughing foam, hands high in surrender.

That was forty years ago, the real war
still to come. We believed citations,
the distinguished cross of heron over smelt,
adoring women, the deep meaning of taps
across the water sad on a minus tide,
flag at half mast and roses floating where the hero
took his green chill place among the ratfish.
Three wars later, one win, one tie, one loss,
the guns never fired hung limp in their mounts.

Any war could be called off because of weather.
Rain's not good for ammo and one glint of sun deflects
confident rounds off target. The alert goes out:
salmon in the camp! and candlefish close ranks.
Danger below the surface it is wise to know
how silly we look in uniform saluting the ship
that passes too far out to tell us where it's from,
has no interest beyond instrument readings and charts
that help it through the straight, then help it cross
the blank enormous water, the only check point
music from the port picked up days out.

Fairfield

"A guy I used to know—he taught me all about the sky."
HUMPHREY BOGART in *High Sierra*

I wanted it depressed, one dusty road
and two cafés both with 'help wanted' signs.
Where I ate, the waitress was too in love

with the cook for things I wanted to say.
The canal passed through town ripe green
and grain, I had to admit, grew assured.
A dog slept fat on warm gravel. No trouble foreseen
raising funds to build the new gym.

I'd expected hurt, the small town kind everyone
knows and ignores, a boy who tried and tried
to leave home, sobbing his failure alone
at the mirror back of the bar, still wearing
his '39 letter sweater, still claiming
the girl who moved to Great Falls will return.
I wanted to honor him in this poem,
to have the sky turn dark as I drove off
the town in my rear view mirror
huddled with fear white in black air.

The drunk I saw seemed happy. I drove empty away.
What if Fairfield sent signals to Mars
and signals came back saying all weather is yours
no matter how vulgar? I imagined cruel sky
left every bird orphan. When I passed
Freeze Out Lake I saw herons accepted that refuge
as home, and I knew the water was green with sky,
not poisoned green with resolve.

To Women

You start it all. You are lovely.
We look at you and we flow.
So a line begins, on the page, on air,
in the all of self. We have misused you,
invested you with primal sin. You bleed
for our regret we are not more.
The dragon wins. We come home and sob

and you hold us and say we are brave
and in the future will do better.
So far, so good.

Now some of you want out and I don't
blame you, not a tiny bit. You've caught on.
You have the right to veer off flaming
in a new direction, mud flat and diamond mine,
clavicord and dead drum. Whatever.
Please know our need remains the same.
It's a new game every time, one on one.

In me today is less rage than ever, less hurt.
When I imagine some good woman young
I no longer imagine her cringing
in cornstalks, cruel father four rows away
beating corn leaves aside with a club.
That is release you never expected
from a past you never knew you had.
My horse is not sure he can make it
to the next star. You are free.

How to Use a Storm

Where did the storm come from? No warning
on the forecast and no warning wind.
We'd put off putting the storm windows on
and insulating the attic when
bang, rain on glass, and now we can't name
the brown form cringing under the cutbank.
Trees go wild in protest and dogs crawl
sullen into the past. All plans are off.
One cloud covers the world pole to pole.

•

In these moments, each to his life and each
alone in himself. I ride rough water
under dark skies more than forty years back.
My cousin is rowing. I am going to die.
I am alone on a prairie
waving hello to bison miles off and blind.
Men work hard in a barn. Because I'm open
and warm they disdain me. Women
disdain me because I warp in their glare.

The storm is over. The brown form under
the cutbank's a badger. What hope's open
to him? He makes us sick
the way he near slithers, his hair wet
and flat like a villain's, his every motion
faintly intestine. We say wherever
he lives it's not fit for others.
Sun fills our kitchen. Tamaracks ask
for this dance and dogs beg food at our door.

The trouble with weather, what's happening now
we think will go on forever.
Moments are slower than days.
Between storms, we believe our weather ideal,
our home safe from those we can't stand.
Better we plan our kitchen to trap
whatever light arrives, and whatever creature
huddles in the blue, a storm's a good time
to remember home is where he says hello.

How Meadows Trick You

I said the glint was thistle. It turned out tin.
The place had a history of picnics.
Include the last sad hour, others left for home,

paper scattered, the long long angle of sun.
In games, children took turns dying
in the run-down barn, and whatever animal
roared in the woods that ringed the meadow,
in time he grew tame, his roar was part of the play.

And what would it matter now if I found it,
was reassured it all happened once, even
the women who, given these years, I'm convinced
I invented. Or was that earlier, in snow
where I'd fallen and one was smiling above me
saying her name: Laurie Roy? That can't be.
I used to remember everything that happened
plain as the love on her face. Now it mixes
and fades. A jungle. A blistering day
in the desert. Typhoon. The Taranto docks.
Grim G.I.'s on the ship sailing west.

If I say thistle and the glint is tin
and picnics never happened, you can believe
something in me is modern. I am no longer
always the last to leave. When I find that meadow
I love and drive off certain some places remain,
I take stock of the light. You can believe the dark
on its way and the durable women
who hover ahead of your car and pilot you home.

Snow Poem

To write a snow poem you must ignore the snow
falling outside your window.

You must think snow, the word as a snotty owl
high on the telephone pole

glowering down and your forehead damp with fear
under the glare

of the owl who now is mating. On rare days
we remember the toy

owl we buried under the compost heap,
white sky passing above, warm chirp

of wren and the avenging hawk.
That was summer. Let us go back

to snow and forget that damn fool lecture
I gave last winter.

Well, then: here is your window.
The storm outside. Outside, the dead dove drifting.

The Carnival Inside

I went timid to that town
where banners welcomed strangers and the mayor
sang halleluiah in the park. It was warm and foreign.
All I knew seemed shaken, long days of toil
in heat and the petulant river carping
at the edge of the field, grim moon. The town band
played such lively tunes, I danced.
The first time.

I said, I'll never go back.
Then Sunday and the music died.
I asked what's wrong. This is the day for worship,
not fun, the police explained. On this day
we give thanks for fun. We honor land

and the food it grows. Boys give thanks for girls,
girls boys, and so on. I stood empty in the empty square.
That won't happen again.

I went home sad. I said
you interrupt music for purpose you are dying.
I went on working, sun and river the same.
Once I started back alone to town. A man along
the road said the town had been destroyed.
I sing in the fields and I've decked the scarecrow
in satin. The moon is a grand comedian.
I laugh so hard I hurt.

From Altitude, the Diamonds

You can always spot them, even from high up,
the brown bulged out trying to make a circle
of a square, the green square inside the brown,
inside the green the brown circle you know is mound
and the big outside green rounded off by a round line
you know is fence. And no one playing.

You've played on everyone. Second base somewhere
on the Dallas Tucson run, New Mexico you think,
where green was brown. Right field outside Chicago
where the fans went silent when you tripled home
the run that beat their best, their all-season
undefeated home town Sox. What a game you pitched
that hot day in the Bronx. You lost to that left hander,
Ford, who made it big, one-nothing on a fluke.
Who's to believe it now? Fat. Bald. Smoking your fear
of the turbulent air you are flying, remembering
the war, a worse fear, the jolting flak, the prayer.

•

When air settles, the white beneath you opens
and far below in some unpopulated region
of whatever state you are over (it can't be Idaho,
that was years ago) you spot a tiny diamond,
and because you've grown far sighted with age
you see players moving, the center fielder
running the ball down deep, two runners
rounding third, the third base coach waving hard
and the hitter on his own not slowing down
at second, his lungs filled with the cheers of those
he has loved forever, on his magnificent tiny way
to an easy stand-up three.

Bay of Sad Loss

For fifty years the bubbles marked
where the ship went down. The romantic one,
sails like summer clouds, the lusty "land ho"
from the crow's nest and the cheering on deck.
Wild times, looking back. We study
the blue sweep of the bay over a vodka tonic.
Remember the albino blue shark we took
off Chile and gave to the zoologist in Vis?

Didn't we burn once, burn in the glare
of sea, in the winds we dreamed, the women
we dreamed in those winds, over our
geography lesson (why was China yellow?)
insects humming outside, prop plane humming
the warm day open, girl in the warm dream
saying "Go to Iceland. Come back and I'm yours."

And what the hell happened? What went wrong
1927? The captain who issued
soft bizarre orders. The first mate suddenly

sobbing and screaming, "It makes no matter.
It makes no matter at all." We sailed
into this bay, our cargo damaged by storm
and said we'll try it again. One more time.
And we still say it. The weather station
gets better predicting the wind.

Bay of Resolve

Think how we touch each other when we sight land
after two years at sea. How we say, "It's still there."
The gulls weren't lying who came to pilot us home.
No matter what happens inside them, the houses climb
lovingly tight to hills, and the smoke rising
above the houses takes the sea chill out of our bones.
When we make out women, the form of them certain
against the white seawall, we stand on the rail and wave.

What holds us back? The shore boats are waiting.
We sit glum in our quarters and sweat. The mate
yells, "going ashore" and the pink girls in the corner
with wild lemon hair cry "farewell," our bite marks
still clear on their necks. How they fought for our kisses
south of Australia. What dishes they cooked
Can we ever leave them? Those bright days they flew
ahead of the bow singing "on," every red inch
of their bodies stung by the shark spray, their faces
shining alive with our love under the pulsing sky.
Our first kiss on land is cold. We turn away.

This bay never gets wild. The harbor is ideal. We need
not anchor our boat. Three months of summer
the water lies flatter than dawn. In this calm weather
we have no reason to mock the captain or sneak
back of the bilge pump to study worn photos of girls.

Long ago, didn't we read how all journeys end?
The man in that story, his name lost now, came home
tired from the raw world of dragon and flame
and developed a coin, still in use, a salmon on one side
under the words "Good As Water." On the other
a woman firm in silver relief.

Bay of Recovery

This water started it all, this sullen arm
of gray wound loose about the islands
whipped in patches by the north wind white.
The girl on the cliff exposed her body
to wind and whispered "whip me whip me."
I was less than bird, awkward on my bad leg,
half drunk from last night, and maybe
you don't think I'm telling it all.
                                        All right.
There was this sullen girl in tight pants
on the shore who whispered "love me"
at the stumps of broken pile.
                                        All right.
There was this girl I could barely make out
alone in moonlight on a passing ship.
Sequins, I am sure. Even now I see the sparkle
of her skin.
                        No. No. Let me try it again.
There was no girl and I was in good shape.
This water started it all, the dazzling arm
of blue blue promise and the dazzling gull.
Gull. Not girl. And it was less than dazzle,
it was more than being alone on the beach
young under the moon, started it all.

The Sandbanks

We went to the moon those empty Sundays,
air purple with chill. Once, we found
the jawbone of a horse. Another time, a creek
no one had heard of, a creek without a name
and that close to home. And though the cliff
had been cut by man, and first avenue south
was near, we were the first men there.

I remember it cold. Cold strata of sand
and cold fern. The mysterious cold air
that hung in the pit. The cold rim
of the sandbanks above us. Cold sky.
I remember the way the nation broke east
yellow and cold, and the Cascades
hiding the nation, snow and blue stone.

I took the jaw home. Where have you been?
There's a way of knowing why we go
to places others pass by. It has to do
with water we discover and bones.
It has a lot to do with rehearsal,
having the right lines to say in that country
we may find ourselves, the grass
in despair and no one friendly in sight.

The River Now

Hardly a ghost left to talk with. The slavs moved on
or changed their names to something green. Greeks gave up
old dishes and slid into repose. Runs of salmon thin
and thin until a ripple in October might mean carp.
Huge mills bang and smoke. Day hangs thick with commerce

and my favorite home, always overgrown with roses,
collapsed like moral advice. Tugs still pound against
the outtide pour but real, running on some definite fuel.
I can't dream anything, not some lovely woman
murdered in a shack, not saw mills going broke,
not even wild wine and a landslide though I knew both well.
The blood still begs direction home. This river points
the way north to the blood, the blue stars certain
in their swing, their fix. I pass the backwash where
the cattails still lean north, familiar grebes pop up,
the windchill is the same. And it comes back with the odor
of the river, some way I know the lonely sources
of despair break down from too much love. No matter
how this water fragments in the reeds, it rejoins
the river and the bright bay north receives it all,
new salmon on their way to open ocean,
the easy tub returned.

Sound Track Conditional

Say you're drunk or drugged and something hums
far off. A factory. A storm. The sound
reminds you how you thought life would be,
Fresno, alone, thirty years back
on a mountain outside town, green valley
flaring away below you like a tune, Oberon's
slow death in *Wuthering Heights.*
You think about time, how your life runs down
one year each day of passing sky.
Clouds tear overhead. A woman dead
is a lot of women, starting with cranes.

Say you're clear and sober and something hums
far off. A carousel. A flume. The sound says
you keep dying like a song and being revived.

The sound says you keep being reviewed
like a movie hit, the critics trying to explain
huge crowds across the land. What to Butte
says something vital also to New York?
Perhaps the killing at the end. You want
her dead after the rotten things she did.
No. That was El Paso and the mongoloid
in the sideshow frowned and batted her beads.

Say this: you're living alone and the hum
has stopped. Ten years of silence. Ten years
of hammering reruns and your cry
directed at no one morning to night.
You cook enough soup to live through July.
You phone every day. Old films projected
on your wall are grainy and jerk. You can't sleep.
Then, one morning, the hum starts. You run
to the door and shout at the sky, "I'm here."
Dead women hum alive on your lawn.
The sky slows down. You win thirty more years.

Belt

I had been on the road before. The first time
in a foreign land. Dead men lay along the side
and a woman sobbed. She offered me wine
and said one was her son. I understood
though I didn't know the tongue, a wild
gutteral grunt that turned the top soil gray.
That language was so harsh there were no trees.
I must have been ten. And I must have it wrong.
No record anywhere. No war in the world that year.

The town was strange, not like the road. Nothing
in it familiar, not even the humor, the way

the local mechanic kidded the waitress
fresh out of highschool, planning her move
to Great Falls, though I knew every American word,
the good-natured presumption behind the barbs,
and I knew the highschool like it was mine,
main road, movie theatre, hardware, drug store,
the bored girls walking nowhere, the boys
leaving town to go fishing. And I knew here
war was where it belonged, hidden inside
like words I wanted the waitress to say.

And I wanted to call it home, to say to someone,
I lived here before. Where's Al, the grocer?
What happened to his daughter? I drove out
and the sky was livid with hawks. There were flowers
I hadn't seen coming in and the road slanted
a more charming way than it had. White pieces
of cloth left by a surveyor fluttered like flags
of surrender, and the girl I offered a ride got in.
She said, "Wherever you're headed, that's fine."

Bone Hunting

I realized early they were dying like a wall,
the barn they'd never paint again, bird nest broken
and the beaver dam. Skies honored them
by dimming at the burial. Fields back home
went fallow some exact unit of time, day, week,
millennium after the expensive dirt snapped shut
around them and the local creek resumed.
Wind ranted like no one loved the wind.

I buried my love for home, the hard trail
through the woods, the Manards, French
on their porch waving hello when I burst

out of the woods into the paved rich world of car
and turned to the glinting town. I looked at my shoes.
This isn't where the handsome come.
Then the Manards were gone and vivid, the path
wiped out by new housing and I retained every turn.

And what was that movie, Italian, long ago
where a woman died in war in such an offhand way
the crowd thought, 'this means nothing'? The music died
on the sound track. Children ran off chattering to games
and I didn't cry. That's one way to take it: real
and common as rock. Another: to multiply hurt
drink after drink in Las Vegas where showgirls I dream
hint in vain for the key to my room.

I hope I'm right when I say sun gives dirt some odor
it can't find anywhere else in March. A block
from our house, a meadow climbs to a forest
and our dog plays there where my wife and I walk.
Geology says the rock above us will hold
a million more years. We trust that claim
and our dog tearing off like bones are buried
for storage. No shabby reason like song.

Houses

The house you're moving from is not this house
in the sketch, nor that one over there,
your furniture on the porch and your nameplate
weathered fast to the door. The picture's
too idyllic, shade trees rooted strategic and firm,
roses crawling ivy crawling the walls,
leaded windows that double the sadness of rain.
And the real one's too run down. The van
moves off with everything, even the girl
you could not find the courage to ask home.

•

Some say, 'where I hang my hat.' Some say, 'where
the heart is beating though hurt.' Whatever
you say, make sure it's alone in a cold garage,
the mechanic's hammer banging you mute.
Make sure only you hear the address.
Make sure your car when fixed
will not break down between the home in the sketch
and the home you deny, the boy with your mouth
who shouts goodbye from the roof.

Sail easy on the freeway. Your next home
has never been photoed. Your next home town's where
so little goes on, the hum of your refrigerator
joins the slow river leaving for home.
Isn't it familiar? Rain hitting the south window first?
Dark corner where the warm light can cringe?
If you go with rivers, not roads, the trip
takes longer and you weave and see a lot more.
When you say, 'I live here,' animals
you hadn't thought of for years live on your lawn.
They insist you remember their names.

White Center

Town or poem, I don't care how it looks. Old woman
take my hand and we'll walk one more time these streets
I believed marked me weak beneath catcalling clouds.
Long ago, the swamp behind the single row of stores
was filled and seeded. Roses today where Toughy Hassin
slapped my face to the grinning delight of his gang.
I didn't cry or run. Had I fought him
I'd have been beaten and come home bloody in tears
and you'd have told me I shouldn't be fighting.

Wasn't it all degrading, mean Mr. Kyte sweeping
the streets for no pay, believing what he'd learned

as a boy in England: 'This is your community'?
I taunted him to rage, then ran. Is this the day
we call bad mothers out of the taverns and point them
sobbing for home, or issue costumes to posturing clowns
in the streets, make fun of drunk barbers, and hope
someone who left and made it returns, vowed
to buy more neon and give these people some class?

The Dugans aren't worth a dime, dirty Irish, nor days
you offered a penny for every fly I killed.
You were blind to my cheating. I saw my future certain—
that drunk who lived across the street and fell
in our garden reaching for the hoe you dropped.
All he got was our laughter. I helped him often home
when you weren't looking. I loved some terrible way
he lived in his mind and tried to be decent to others.
I loved the way we loved him behind our disdain.

Clouds. What glorious floating. They always move on
like I should have early. But your odd love and a war
taught me the world's gone evil past the first check point
and that's First Avenue South. I fell asleep each night
safe in love with my murder. The neighbor girl
plotted to tease every tomorrow and watch me turn
again to the woods and games too young for my age.
We never could account for the python cousin Warren
found half starved in the basement of Safeway.

It all comes back but in bites. I am the man
you beat to perversion. That was the drugstore MacCameron
flipped out in early one morning, waltzing
on his soda fountain. The siren married his shrieking.
His wife said, "We'll try again, in Des Moines."
You drove a better man into himself where he found tunes
he had no need to share. It's all beginning to blur
as it forms. Men cracking up or retreating.
Resolute women deep in hard prayer.

•

And it isn't the same this time. I hoped forty years
I'd write and would not write this poem. This town would die
and your grave never reopen. Or mine. Because I'm married
and happy, and across the street a foster child
from a cruel past is safe and need no longer crawl
for his meals, I walk this past with you, ghost in any field
of good crops, certain I remember everything wrong.
If not, why is this road lined thick with fern
and why do I feel no shame kicking the loose gravel home?

The Right Madness on Skye

[1980]

The Semi-Lunatics of Kilmuir

And so they cheated and wandered and were loved
throughout this island. If that's too mythical a tone
consider those who conform and know something's wrong
and need a zany few who won't obey.
Granted, without obedience most of us would die,
and it was worse then, year eighteen whatever,
the crofts in feudal domain. Think of losing your home
on a Duke's whim and look at the home you lost.
Imagine this lovely island warped ugly by tears.

Yesterday in Glasgow some magistrate ruled
feudal rights prevail. Crofter reform turns out
a cruel joke. You pay and pay and own nothing.
Wouldn't we welcome them back this minute,
those clowning con men from Kilmuir?
They were crazy like dolphins. When Gilleasbuig Aotram,
most dolphin of all, met a real crazy
raving in chains, headed for the asylum, he said:
"Had you the right madness bread would be secure."
Have the right madness. This land has always passed on
and, like you, is still here.

A Snapshot of Uig in Montana

Children take longer to die
where sea hooks blue behind the headland
and the hooked dock longs for the next boat.

We will live there soon. The headless specter
moans the music all moan dispossessed.
Montana wants to be warmer and forget
how many farmed too hard and failed.
Most of all, here we want the self discarded
left unresurrected and wind resolved to move on.

There, we'll welcome both wind and dead air.
Look how hayricks though erect in rows
can't be soldiers and sky fights to stay blue.
To be old and charming as those fields
we must survive sad moments, must go on ploughing
after the invaders sail, all we love left broken
or dead: lamb, hut and barbarians' wake.
No sense waiting on the shore, fresh bread,
fresh tears. They're not coming back.

April and our snow hangs on. Whatever's
delaying spring rides high in arctic currents
and can't be controlled or explained.
In this shot of Uig, we can see all cause is local,
all effect. When we ask the way to Loch Sianta,
even if we've stopped the water horse
returned to terrorize the village, when he sees
we're foreign he'll put on his crofter's face
and where he points that will really be the trail.

A Map of Skye

We'll be confined and free. Roads end fast
and water leads slow ways to open water.
The harsh names on this map are Nordic,
the soft words Gaelic. We can love there well
grateful what is cruel ran out.
Even ruins will be civil, moss on ruins,

anger drained from ghost.
The only irritants, a soft longing for mist to clear
and a nagging feeling more should happen.

It's happened already. That will be the charm.
Not one isolated Indian war, relatively recent
and forgotten, but Celtic memory way back,
primal things to hate kept smouldering. . . .
England, Viking, the ninth century storm
that leveled farm and tower, and the tower down
the day of the invasion. It is all here
in the names, the sound of broken bone and blood.

We need that land of slow recovery, the grief passed
wife to daughter, some continuum of song
and we need bays that contain,
that promise a wider world beyond
the final promontory, as if travel
still involves the unknown. Read the roads.
A lots of switchbacks and a lot of time to find Portree.
And read the water, how salmon glow like swords
and checkpoints never run out.

Clachard

Maybe they believed anything that solid
and big must have eyes and would warn them
when Vikings sailed into view. We know
nothing about it, this stone stood on end.
Why on this spot? That much weight
took many men to erect we are certain.
In hard wind we imagine men crushed
under the stone and the trying again.
In soft light we see horses and rope.
When modern and think we think ancient,

we say phallic symbol or breast.
Tired we say God and tower guard.
Let them know we are strong. After we love
we say it's a signal to birds: come home.
It occurs to the poor, this is a sign
of surrender. To any invader, it said:
sail in and take me. And says it today.
After awhile you'll forget why you came.
In time you won't know what I say.

Greystone Cottage

Some days the tick of two protestant clocks
in the cottage, related in some nebulous no less
real way to one long ago, put me again
at the kitchen window waiting for rain.
Open bright sky, and I look across Uig bay
and *ru Chorachan* to the river cascading
nine miles away down the Waternish cliff
into Loch Snizort. At one time, Iain,
our neighbor, our friend, tells me, salmon
clustered under that steady pelt of fresh water
on salt year long for the illegal taking.
I dream myself poacher. I dream myself
benevolent wealthy invader, nothing on board
but my need to be welcome ashore.
I bring you songs from a glamorous planet.

The rooms are small and built so that sound
cannot carry one to another. Alone in a room
as I am now in the kitchen, the house seems empty
and I hear only one clock. Anger cannot carry
nor laughter. How I feel is locked in with me.
I could be dying and no one would hear my cry:
'Call Doctor MacRae.' I could spot a ship of threat
sailing in, ancient Viking, modern American oil.

No one would hear my warning throughout the house,
throughout the island. Like salmon
we wait to be taken. Nothing will save this peace,
this near sacred space between people and homes.

This is the season hayricks dot crofts
and hotels shut down and the English tourist
goes back to London. We're staying on, snug
in our cottage, snug alone in each room.
The clock in the kitchen reminds me of a time
few people dropped by and all mattered.
Rain on the window reminds me when
a vagabond in rags came looking for odd jobs.
He sang to himself and I still remember the tune.

The Clouds of Uig

for Johan Ross

Over the years these clouds have colored much
cloud white and blue: horse, house and fence,
the recent tower already in ruin.
They change the green of Skye apple to Kelly
and back a hundred times a day.
They never stop changing the distance to the pier
from your front door.

They have no form. No one would mistake
the shade of one on water for a boat.
They never slow down and they never run out.
When one sky leaves, taking with it the rain
that couldn't make anyone wet or leave grass
dry very long, another sky follows close behind,
the loud blue interval between. . . .
recess in a crowded school.

They move on like your students, sixty years
of them and still they come
like surly children, like amorphous rules of light
we can't quite understand and have to obey.
A new set of rules this minute, faintly the same.
We can live under them.
They move certain as blood. Under their shade
the bay locks complete and, deep in that cloudy water,
many lives go on.

Graves in Uig

The dead are hidden from the sea. The sea
can't find them on this high moor over
on the inland slope where stones aren't kept up
and grass goes uncut and sheep wander where they please
among the stones dropping their olive pit black turds.
Sixty-eight stones in all counting blank markers
and no more than nine names, most of them
starting with M. Some stones count for more than one
and one spans decades between
the first name on it dead and the last.

I have a theory. It's not good but hear me.
East and north are the cold winds. Right?
And the west wind brings rain and holds
temperature in check. I say they put the dead
here where north and east gales can find them,
knowing in death we are tough, and leave the living
on the west side protected from cold.

I admit one fenced off large stone is obscured
by brush and the iron grillwork around it
has rusted, one section already down. That
makes you think, doesn't it, someone lost interest
over the years, or the dead left a last request

to leave them alone? One other theory I have
involves women never heard of on this island
and has nothing to do with the dead.

We walked here, my wife and I, this day
vivacious in sunlight. Last night
we heard about the death of Robert Lowell.
You pass through two gates to get here.
Both are very much in working order.

Hawk in Uig

Every good wind he hangs over the field
in front of our cottage. Head on he looks like a bat.
Bela Lugosi's returned, I say. My wife
doesn't laugh, nor my daughter. Twelve minutes
almost to the second he hangs
then veers off
back into his life of circle and search.

The wind up, if he's not here by ten
I know something's wrong with the current,
water or air. When he dives he seems to have
no mackerel in mind.
I suspect he's always at play, like a swallow
no reason for his movements other than fun
despite his stern face and his eye full of hot hunger.

I knew a family back home so ugly
I still think of them. I was young and cruel
and made fun of the daughter's bad looks
and her three dumb looking brothers, mouths open
in effort to understand the nothing
and bad something that were both bound to happen.
I don't remember their name. I remember
it sounded shabby and poor like them.

•

The hawk hasn't shown today. The wind
doesn't seem weak and the sea bangs the cliff
as it always does when he comes. Past two now
and no sign. Rain hits the window
with an empty sound and runs down
obscuring the view. Clearing now
and still no hawk. I'm weak waiting.
I promise the sky tomorrow if he comes
I'll call him something better than Bela
and I'll offer him meat.

Uig Registrar

for Chatta MacLean

No in-between. The news is good or bad
and hard to write in a neutral hand—
died of exposure, 4 A.M., 40 yards from home—
body not recovered—cause not ascertained—
wed, church of Scotland—19 and 22.
Cold in words. Flat in lasting ink.
Some come elated, the sad long history
of Scotland shed for the moment. Some
come heavy with recent loss and with
that dignity they took from Celtic stone.
You write it down. Below, the Rha
and Conan enter the bay. You try
to catch the hum of their steady entry
beyond the choked phrase, the bridal smile.
You write it down, the way it has to be
for the record, the way it has to be.

Piping to You on Skye from Lewis

for Iain MacLean

Pipe the Gaelic back for one last dance.
One long war over, you took a private vow:
say goodbye to islands only once.

Honor them daily with music, those dead attendants
of the fate of living Gaels: to lose.
Pipe the dead Gaels back for one more dance.

In war you might die English, might get buried in Provence.
Best concentrate on what the Skye dead did and do—
say goodbye to islands only once.

Goodbye home you said to Bragar, there's a bony chance
bones stay whole in cairns. From Stornoway, your radio
pipes the dead Gaels back for one more dance

and you bend close to the static, convinced
you'll find in bagpipe overtones the drumming reason to
say goodbye to islands only once.

War's tough on personal reconnaissance.
Spy from this green distance on your life and pray you
say goodbye to islands only once.
Gaels who die at home show up for every dance.

The Clearances

Lord, it took no more than the wave of a glove,
a nod of the head over tea. People were torn from their crofts
and herded aboard, their land turned over to sheep.

They sailed. They wept.
The sea said nothing and said I'll get even.
Their last look at Skye lasted one hour. Then fog.
Think of their fear. When you can't read, not even a map,
where does home end and Tasmania start?
Think of loss that goes stormy knots beyond bitter
and think of some absentee landlord home in his tower
signing the order and waving off a third ale.

Want an equation? O.K. The lovelier the land
the worse the dispossession. I know that's not right.
Blacks weep when put out of a shack,
Puerto Ricans to see the slum town down.
We've all lost something or we're too young to lie,
to say we hear crofters sobbing
every high tide, every ferry that sails
Uig for Lewis, that vague shape out there in haze.
We don't hear them sob. We don't know that they did.
And that form in the haze might be nothing,
not a destination, no real promise of home.

Some afternoons when pressure builds in the bay
and I think the sea will explode one more
mile per hour of gale, I wave my hand
and have the ship abort. I bring them back
and say it was a mistake. The landlord was drunk.
He's happy you're here. Don't worry. I'll find room
for the sheep. They laugh loud as money
and sing back to their crofts. When water relaxes
into a lazy roll home, Lewis stark in clear air,
I know they'd come ashore the way they left,
numbed by hard labor and grim
and I'd be no friend in their flat eyes.

Glen Uig

Believe in this couple this day who come
to picnic in the Faery Glen. They pay rain
no matter, or wind. They spread their picnic
under a gale-stunted rowan. Believe they grew tired
of giants and heroes and know they believe
in wise tiny creatures who live under the rocks.

Believe these odd mounds, the geologic joke
played by those wise tiny creatures far from
the world's pitiful demands: make money, stay sane.
Believe the couple, by now soaked to the skin,
sing their day as if dry, as if sheltered inside
Castle Ewen. Be glad Castle Ewen's only a rock
that looks like a castle. Be glad for no real king.

These wise tiny creatures, you'd better believe,
have lived through it all: the Viking occupation,
clan torturing clan, the Clearances, the World War
II bomber gone down, a fiery boom
on Beinn Edra. They saw it from here. They heard
the sobs of last century's crofters trail off below
where every day the Conon sets out determined for Uig.
They remember the Viking who wandered off course,
under the hazelnut tree hating aloud all he'd done.

Some days dance in the bracken. Some days go out
wide and warm on bad roads to collect the dispossessed
and offer them homes. Some days celebrate addicts
sweet in their dreams and hope to share with them
a personal spectrum. The loch here's only a pond,
the monster is in it small as a wren.

•

Believe the couple who have finished their picnic
and make wet love in the grass, the wise tiny creatures
cheering them on. Believe in milestones, the day
you left home forever and the cold open way
a world wouldn't let you come in. Believe you
and I are that couple. Believe you and I sing tiny
and wise and could if we had to eat stone and go on.

Sneosdal

What a walk. First mile uphill. The road
went rock to peat to mud. The final
five hundred yards we floundered through lumpy swamp.
Whatever we've read in old novels, it's no fun
to walk in heather, and we'd have to cut this wind
in half to enjoy a kiss on the moor.
We believe him worth it, the legend
of this loch: *Each uisge*, water-horse.
Hasn't he kept us in terror all our lives?
This is where he lives, in this eerie black water
tucked in behind the crag
that rises like a bad past between our faces
and all of the afternoon sun. We know his disguises:
gentleman of the evening, sheep dog, normal horse.
And we know he comes to our village for no reason
other than to frighten what we used to call maidens
or to kill the mayor
we've never been organized enough to elect.
He's not drunk with power. He comes
just now and then when least expected, when
we enjoy an innocent picnic
or go to the store. Sometimes
we think we see him and don't. A dog looks wrong
in certain light or one horse won't run with the others
exhilarated by gales. When we see a man,
white tie and tails, given our lives we know

that much charm is suspect. We lock our doors
when a lone hawk seems to enjoy the storm.
He hasn't come for so long, today we've tracked him
to his home. We had a hard time finding you.
We are wet and cold. The blackface sheep resent us.
The shepherd won't return our wave. With the world
on its way to certain disaster, can't you reappear,
rise slimy and majestic out of the loch and snort
at least one minor threat to keep us in line?
Or are we out of monsters? Are we now reduced
to sensible conclusion like empty water,
with no one more interesting than ourselves to fear?
We take the long walk back, mud to peat
to rock, the last mile easy downhill.
Our car has never waited for us this long before.
We are embarrassed by what we hold in,
the hopeful and hopeless child that wants to cry—
We saw him. We saw him. He is really there.

Kilmuir Cemetery: The Knight in Blue-Green Relief

The rotten thing is after you've been pushed around
so often over the years, moved near the gate
for visitor convenience, moved near Flora MacDonald
in effort to have all brave ones united,
not scattered here and there like in life,
and the current whether or not to keep you safe
in a museum, I can't be sure you mark the spot
the one you represent is buried: Angus of the Storms.
It shouldn't matter, but he was a knight in life
as you are in stone and we've run out of knights.

Is this where you belong? And were you really
that brave? Didn't you come home nervous

from war and have bad dreams loaded
with sobbing children and dead innocent sheep?
Didn't the tinkle of a far off cow bell though faint
explode you out of sleep?
Or were you always this resolute, the way you look now
on this slab flat in the grass, and were you always this
noble and aloof, paying no attention
to rain that pools in your eyes?

I knew a man so brave he flew extra missions
because he believed in the war. We called him
Screwy Jew, and his odds stretched thin until
one day he exploded into fine sand and fell
five miles in a trillion leisurely trails
no one cared to trace. Do you know him now?
Is he one of you? I imagine you asking for trouble
wherever you rode and cowardly peasants like me
moving out of your way. And I imagine you dead
on a beach and gulls collected to shade
your blood from drying too fast in the sun.
That was a great moment. We went on ploughing.

You here smug in blue green stone relief
may represent no one. If you were really that small
and took off your mail, put down your sword
and shield, I'd break your goddamn puny arms, I'd
knee you in the balls, I'd kick your ass north
all the way to the pole. They wouldn't carve me in stone,
nor call me Dick of the Storms. Something right goes wrong
with brutality when it loses history and style.
These days, however many dragons we kill
we are sand falling home
leaving no trail.

Kilmuir Cemetery: Stone with Two Skulls and No Name

Probably two thieves, but why a stone this big,
this thick horizontal slab? The time it must have taken
to carve those skulls. Who paid for that? Surely
it was not an elaborate lesson to other: don't steal.
And what could anyone steal that others would honor him
this much after he's hung? Doesn't work out at all.

Maybe one killer. The second skull his victim. There.
Remember the victim twice, once in his grave
and once here, and the murderer a brief once under this slab
heavy enough to hold him down forever. The problem remains.
Who paid for all this? Why not put
the killer's corpse on the beach and tell the sea-birds,
"Start picking." In this fresh air he couldn't reek long and in no time
his bones would be clean.

"And these two never touch in the air so full of summer"
a poet once said of two stones. One marked a woman.
The other a man. What if two lovers left a stipulation
in their will: they refused to die unless buried together.
And the state, not bright in those days either, agreed.
This is a northern island. There's no air here
so filled with summer we're better off in death alone.
The moon is never not always sometimes in Scandinavia
no matter how simple it sounds.
When you're a skeleton, it's hard to find a lover.
Take it with you, brother, sister. You'll find days
any old bony kiss will do.

Duntulm Castle

1

Those knights had an eye for strategic location.
One look at the sea and they knew the way danger
would come. What better than this, the ocean open
all the way to the sky. Only one island nearby
Tulm, and that with no cover. In this harmless
dramatic weather, what better place to wonder
what I would have been, cook or castle clown
or knave who stole out of need, a captive in the dungeon
scratching on stone one more year of the hundreds
I lost dying of slow darkness.

2

If you hear anything bad about me, believe it.
Given a choice, I'd be crofter, friend to anyone.
To the army that went out and the other army
that came back I'd wave the same good luck
and go on turning the dirt and planting. Time
for conscription, I'd say: look, without me, no food.
I'd manage to always stay here, my world cut short
by the stone fence I must not plant beyond.
Think anything you want in your castle
perfecting good manners. Old as I am, something
happens inside when gannets collapse their wings
and free fall into the waves like dead stars.
I excuse myself from wars.
You stand before me ferocious in armour and mail
and ridicule when I tell you the raven comes here
because damn it all he's a raven and this
is a castle in ruin. Sure, I'm afraid of your sword,
your unforgiving eyes. Haven't I begged
and begged at your gate for scraps in bad winters?

3

The same two herons flew the same formation then.
To me, that's fun. To knights it meant spies
and a means of attack they'd not counted on.

Did I tell you I've flown and dropped bombs?
Buildings looked like you do now then.
I was handsome in my uniform.
That's about the time you gave the traitor
salted beef and salt water and laughed him dead of thirst.
I wish I was poet enough to hear his final gasp
from the dungeon, and man enough to admit it's just me.

4

Hard wind hates imagination. I come from a land
where without half trying we create
a thousand reasons to say goodbye. In this wind
I'm afraid to lean over the rim and watch the babe
fall inadvertently bye bye into the sea,
the nurse beside me begging "Don't tell them"
and the same nurse below tied to the prow
by her hair and tide coming in for an all time high.
Don't tell them over tea at the Duntulm Hotel.
I'm the one who told.

5

Once a year a poet came
on foot over the moor.
He read and they listened hard.
Year after year he came,
every time a little more welcome,
a little more polished.
In time he ate with the knights
and had his choice of the women.
Gradually, he relaxed.
One day he read a poem
that sang a way to get here
no knight had considered.
They banished him to Tulm.
Gulls took his bones
and one by one
dropped them into the sea.
So help me.

Mill at Romesdal

for Dr. Calum MacRae

One look at this mill and the adjacent croft,
the local intimate way grass slants to the mill,
the sea beyond the broken water wheel, and we know
here we could keep some private promise to improve.
We could reinforce the floor
where grain was milled, repair the tracks
for the grain cart, redivert the small stream
back into the flume and start the mill again.
Send the word out now: your miller
is open to all who bring raw grain.

If we could turn our lives that way, the way
the mill stones turned, slow and even,
the milled grain falling dreamy all day
every day but Sunday into carts, we'd find
some recent peace, a composure we never quite trust
in family portraits. We'd be wise to allow
for the loch that hammers inside
and that man not on record who broke one day
in the byre and demanded the cattle say thanks.
With this loch pale in our faces and money
collected last year for milling turning
to dust at the touch, we really are happy, are happy—
our voices run down late summer,
the stream without pressure and the water wheel limp.

If we count bones found on Skye, we get
Celtic, a lot, Viking, very few, despite
three centuries of occupation and Nordic names
that hang on: Hinnisdal, Monkstadt, Eyre.
The Viking bones found here
don't care what we or the man they belonged to did.

They don't blush for their part in oppression,
innocent women in shock.
There's a way of saying, "Yes! We were rotten, so what?"
Of saying it any time we want to the sea
that answers softly in Gaelic and doesn't indict.

We won't restore the mill. The water wheel's
broken beyond repair and, if we got the two stones
back in gear and grinding, no one raises grain
today on this island. The modern Norwegian ship
needs papers to sail these waters. The Viking bones
are in Glasgow for date and classification.
We own the mill in the warmest sense of own.
Let's keep it run down. Let's keep the crofter's cottage
empty and cold. If anyone asks for a miller
we'll say, that's what we were once, and worse.
This is what we are now.

Druid Stones at Kensaleyre

I imagine Druids timeless, so lacking
a sense of time that, like animals, they found
every moment loaded with now, and no future,
no, or too much, awareness of death. These two stones,
woman and man I'd guess, will age no faster
than the bay they overlook. Like all stone
they will stay young and know nothing.

Driving north from Portree, from a certain point
on the road the church at Kensaleyre
looks higher than the stones I say
are woman and man, and that seems wrong.
Sundays, a cleric lays on stone ears
modern concepts of sin. Stone throats don't tighten.
The sea doesn't listen. I, who don't go to church,
live alone with what I've done.

•

Some day I'll bypass the church and keep going
across the brief moor to where they stand,
that young couple, beautiful, poised.
I'll put out my hand and say my name.
They'll say "Welcome" in stone. If you pass
in your car and see three of us solid
forever above and one with the sea, despite the wear
of weather and the way indifferent traffic
hurts even the stoniest heart, know one
came late, is happy and won't be back.

The Braes

for Sorley and Renee MacLean

I would have taken this road on sight
not knowing who lived along it,
not knowing where, if anywhere, it goes.
I'd drive unaware Celt blood flows
even now in the grass, the result of violent gesture
against the injustice of seizure
by a callous feudal gentry,
imagining my entry
foreign, modern American, tame.
I'd drive this road for the same
old reason, to find a poem, drive
slowly by crofters who don't return the wave
of strangers, then use feeling alone
to follow some personal line
that won't do here where the first resistance
flared up and got the instant
result they fought for, the men and women.
They won and they won later in London.
Better I put a curse on Ballingall.
Roast, roast in the fires of hell.

Nothing here more than any place
else on this island says we faced
them here and bled. You have to know
this is where the poor woke up a nation.
Same time, back home, in sand, in snow
where nothing grows
we started Indian reservations.

St. John's Chapel

All debris ends here at the north end
of Loch Caroy where St. John's chapel
and a dozen graves sit below the road
unnoticed and summer traffic pours north
to Dunvegan, the clean castle there,
the informed guide. It must be wrong
to bury your dead where the sea forgets to be nice,
sits there sullen and every day deposits
one more afternoon of waste.

Wouldn't this try belief?
Could we fake faith when needing one word
of comfort we find the chapel locked forever,
our dead child's marker fallen over,
this sad beach littered with acres of trash?
And what good are flowers growing from graves
when we need to cry 'forget forget'
loud in this forgotten spot.

And we need to take note of the grillwork.
The iron fence that should surround the dead
broke apart like an afterthought.
Rats have their way at night.
Names on stone got lost in the gnaw and crawl
of moss. If we clawed a faded name

and sobbed 'is this, is this the one?'
it would come out flat.

We want severed connections.
We want the ocean trailing off out
of the void of lost promise and rage
into this bay and that, some lovely,
some, like this one, sick. With water, with number
of graves we feel the urge to be finite.

No telling why we stopped. Our dead
are buried continents away, in cemeteries
well kept up with money, stones relatively
recent, names in clean relief.
Maybe the stairs seduced us, the climb down
out of sight of cars that catch the sun
once and move on.

Trumpan

It just says 'church' on the map.
No mention of fire, the MacDonalds gloating downwind,
the MacLeods in mid-hymn burning.
Their screams ran away
to silence in the west roar of air.
This is that same loud air. This day,
despite the storm seems quiet, the view pastoral
even where land falls off
sudden as life and sea snarls below us like white hair.

The sky's a calendar shot: clouds
rationing light and light streaming down
one shaft to spotlight one green patch
of water in the dark forever. Sing
herring boats home, good wife.

Your voice, quiet as love, rides the right wind right
to where the radio waits for the forecast,
the rare true heading to port.

With no towns, with villages so thin
vacant lots outnumber homes fifty or more
to one, and fences try to convince the deafening storm
they know the property line, all we brought,
food, wine and attitude, must be consumed
in a quick chaotic picnic. We can't talk
until we're in the car and in the car we don't.

Home in Uig, we count the boats. All here.
All men accounted for. In the whole of Skye
no one died today. Make room in dreams
for Trumpan. Remember a road that goes to murder
and comes back friend.

Langaig

We are what we hear. A well known singer died
yesterday in Spain. Thirty-five years ago
I got fired for sneaking off to hear him. I sobbed
"sorry" at the foreman, fired days later himself.
I cast blue nylon high over water turned black
by peat and light diminished by heavy Highland low sky.
I heard music and lost my job. I've not worked hard since
on anything but words, though I fish all waters
devoted and hum old songs when I fish alone.

I hum "My Heart is Taking Lessons," a song
the dead singer sang. I hum "I Had the Words and You
in My Heart." I remember him singing that.
I hum flat and off key, but that's hardly my fault,
the lack of gift, of training. In this lake (read 'loch'

to be local) trout run black as the water though Scots
like us call them 'browns,' the old Scots, 'Loch Leven!'
I hum "Makes No Difference Now," the best recording
the dead singer made and he left lots of good records.

To relax, to slide with, ride the forces of whatever
sweeps us along, jokes well timed, phrasing under control—
that was my ideal. I didn't come close in real life.
A soft impulse was proof I was weak. I laughed
at any weak joke, still do, and believed our purpose
to lighten the day, to be tougher than fate.
In reaction to that, I believed we should give in to pathos.
Today I believe: fish hard and hum every tune
I remember hearing the dead singer sing
and leave believing in being like him to others.
Does that make us brothers? Let's be. My bobber
jitters and I know it isn't just wind. I set my line
too soon and lose the black brown. The eagle yells
from the Quirang, "Go easy. Give him time to take it."
I hum "White Christmas," though I never liked it.
Snow on mainland mountains across the minch (if you're
American read 'strait') reminds me I'm fishing
late in the season. I may be breaking Scot law.

Christ, what rain and no real Jesus in it.
No real king. No friend. What lover first inserted a tongue
in a lover's ear? And where? It must have been pre-
Peloponesian war. It must have been pre-all
language and hunger, and located song prior to lyrics.
Fishing preceded song. We know that from instinct,
not records. I've fished this loch often before
and alone with my ghosts felt free to sing.
I've got a brown on. My line is writing a song.

I'm fishing. I'm singing. My heart is not exactly
giving lessons though I've been lucky enough in rare

moments to take heart in some words, and to have
a job teaching others to sing, to locate by game
some word like 'brown' in black water, to cast
hard for that word, then wait a long time to set.
Now the reeling in, the fight, the black trout lovely
on heather, the dead singer in songs
we recover, and hum when alone, and hum wrong.

Ayr

You might die anywhere. You will die in Ayr
north of the river, in the Newton Cafe.
You'll die to no notice in the Orient Cinema
in the balcony.

When you die in Ayr, if you die
in the Newton Cafe, jars of good cheap candy
on shelves back of the counter
will remind the investigating officer of home.

If you die in the Orient Cinema
George C. Scott will not be on the screen,
not at your final moment.
The janitor will find you. No reaction.

South of the river the town of Ayr's alive.
New shops. New shopping center. The tongue
will be braid at the inquest.
You won't understand.

The next town north is Prestwick. Big international
airport. BOAC as usual, late.
Whoever was coming to visit will say
he's not here. Where is he?

•

You'll die in Ayr
where warehouses rent for next to nothing
and rats complain, no rats other than them.
The report will read: not from here.

The report will read: foreigner, deceased.
The investigating officer
will ask the girl back of the counter at the Newton Cafe
to a movie.

Visitors will make their way to Glasgow.
Scotland is not bewildering.
People are helpful. The food is uninteresting.
Lots of castles in beautiful ruin.

Try Ayr in the off-season. Try
the Newton Cafe some early winter evening.
Scampi and chips. Try staring
out the window at some earlier street.

Don't try dying. I just said that to mention
Ayr. In the Orient a couple holds hands
and George C. Scott shows them how to act.
Try Ayr north of the river. Try some earlier home.

Ferniehirst Castle

for Chester Kerr

This was our first line of defense. It held
about five minutes. What could we throw at them?
A few chickens to trip over, a cow to block the road,
and one farmer who didn't want anyone hurt.
Sheep and maze remained neutral.
The priest who worked the chapel changed a few
key names in the sermon and went on.

Was there ever a better place to let the enemy through
and years later when he came back enroute home
to act as if nothing had changed?
Nothing has changed. Did you have trouble
fording the Jedwater river? Was there
a one eyed farmer, not quite right in the head?
He died. Come in and get warm.
Stay here until you are strong enough to go on.

Centuries have passed since then, all of them
just as bad. The sermon changed this way
and that and couldn't keep up with the times.
Despite architectural plans, rooks know
this castle will go to ruin. When they come for good
as they always do when they find broken stone,
they'll spend their lives on basics, searching for food
and flapping dark signals to the man taking notes.

We do best with short range plans,
so limited rooks take off bewildered.
In any century, to stay humane we lived
in one or another kind of isolation, far as we could
from highway and harm. Even then,
too much ocean too long or forest, our eyes
started to see things and our blood turned to rain.
This is very old mortar. If we do this and not that
to the floor and don't get too smart with the ceiling
all who return with very old hurt in their eyes
will know they are welcome.

Culloden

Nothing seems right, not the monument too close
to the road nor the road that seems misplaced.
We'd have everyone fallen named, not one stone
per clan, hidden in fern or behind a cedar,

even the clan name faint, and trails that wander
the woods better for lovers than for tribute.
We can't imagine trumpets, the steel clash of men,
the bonnie prince riding away. If anything
we think of picnics, cold salmon and wine.

If a hill isn't rounded some filmatic way
could anyone bleed there, could a fifteen year
old boy cry 'Mother, I'm dying' then die?
We need wind to fight wars. No wind here.
The air's too dead for the dead. The trees too solemn
for contrast with a serious tear of defeat.

We have to trust books and the handed down
stories of loss. Otherwise, given this sun
breaking clean on the grass, museums meant
to commemorate mean nothing. We have to trust
the faces of Scots today, the pulse of blood
in those faces. And we have to trust the sad
memorial tone of anyone who volunteers
to guide us through this field not right for battle.
We say, yes, yes, we hear the pipes, the drums.
We see the charge. We hear the fatal screams.

We are simply being polite. No topography
lends itself easily to war. To animals maybe.
To birds. To clouds. A grave we hope to outlive.

The Standing Stones of Callanish

See them in snow under a full moon they told me.
The shadows will take you out of yourself to when
the Stones were erected, the time it took and the reason
we try to guess today. Some claim, a way to tell time.
Others say, religion. I guess pattern itself,

the delight of pattern and, if we ride birds,
center, circle and spoke looked down on lovely.
Contrast it with uncertain currents of sea,
gales that rip up what seemed
well rooted rock and send flying like suicidal stars.
These stones wear better than sky. See
the clouds in tatters and blue faded to weak cream
at noon with no explanation. Gales clear the grounds
of brochures torn in frustration at phrases—
'the dates are unknown'—'Herodotus states Abaris
told Ptolemy'—when? I try
to remember history and can't get past World War I.
I've walked around them twice, December in my bones,
knelt to get an angle on the two long rows
going north from the hub, one direction I've always believed.
And I've calculated the weight of the big one
and guessed the number of men it took and the work
to bring it from Wales where some say it's from,
a special barge that wobbled and rode high without cargo,
and that special day they put it in place and it settled
the way they'd hoped and it held. That was long before
people knew how to cheer, shake hands or offer a toast.
I imagine them resting a moment, then grim with resolve
starting down to the sea to get the next stone,
and one woman thought strange but obeyed,
urging them on and muttering hard at the sky
a word we've lost. It sounded like 'shape.' It meant 'world.'

Ness

This is where those who hate monuments
pay last disrespects to the world. They've wrecked art,
cities, the language passed woman to man and back.
They've destroyed personal records, birth, school, marriage
and divorce. With luck they'll board a final ship

that flies a flag no color on earth.
They'll bribe the captain to destroy the record of death.
For them the horizon is a pass.
Beyond it the glamour and thrill of ignorant waste.

And I'll be one of them, no shame. I'll tear every poem
and toss lines in tatters to that great God, wind.
I'll leave laughing. Everything ends here: life,
hope, civilization, love, loneliness and regret. The end
promised children. The world on medieval maps
that drops off blue for water into white for void.
I'll give up whatever's hard, saying the plural of ghost,
the singular of girls.
I'll shed my life and sail counter to breakers.

The ship will tire far out and lose stroke and start back
in the wash. On my way home I'll dream it again,
something like history even if wrong, starting with sun
and coming down the ages, unclassified tooth
to computer, star to diamond and back. If you find me
broken and babbling on rock, listen very hard.
The tongue may be dated. If you pick up a phrase
you can match it with words on that scrap of paper.
You found it in Wind. You don't worship wind any more.

Carloway Broch

Park. Let's walk the brief path back
1600 years across the field
to where we once lived. When we left we carefully
left no record. To reach old age, 25,
we built the doorway low and posted a guard,
rock in each hand, over the entrance
the enemy, whoever he was, would have to crawl.
If woman with child, you slept high
on the elevated tier of stone slabs we wedged

between the two walls. If man, on the ground
in case of attack. No attack came.
We grew up guessing which man was father.
That didn't matter as much as fire
or fish we took from the sea.

By 400 A.D., we'd gone. Most of us
dead and the few who remained called Celt.
We were innocent prey to concept:
God, family, cross. Within two centuries
we'd upped the ante to 30,
moved out of the broch and into stone huts.

Let me skip 14 centuries or so.
You can find those in books.

And you can see what happened to home, most
of the old stone gone, at least two thirds
of the double wall down and what remains,
some tribute to our skill, we call "ruin"
or "historic shrine." By now the fish
we called "food" swim named. Local animals seem
too small for those skins we slept on and this sky
full of rockets and space program debris
tightens the eye. After we lived here we lived
many places and lives—none of our doing really—
mostly result of war. This century alone one war
took 50 million. We could not believe it then—
that world with so few souls and we huddled here,
one community, 20, every hard gale.

Bastard, also a concept, is considered obscene.
Given my genes, my medical past and my recent
ability to control bad habits
I expect to reach 83. Wife, children, friend—
I want you along all the way. Let's walk
the stone hard trail ahead to where we are now,

beside the car looking back at what we were.
The broch towering over the farm
silhouettes itself against the ever climbing sea
and the ever diminishing sky.

We say "beautiful" and don't know why.

The Cairn in Loch An Duin

Is this all we will know of the dark,
bone dark under rock and just out
of dry reach? This black water lake
that supposes no trout, now and then catches
blue fire under a quick passing gap in the clouds.
It must have been planned, the cairn
set just beyond our wading range,
some message understood: leave us alone.
Leave them alone. Don't ask in Bragar
the date of the cairn.

We guess a spirit wants out from under
the rock. One aching jawbone cries to come ashore,
to climb the short hill to Bragar
and sit there with other old Celts and chat.
What would he tell us of time, of long days grinding
across the sky without us? Do some clouds repeat
like planets? Any improvements in food?
And we'd ask him one question that burns:
Dead, will we, without going mad
envy the town we see every day and can't enter?

Death may be weaker than sleep. We know flesh
rejoins water and dirt, and for centuries believed
the soul unites with the sky. The memory
would find some special other place, a gold cottage

that houses all we were, are and will be, high on a moor
over the open ocean, where wind slams home
and a child cries excited.
Can't we be more than just bone under this plain pile
of rock in a lake close to shore,
the living tauntingly near?

In Bragar a whale jaw forms an arch
and through it the living pass to market.
That giant bone reminds us more than the cairn
of what's left behind one darkening moment—
rain, music and tongue.
This is where sky bears down
year after year and light ranges dim
to dim blinding. We're left with whatever
we find inside to keep going.
Bones mix in the cairn.

The water flames blue and beyond the cairn
one ripple. We can bait a hook,
can cast and wait. This is no song of reprieve.
The small jaw stays locked in stone.
The whale jaw opens wider in the town.
The surface fills with ripple. We cry
"trout, trout, trout" to each other. Hard. Honor the trout
this season honor goes lonely as bones.
They play the surface like children,
what we have been.

St. Clement's: Harris

Lord, I'd rehearsed and rehearsed your loss.
You died and my rehearsed face, the words
I'd planned to say over your stone were ready.
I set my face. I said my words. The sea I worship

did nothing to relieve the grief in Rodel.
This day, December 28, 1977,
the church locked, I bang the door and no one comes.
Happy New Year, Lord. Almost that time.

We were something else that age of reptiles.
The triwinged dragonfly drove us to caves.
There we huddled and shook. Those days, all
huge creatures, dinosaur and those that end in -saurus,
no matter how imposing meant less than land.
For one example: white cliffs climbed
so straight they seemed geometry
and high high when we looked gave off
gratuitous white light that formed, fragmented,
floated and was cloud. I'm afraid
the introverted palm leaves even then
threatened to open and smile. The world would bloom
with or without us. Every dawn, the sky
turned pink like special places on girls.
No Lord then, we were something else. O.K.?

Three days and this year ends. Nothing's touched
after five hundred years. Brochures with photos
taken in some rare good weather
don't mention dead reptiles. Here it started
with man, woman and with what they believed
and couldn't understand. Christ came on so northern
he wore skins. Believe and fish will come.
If I was terminal and had six weeks and knew it
I'd fish every lake on Harris. That's a lot
of water. And I'd fake faith long enough
to leave room on my stone for favorable words.
I'd fish the ocean hard my last day on this page.

To get down to earth, if buried here
with faith—even in death we love beauty—
I'd be buried redeemed. Look,

the ocean below and forever, the wide void void
of eternity's nightmare, the lovely way
graves are spaced to leave room for grass.
The date of my death would endure
given good stone and some artisan's fine tools.
May he carve "decent" despite what came out at the inquest.
Please understand, that was just a bad time.
If I can't enter the church, at least
I can go on peeking. Inside, shadows
fall like jail from leaded windows wrong onto stone.

Lord, you're dead. Imagine five centuries gone
and me far as sky from ruin. Imagine
this locked church and my pounding, my hope
to study six hundred year old carvings inside.
Like anyone
I come from a monstrous age, white cliffs
climbing and climbing out of whatever painting
I saw once, climbing out of the frame
and somewhere above
issuing light that released became
some aimless immediate plural.

Letter to Garber from Skye

Dear Fred: I hope this finds you, Marge and children O.K.
We're living on Skye, in Uig, in a homey cottage
high over the bay. Below us, two rivers, the Conon
and Rha enter the sea. Both look trouty and aren't, a trick
peat plays staining the water dark brown and mysterious
where the rivers begin high on the moor. It's windy nearly
all the time, and when you look out the window you think
it's cold. You go out and it isn't. The people too are like that.
Warmer than you think on first sight, with no throw-away charm
like in cities. The sky, water, vegetation and wind are Seattle.

The panoramic bare landscape's Montana. For me, two
homes in one. More than that, consider how many here live
silent inside like my surrogate father. Don't laugh but
today I told my wife if I die here here's where I want
to be buried. She said, me too. I wish I could explain.
Something young inside me says when they visit my grave
I want grass moving sadly and the prolix sea in sight.
On the other hand, dead I won't give a damn. The Scots
are good at that too if that's what you prefer. They are
most accommodating, the Scots, most given to accepting
fate. To be good as these people, are, you must have cruelty
deep in your history, must have tested your capacity
for hate long ago and know how bad it can be and what
it can do. There are castles of the cruel in ruin
and megalithic forts. The blood of our mothers has dried.
An old saying: The fate of the Gael is to lose everything.
From my upstairs window where every morning I write hard,
I see Uig pier across the bay. It reminds me
of a small dock years ago on a lake that didn't look
trouty and was. Remember? All these passionate gales
that stunt trees and leave grass bent permanently east
are the same force that took your dock. They're still taking
and still worth it. So what if it all burns out? It burns.
It is the fate of the Gael. It is the fate of the headless specter to be
forgotten by all. Once his howl was legend
on this island. Now I can't find a soul who knows him.
Not one. They stare at me when I ask. And only a few
old timers remember the water horse. And now what shall become
of us without monsters to pity and fear? The quest
for the autonomous man must have ended in this place
the day before the first tourist arrived. It was, as you
can't imagine, not the failure some scholars maintain,
you included. But you'd have to meet this wind head on
every day with no friend and no family and no
critical vocabulary before how alone we become
would hit home. The fate of the Gael is to lose. Everything
matters because everything dies and that includes storms.

It is calm. The sea does not stir. The hawk has no hard air
to hang on. Up on the moors, the autonomous man is lost
in this autonomous land. He does not answer our cry
to come home. When we light fires, he replies with the dark
silence of early warriors. Until he returns
he remains a threat to all of us who need others, who
need a good time on a dock catching trout, in a cottage
writing a poem for a friend far away. A new saying
I just made up: it is the fate of everyone to lose
the Gael. Five months to go and already I'm rehearsing
good bye, setting my weak mouth hard in the mirror, keeping
tears in check by thinking bad jokes. Did you hear the one
about the American who found so much quiet inside
he couldn't shut up, the way the lonely can't. I can. Dick.

Villager

What's wrong will always be wrong. I've seen him lean
against the house hours and glare at the sea. His eyes say
no boat will come. His harsh throated seemingly
good natured mother bends her back to the soil
and there at least all grows well. When I speak with him
his eyes move away to the sea and I imagine
the red in his face from drink is also from
some ancient tribal shame. To him I'm wealthy.
When we talk I know how wealthy I am.

The police have him on file: petty theft.
I'm certain he steals to make up for the nothing he finds
every day in the sea, and to find money for drink.
Some days a woman picks him up, a sister I'm told,
takes him away and hours later delivers him back
passed out. Next morning again he's propped against
the house, the tide out in his eyes. I imagine
his sister, if that's who she is, knows oblivion
is what he must have often to survive.

•

I have much to tell him. And nothing. I'd start
with the sea. I'd say, there was another sea something
like this long ago, and another me. By the time
I got to the point he'd be looking away and be right.
No two hurts are the same, and most have compensations
too lovely to leave. At night, a photo glows alive
inside him when his mother's asleep and the cops
aren't watching. It lights up in the dark
whenever he looks hard and by dawn has burned out.

I almost forget: he'd do anything for you. Love him
for what you might have become
and love him for what you are, not that far
from him. We are never that far. Love
everyone you can. The list gets longer and shorter.
We're seldom better than weather. We're nearly as good
as a woman we met in passing once at Invergarry.
Don't be sorry, for him or for self. Love the last star
broken by storm. And love you. You hold it together.

The Right Madness on Skye

Now I'm dead, load what's left on the wagon
and have the oxen move on. Tell absentee landlord driver,
Harry of Nothingham, slow. I want my last minutes on earth
filled with this island. For a long time
my days were nothing. My remarkable late surge
I attribute to fanciful chefs: cloud in the salad.
My dramatic reversal of fate insists on this will
read aloud in this poem this day of my death.
Have the oxen move on. Tell Harry of Nothingham, slow.

Take my body to Kilmuir cemetery and adorn
according to instructions. Don't forget the mint.
Carve any lines you want on my stone. If mine

double check spelling. I'm dumb. And triple check
high birds. Bring them down and make them state their names.
If none says 'Rhododendron' you know they're fakes.
Throw them out. Give the piper and drum five minutes
and explain to them, dead, I tire fast.
Have the oxen move on. Tell Harry of Nothingham, slow.

Alive, I often wounded my knee begging response.
My turn to put out. I will one eye to the blind of Dunvegan.
I will one ear to deaf salmon climbing the Conon.
And to the mute ocean I leave this haphazard tongue.
You might note on my stone in small letters:
Here lies one who believed all others his betters.
I didn't really, but what a fun thing to say.
And it's fun to be dead with one eye open in case
that stuck-up twitch in Arizona mourns my loss.

Toot, toot, lovers. Now that I'm moving ahead
you eagerly line the roadside to cheer these remains.
Some say, first, get rid of the body. Not me.
I say let the corpse dance. Make the living lie still.
I told you before, five minutes for piper and drum.
I leave vivid instructions and no one, no one listens.
Let's try it once more. I'm dead. I want to milk that wild
for all it's worth to the crowd already turning away.
Have the oxen move on. Tell Harry of Nothingham, slow.

By now you're no doubt saying, "We've got you to rights.
You can't write a poem from the grave."
Remember, I'm not buried. Only cold on the slab.
There's a hell of a difference between being stiff
from rigor mortis and being held rigid by peat.
Harry of Nothingham knows. Don't you, Harry old chap?
And oxen aren't as dumb as you think. Just because
I've no religion don't say heaven can't welcome me back
under the new majority quota now in effect.

Don't back up for cars. Clear the road for the dead.
Cry 'Fat bag of bones coming through.' I heard that note.
I told you, no trumpets. I told you, five minutes, no more
for piper and drum. Who's mouthing that organ for nothing?
Who's humming along and stamping the right time?
That's the wrong madness for Skye, I say. Wrong
for dispossessed crofters who didn't want me to die
and wrong for comedians waiting for final returns.
Have the oxen move on. Tell Harry of Nothingham, slow.

It's a long road that has no break in the blacktop.
It's a crock to say it. Are they really preparing a speech?
He was this, he was that, lies about me over
the open dirt? If so, have the oxen reverse.
Bring Harry of Nothingham back. I was rotten
in Denmark long before something caught the boat,
and I'm still non grata in Venice. Everytime I level
the piper and drum drown me out.
Have the oxen move on. Tell Harry of Nothingham, slow.

If I'm allowed to digress this way, take me on tour.
What the hell. The hole that's waiting can wait.
I want a last look at Seattle and the way light
subtracts and adds miles to the journey.
And I want to ride again the road on the upper Rha.
If you've got a map you think I'm skipping about.
Listen. All places are near and far selves neighbors.
That wouldn't set well with scholars. Don't tell Harry.
Bury my wounded knee at Flodigarry.

Are we on course again? Good. Isle of Skye, right?
This the day of my death. Only feigned tears, like I ordered.
Make sure the flowers are plastic. Five minutes, remember,
piper and drum. Tell the nearly no mourners remaining
I was easy to mix up with weather. The weather
goes on. Me too, but right now in a deadly stiff line.

Tell the laird who tricked me into being a crofter
I never worked hard in my life except on a poem.
Have the oxen move on. Tell Harry of Nothingham, slow.

Tell Harry of Nothingham stop and have the oxen relax,
I want off at the crossroads. That's far as I go.
I was holding my breath all the time. Didn't I fool you?
Come on, admit it—that blue tone I faked on my skin—
these eyes I kept closed tight in this poem.
Here's the right madness on Skye. Take five days
for piper and drum and tell the oxen, start dancing.
Mail Harry of Nothingham home to his nothing.
Take my word. It's been fun.

New Poems

Last Words to James Wright

I'll call you Bedford, Ed. That's what you called me.
The plane lifts off the runway, circles left across
the mountains, straightens and heads east.
I'm reading in New York and Zetta's coming.
Ed was you, was me, our private ploy.
He lasted 30 years. Now one of Ed is gone.
And what's one Ed alone? You told me January 3
they'd operate in time and damn it, Jim,
I took that as a promise. I really did.
Ed Bedford, you bastard, you lied.

This time, the branch is broke. In early work
you urged the criminal, the derelict,
the dispossessed to run between the stars.
You wanted words to sing the suffering on
and every time you asked the words came willing.
I'm toasting you in heaven, four miles over Billings.
When I see Zetta, your wife
I'll kiss her. I'll call her Annie for luck.
I'm scared as hell nothing's going to work.
Ed Bedford, you bastard, you lied.

You're the only man I knew outside of me
quoted Robert Benchley, same passages in fact.
You need every laugh you get
when your home town's stocked with broken souls.
You left and couldn't leave that dirty river town
where every day the dirty river rolls.

I'll toast you on the Minneapolis layover.
As Rodney Dangerfield puts it, Ed:
"It's not easy, life. Not easy at all."
Make it scotch and dirty river water.

Now the New York leg, non stop. The midwest
moves back in the dark, now and then
the dull electric burn of town, the dark again.
Off left, some shining major city. Remember, Jim,
when they seemed glamorous, filled with magnificent women
you'd never find at home. That and the need to run,
the gift that sent a raw boy non stop
over a green wall, over a green world,
star to star, buddy to dubious saints.
What poet ever found a synonym for shame.

Those saints in solitary where the dirty river rolls,
they know each life clicks off and on,
the off darker than a shabby habit,
the on more blinding than a stray star in the kitchen.
Jesus, Jim, the starker the fact I'm facing
the less I want to sing. Sorry, Ed,
to be so godddam serious. We've got your poems.
We've all got at least two names.
But which one gives and keeps his word?
Ed Bedford, you bastard, you lied.

Ed Bedford, you bastard, you died.
What a chill. We circle the Statue of Liberty.
I feel no liberty at all on the final approach.
I feel a little drunk and a lot more empty,
like passing through some unknown factory town
knowing it must be home.
Be glad of the green wall you climbed across one day.
Be glad as me.
I forgive you, Ed, even if I did swear never.
What's a lie between Eds? What's one more dirty river?

STONE POEMS

Green Stone

All stones have luck built in. Some
a lucky line that curves a weak green back
into some age prehuman. If stones
could talk they'd tell us how they've survived.
They've been used in beautiful fences,
been weapons hurled.

The luck of a stone is part of that stone.
It's not mystical, does not exist just *on*
the stone like a spell put there by some spirit
in some awkward moment—say the picnic's
on the verge of disaster, then good wine opened
and the sun suddenly out, and oh the laughter.
But why am I digressing?
These things have nothing to do with stone luck.

I'm speaking of real stones. You understand.
Rocks. Not symbols for testicles and not
some lay philosopher's metaphysical notion
of an indestructible truth. Real stones, the ones
you find lining ocean floors or creek beds
or lying lonely on roads. Probable colors:
blue, yellow, gray, red, green, white, or brown.
The luck of each is the same, but each suited
to a different situation. That's why December,
told I was dying of cancer,
I picked up a green stone I liked the look of
and carried it in my pocket.
I fondled it just before I took the plane to Seattle.

425

I kissed it often, both sides before the plane took off,
before biopsy, before major surgery. And now
that surgery seems to have gotten every flake
of sick tissue, I keep it on a ledge,
where every morning sun warms the stone.

When I'm totally recovered, another three months
they say, I'll throw the stone back where I found it.
I won't tell you where that is.
The same rock would not work for you no matter
how trivial your problem, how little
luck you need. Please know
I want your life to go on same as mine.
It's just essential you find your own stone.
It lies somewhere near you now, innocent,
and your eye will spot it in one right moment.
You must hold it close to your ear, and
when it speaks to you, you must respond.

Gold Stone

When you find a gold stone know
it isn't gold. If you find it where you should,
under flowing fresh water you'll find it
pulled out and dry pale cream or maybe beige
trying to look splendid. If you find
it on a dry road it was probably
recently painted gold as a joke though you look
and look and the road stays empty,
no snicker of kid behind gorse, nothing worse
than a golden eagle and he has far more
sullen anti-social matters in mind
than fooling you miscoloring one stone.
Now you hold the gold stone. Granted
it doesn't look so gold, the water that made it
look gold dried off and the sun gone down.

Whatever color it assumes deep in your pocket
or purse, give it a chance. If woman
with gold stone, that stone may promise
at least one more golden affair. If man
and lonely, a gold stone will find you a lover,
a woman you saw once in a railroad station,
Berlin, that wide warm easy mouth.
Never believe a gold stone forever.
Just long as you can.

Gray Stone

A gray stone does not change color wet
or dry. Baked on a scorched road or shaded
by cedars, underground or tossed
into a bright green sky, it's always gray.
It is the stone of earth, of the down-to-earth
no nonsense way of knowing life
does not often of its own volition provide.
A gray stone will not
change your luck or shorten the mortgage
or make you young again. It doesn't say
"now" to investments—money or love.
It doesn't say "no" when you plot wrong things
you are sure you must do with your life
or die from the drone. Keep one gray stone
in a secret place, and when those you love
are broken or gone, listen
with a sustained, with a horrible attention
to the nothing it has always had to say.

Red Stone

If underwater and glowing, a red stone
is always good luck. Fish it out, even

if you must wade and wet your good shoes.
It will dry flat red like a new potato.
You should rub it and remember the way
it sparkles underwater, like a red haired woman
curving troutlike through moss.
A red stone will get you through divorce, rage,
sudden attacks of poison and certain diseases
like ringworm or gout. A red stone will not
reverse Alzheimer's disease, or get you past
cancer of the colon. Use it for what it can do.
When it has done its work, return it softly
where you found it, and let your wet feet
sting a moment in the foam's white chill.

Brown Stone

A brown stone if brown a certain way
and held up to sun glows a healthy bronze.
Keep a brown stone in plain sight always,
on your sill, or a paperweight
on your desk. Act friendly to the stone.
Smile. Touch. Even pat its brown hand
and say "good stone, good," though of course
be alone when you do. Don't get a reputation:
"Creep with pet rock," or "Passing
around the bend and not coming back."
A brown stone is also the name of a kind
of house in the eastern U.S., built once
for the wealthy and still in high priced use.
Don't be confused. The brown stone I speak of
is a brown rock about the size of your ear.
It has a subtle magic. If you rub
and compliment it it will turn you
handsome and, like the stone,
you'll want to be where you can be seen.
Get a sun tan. Swim your body hard.

Blue Stone

A blue stone is only one piece
of a huge blue stone no one can find.
A blue stone is anything but
a blue stone. It is a speck of sky
in your hand or a tiny bit of sea.
Of all stones, it contains
the most magics. It can veer your life
away from poverty to riches. It can grow a tree
exactly where you need shade. Just rub
a blue stone and make a wish. A blue stone
becomes the blue marble shooter
you won all those marble games with.
I always act indifferent
around blue stones, sort of nonchalant
like I feel they're nothing special.
That way they work best for me.
I avoid cold faces and cruel remarks.
When I sail a blue stone downwind into
the long blue day, armies start marching.
When I find the stone, armies stop.
When I sail a blue stone into the wind
that always precedes a rain in Montana
and then find the stone and pick it up
a bird sings blue rain.
Days I can't find a blue stone
no matter where I look, I know they've returned
every one to the big blue stone they came from
somewhere in blue mountains,
somewhere unmapped and roadless
that can't be seen from the air.

MAKING CERTAIN IT GOES ON

Where the House Was

is now a church parking lot, the church
not one you've heard of but you presume legit—
National Church of Christ, something like that—
and all trees down except the old holly.
You can't believe you're old enough to feel nothing—
the cherry tree gone, the monster pear gone,
dogwood and plum—old enough to not miss them.
You shut your eyes and you see them.
Your vision must be late autumn.
They've bloomed and produced and shut down.

The parking lot runs the full block, exits,
on both streets. You drive in one end
and out the other. No song you wrote, lyrics
or music, pops into your head, though once
you wrote plenty of songs and sang them
down holes to cringing gophers.
Days you waited. Finally your music came back
from somewhere deep in the earth,
somewhere deep where fires still burned.
Today you found it all gone.
You heard nothing to remind how it had been.

And you heard nothing to remind you how
it had been, robin and wren, and one dog so decent
it loved the mean children who hurt it,
loved the mean kids who grew old and mild
and settled all over and died.
and settled about one in Rangoon, his name

Robert Edwin, raving in fever,
who left a house here and never wrote home
to reclaim it, let the state take it for taxes.
Robert Edwin, dead. He never wrote home.

You remember. Bob Edwin. A purple left hand.

Elegy

in memory, Harold Herndon

I expected him to look dead in the casket,
you know, waxy, blue tinge, but he looked
dozing and tanned, and I wanted to poke him
in front of the crowd and say, "Harold, time
to get up. No train to drive today. I brought
you a drink. I heard a new joke. Look. Outside, the sun."

I tried to remember his life. He gave
it to me in pieces over the years: parents
dead early, some orphanage in Belgrade,
Montana, or Manhattan, Montana,
how he came to be a train engineer,
how he came to own the dear bar.
I remember the unobtrusive, tentative
way he introduced himself 17 years ago
and how, my life seemingly a wreck, I wanted him
to be there like a boulder beside the river,
put there by experts to lean on,
to sleep in the shade of.
I used him plenty. I paid him back
what I could, mostly a poem, and now and then
drinking our way right into dawn.

•

He sold the bar when I was in Scotland.
He went on driving the train, the Helena run,
long leisurely freights. My need of him
had run out and I felt better, felt now
when we met I could give something to him.
I need ask nothing, but this morning I feel
like asking someone a hell of a lot
before the freight pulls out, the freight certain
to be tough going and slow, loaded to the limit
by the heaviest star in the firmament.

O-Mok-See at Nine Mile

In the stands, one old man tries to remember
where he saw horses running out of clouds
straight at him. He didn't cringe or cry out.
He remembers he smelled crayola, and the black locks
of a girl in front of him fell across the horses.
Now he can't comprehend that were he young
and handsome, the lovely girl on the gold stallion
is too drugged to notice his hungry gaze.
The wind's not strong enough to excite the horses
though they romp in cool cloud shade and grow
silent when coated suddenly with sunlight.
To the old man, the events seem silly: pole
bending, barrel racing, the key hole. The children
seem silly accepting ribbons. He feels the cold
when a cloud crosses the sun. When the sun returns
he blindly tries to spot the beautiful girl he
does not know is high. He's certain she's gone
to high pastures with a carload of young men.
Then he spots her accepting a ribbon from the judges.
She's placed in another event. The ribbon is white.
"Does white mean third?" he asks. A voice says
"Fourth. They shouldn't give anything for fourth."

The old man looks at his shoes. They are new.
He forgot he's wearing new shoes. "I've new shoes,"
he says to no one in particular. No one answers.
He wants to tell someone he's sorry wild horses
no longer pour out of clouds.

Tony

His energy did him in, came flooding
his heart with dark adrenalin. His fine book
of Mexico poems for whatever unjust reason
had gone unnoticed. He threw himself into gliding
and he died climbing sand, the wind acting as if
nothing had happened moved alive the dead ends
of his hair. We live thinner now in that wind.

He had that first generational hope we could be humane
and still get things done, his parents from Russia,
the new world opportune. He believed in the soul
but would never bore us with that word.
He'd write the lines of some obscure cathedral
touched by an obscure sun and we would know
it was real and someday we'd find it if we ranged
like birds and gave the world the vast loving chance
it deserves. He made us bigger. He made us
want to fly. I saw him the last time in Denver.

I remember his good nature, his tacit belief
we should take seriously only what we love
and each other. Anger? That was left behind
in Russia, in soil that went wrong, the failing
price of wheat. Somedays I wade wheat
under a burdensome sky, and, fat or not,
when I reach the horizon's ultimate rim
if the wind is right, I lift my arms
and think of a way I could be. Then I fly.

Distances

Driving a prairie, we see a mill far off
and though clouds climbing out of the stack
pollute the air we find the sight lovely.
Horses on the rim of a distant rise
move faintly. We barely see them move
though they run wild. Or when a mile offshore
whales romp and spout, we admire
fountains in Rome, and the distant cathedral
that makes all daylit hours dawn. Artillery
lights a glorious horizon too far for us
to hear the thundering guns. We remain
out of earshot of scream.

Clouds bring rivers closer, bring closer
the homesteader's cabin, the antelope herd.
Clouds move on and the day opens to distance.
Animals are dots. They could be cattle or sheep.
Whatever, they no doubt graze safely and sky
drums wide. Whole symphonies live between
here and a distant whatever-we-look-at.
At night, what we can't see advances
fast and armed over the quaking plain.

All things came close and harmless
first thing this morning, a new trick of light.
Let's learn that trick. If we can, it will mean
we live in this world, neighbor to goat,
neighbor to trout, and we can take comfort
in low birds that hang long enough for us
to read markings and look up names
we'll whisper to them from now on.

Here, but Unable to Answer

in memory, Herbert Hugo

A small dawn, sailor. First light glints
off water and it rays across your face
some ill-defined religion. I see you
always on the bridge alone, vigorous
and handsome. Eight bells. You bellow orders.
Your voice rolls back the wind.
Your eyes light numbers on the compass green.

Had I found you lost, I swear
I would have torn the clouds apart right
beneath the north star long enough
for you to fix position, and we'd have gone
sailing, sailing down our boyhood rivers
out to open sea, you proud of my power
over uncooperative sky. What a team
and never to be. You gone to China. I alone
with two old people and in nightmare earth
becoming drier. No new crop. No growth.

Even in war we lived a war apart.
You who desperately wanted combat
stuck piloting new ships from Pittsburgh
to the gulf. Me and my unwanted self
praying the final bomb run out, praying me alone
home safe, then all the others I forgot.
Forgive the bad nerves I brought home,
these hands still trembling with sky, that deafening
dream exploding me awake. Books will call
that war the last one worth the toll.

Father, now you're buried much too close for me
to a busy highway, I still see you up there

on the bridge, night sky wide open and you naming
wisely every star again, your voice enormous
with the power of moon, of tide. I seldom
sail off course. I swim a silent green.
When I dream, the compass lights stay on.

Salt Water Story

He loved his cabin: there
nothing had happened. Then his friends were dead.
The new neighbors had different ways.
Days came heavy with regret.
He studied sea charts and charted
sea lanes out. He calculated times
to ride the tide rip, times to go ashore and rest.
He memorized the names of bays: those
with plenty of driftwood for fire,
those with oysters. He found a forest
he could draw back into
when the Coast Guard came looking, news
of him missing by now broadcast state-wide.
He made no move. He turned out lights
and lit candles and watched his face
in the window glow red.

He dreamed a raft
and dreamed this sea lane out, past
long dormant cannons and the pale hermit
who begged to go with him. A blue heron
trailed him. A second heron trailed the first,
a third the second and so on. Those who looked for him
checked the skies for a long blue line
of laboring wings.
The birds broke formation, and the world
of search and rescue lost track of his wake.
His face glowed red on the glass.

If found, he'd declare himself pro-cloud
and pro-wind and anti-flat hot days.

Then he dreamed wrong
what we owe Egypt, what we owe
sea lanes out of the slaves to ourselves
we become one morning, nothing
for us in dawn, and nothing for us in tide.
What we owe Egypt fades
into what we owe Greece and then Rome.
What we owe Rome keeps repeating
like what we owe time—namely our lives
and whatever laughter we find to pass on.
He knew grief repeats on its own.

One night late, the face in the window
glowed back at him pale. He believed that face
some bum peeking in
and waved "hi." The old face told him,
to navigate a lasting way out
he must learn how coins gleam
one way through water, how bones of dead fish
gleam another, and he must learn both gleams
and dive deep. He learned both gleams
and learned to dive fast and come up slow
as sky every day.

And we might think someday we'll find him
dead over his charts, the water ways out
a failed dream. Nothing like that.
His cabin stands empty and he
sails the straits. We often see him
from shore or the deck of a ferry.
We can't tell him by craft. Some days
he passes by on a yacht, some days a tug.
He's young and, captain or deckhand,
he is the one who waves.

Ashville

The writer was wrong. You can go home again
but you'll arrive one day late for salvage
and you'll find your skin has turned to glass.
When he went home the town no longer
hated him. He napped easy on the upstairs bed.
When he woke to the strange painting on the wall,
the flaking horses, the dark swamp, the dog
without a head, he must have felt he understood
the painter's sense of failure, the desperate not
held together by a trick of passion,
not quite working, not quite failing to work.
And I suppose it's appropriate my guide
lacks deep emotion. I asked him about the painting.
He admitted he'd never noticed it before.

Why should he notice that strange scene now?
Closing time, I'll bet a silk girl
picks him up in her Ferrari. And if say she
loves his youthful cool approach, she will not
love the monster passion we preserve this house
to honor, or the way that passion fed itself
daily hidden from the mother's vicious eye.
Across the street that must have been narrow
back then and must have been widened for traffic
father chiseled the last word wanted in stone.

The guide goes on with his bio-literary facts:
how angels arrived from France and how today
only one angel remains, that on a gravesite
in a nearby town. And I know whatever direction
that angel faces he faces homeward for someone.
How home holds us. How it held the writer
all four directions he looked, how it held him
locked from birth to a headstone designed

4000 years ago in Persia. Every nap
he must have wakened and there it was again—
the odd picture. He saw it again and knew again
it didn't work. The painter had quit too soon,
maybe had given in to the steam and iron clatter,
to the bitter mutter in the kitchen below.
The guide can't issue faithful lies. He sticks
with what he knows and I remain a guest.
I can't complain the picture isn't complete.

Maybe our writer turned from the painting
to a dream of powder, some gold
flour he might sniff and ride, cloud high
and giant white, the patched land green
and yellow below waving goodbye
and one of two gold eagles whispering "north
north north lies home." Maybe he flew straight
into one of two gold suns. And maybe he too
quit too soon, some animal half done, some cat
painted purple, some swamp that forgot
daylight has a way of seeping in.
The guide's voice seeps in and I can't stop it.
Yes. Yes. There are no ghosts. Just fact and fact.

We can find the family intact in the cemetery.
The big stone: father. The next size: mother.
And in death as in life, brother Ben,
by far the smallest stone. And I keep
dwelling on the painting and how bad art
no matter how strange offers a real way out.
Some are doomed to small lives and small stones.
Others drive on in wide fictions. Others with silk girls
in Ferraris. We don't get quite the whole way back.
That's good. There's this grave. Then there's that.
Right now, this odd road north.

Confederate Graves in Little Rock

Far from these stones, in my country wind shouts
but shouts no name. It hustles north
locked on one heading forever, and salmon enter
rivers on the dead run starting that remorseless
drive home to funereal pools. Children
seem forever preserved in youth by a fresh rain
out of the south, and birds ride thermals
with the easy wisdom of wings.

If I can, I'll die in that weather of home.
This air's not mine. The hum of various insects
compounds the heat. Not one cloud, not
one faint touch of wind. I arbitrarily pick
one name, a 16 year old boy, John Brock
who fell holding the banner of battle in hands
calloused on his father's farm. He was home
in this heat. He could say: I'm dying home.

I row among the dead stumps in a lake.
My bass plug settles and I reel at the speed
I believe fish swim. Nothing. I'd carve names
on stumps to resurrect the souls of dead trees
and make sure someone remembers the forest
that cracked off one terrible tornado ago.
That air howled 'rebel' and the name of a family
destroyed by a blue rain of artillery.

In North Little Rock, poverty's shacks
fill with song. They're singing the last rites of one
more victim of murder—the mean word uttered—
the kind gun fired—the usual forms
filled out and filed—the usual suspect jailed.
They're singing from graves created by wrongs
that go back before wars were recorded
or graves marked by stones.

•

Maybe the best graves stay unmarked, the right words
never find themselves cut into stone.
Whatever the weather it could be home for one
blood or another. For certain the best wars
wear down for personal reasons. It's hard
to do battle in breezy country where sun
lights the highway and one cloud shades
your car, whatever speed you drive.

Bannerman's Island

for Chris

We are passing it now. Our boat
will circle it twice. The tour guide is telling
how Bannerman made a fortune in guns
and built a castle on the island.
Downriver behind us
an old man on the ramparted wall
of the armory sits painting the island.
Behind him, gray lines of cadets are marching.
The old man hopes for two more hours
good light. Our boat begins
a barely discernible turn. Our guide points out
the castle in ruin. He speaks of wild game
imported from far off jungles, then hunted down
on the island and shot. He does not say
the bones are still there. We like to think
the bones are. The old painter
can't catch the color of oak leaves
reflected off the river. After they finish marching
the cadets will go to a lecture
and be told they are to be the future leaders
in event of war. Some will dream
Eisenhower giving the order, June 5,
long ago, and the morning of the sixth,

that flash and thunder, waiting for the next report,
a world waiting for the next report.
The old man decides his color of oak leaves
off water is good enough for this time of day.
Twice our boat has circled the island.
Now it heads home. Let's not look back.
Let's keep our eye on The Point. Behind us
a bewildered tiger has run short of cover
and stands alone on the shore. Across the water
the mainland, where miles and miles of woods
offer a chance. Behind him, Bannerman
taking dead aim.

George Stubbs at Yale

for Louis Martz

In land that obviously northern, no record ever
a lion has attacked a horse, not where air
polishes animal skin with light
and storm tears green holes through cloud and flares out
stiff the soft willow branches
and the horse's white mane. In some house not
in the painting, a woman says nothing all day
over a stove. In Africa, where real lions stink
in heat and grow shaggy, their legs tormented
by flies, we might paint polar bears—one more
answer to some vague "they" and some dim
early "don't do that." If a horse seems too perfect—
color and line—we order whatever beast we bore
long ago and kept secret, "kill." We gave him that rage
we found in sky during storm, and his tail bends
the same way tree trunks bend. In some house not
in the painting, a woman babbles day long over
a sink. The lion clearer than any we've known,

we speculate the day Stubbs conceived the painting,
wind blowing clean everything he saw
and he, slightly wild inside, said "why not a cat?"
The lion ended looking at his victim
with lust more than malice. Whatever storm started
all this, we won't find it recorded.
It's a matter finally of where we are from.
We must stay northern to find light diminished by cloud
and to give line a chance to be stark in that light.
We must live threats we invent.
We must stay northern to bring warm lions home.

Pishkun Reservoir

for Bud Guthrie

Think of those big trout, Bud, fifty years
back and more and no limit then, no game regulations
and no sonic booms cracking the dam
or the dam tender's house, mortar and stone.
How those big rainbows danced
on their tails. How fishermen believed skies
full of willing women. This land spreads big
as the big sky and there's plenty of room
for the dead, for enemies who died and dead friends.
I know what poets I'd bury here and everyone's
a king. I'd ring the reservoir with their stones
and all night their spirits would dance over
the waters. All day trout would dance on our leaders.
We imagine a man in the dam tender's house
stationed there decades ago and forgotten,
beginning to crack like the house. If he came
to us asking the year we'd say "welcome,"
we'd say we too forget the President's name.
Here the hard wind blows all hurt away:

the maimed bison moaning at the bottom
of the jump, Indians starving that year
no bison were seen, the sadness of children
and the sadness of none. We would be
hard as that wind. We're lucky enough to cast down it
and just as we guess the high white jet trail
a major run, say Chicago-Seattle, your bobber
moves some right slightly wrong way and we know
no matter how faint that nibble seems
it could be fifty years old, something real big.
Still no limit, Bud. No limit that counts.

Poem for Zen Hofman

We saw him in his powered wheelchair
go downwind across the ice too fast
for my fear, his face against the polar air
a twisted angel's face. I told my wife:
That's Zen. That's Zen. She said "beautiful."
And he writes poems, I said. I tried
to say: and he writes poems for me.
The wind sang Zen away safe from my lie.

When I went twisted into taverns long
and not so long ago, Seattle, Portland
and a dozen towns with (I insisted)
willows bawling rain, my wife would not
have been my wife then, and my friend
would not have been my friend. Now there's Zen
and a winter that won't quit, and all
of us go begging like the sun.

In current dreams I find bad men.
One I took a swing at. He was dreadful
and he poked fun at my fighting stance.

Another (Lord, I liked his looks) was a comedian
comedians disdained. He tried too hard
and he went wild wrong times. I tried to explain
to famous grinning men. They told me
take a hike. My dreams happen on dry land.

Let's say for all this goddam snow
dry days will come, dried by the same wind
Zen will travel downwind home
no chance of spinning out on ice. I'm with him
in my better moments
heroic as a tree root only not that strong
and not that twisted either. My wife
advised me: Be him. Be like him. Pretend.

Death in the Aquarium

Praise him for the place he picked.
He shot himself dead in full sight
of the red Irish lord and the rare
albino sea perch. They nosed the glass
and cried to the outside world of air
"he's bleeding" in some salt water tongue.
The flounder dozed on. The octopus
flashed one disapproving eye at the cop.

The cop found no suicide note. The cop found
no I.D. The gun could not be traced.
They questioned everyone there but the fish
who swam around those being questioned.
You'd have wanted to film it, the visitors
with no answers shaken and sad, the red
snapper behind them gasping, the misfit
rock cod proud of his bad looks
and the yellow shiners turning and turning

like beautiful words going nowhere.
What a beautiful picture.
A year later the case was filed unsolved.

And you? Me? Where should we die given
a choice? In a hothouse? Along a remote
seldom traveled dirt road? Isn't some part
of that unidentified man in us all
and wants to die where we started?
Don't we share way back a cold green past
and wouldn't we welcome dying unknown,
unnamed on the floor of the ocean,
our bones ignored by the only clock there,
that slow unrhythmic waver of kelp—
our bones giving off the phosphorus
that collects in pockets and waits,
then one night washes in glowing?
And lovers, lovers would stop making love
and stand there, each suddenly alone
amazed at that gleam riding sand.

Making Certain It Goes On

At last the Big Blackfoot river
has risen high enough to again cover the stones
dry too many months. Trout return
from summer harbor deep in the waters
of the power company dam. High on the bank
where he knows the river won't reach
the drunk fisherman tries to focus on
a possible strike, and tries to ignore
the hymn coming from the white frame church.
The stone he leans against, bleached out dull gray,
underwater looked beautiful and blue.
The young minister had hoped for a better parish,

say one with bells that sound gold
and a congregation that doesn't stop coming
when the mill shuts down.

We love to imagine
a giant bull trout or a lunker rainbow
will grab the drunk fisherman's bait
and shock the drunk fisherman out
of his recurrent afternoon dream and into
the world of real sky and real water.
We love to imagine the drought has ended,
the high water will stay, the excess
irrigate crops, the mill reopen, the workers
go back to work, lovers reassume plans
to be married. One lover, also the son
of the drunk fisherman, by now asleep
on the bank for no trout worth imagining
has come, will not invite his father
to the happy occasion though his father
will show up sober and properly dressed,
and the son will no longer be sure of the source
of the shame he has always rehearsed.

Next summer the river will recede,
the stones bleach out to
their dullest possible shade. The fisherman
will slide bleary down the bank
and trade in any chance he has of getting
a strike for some old durable dream,
a dream that will keep out the hymn
coming again from the church. The workers
will be back full shift. The power company
will lower the water in the dam
to make repairs, make repairs and raise rates.
The drunk fisherman will wait for the day
his son returns, divorced and bitter

and swearing revenge on what the old man
has come to believe is only water
rising and falling on climatic schedule.

That summer came and is gone. And everything
we predicted happened, including the death
of the fisherman. We didn't mention that before,
but we knew and we don't lie to look good.
We didn't forsee the son would never return.

This brings us to us, and our set lines
set deep on the bottom. We're going all out
for the big ones. A new technology
keeps the water level steady year round.
The company dam is self cleaning.
In this dreamy summer air you and I
dreamily plan a statue commemorating
the unknown fisherman. The stone will bear
no inscription and that deliberate anonymity
will start enough rumors to keep
the mill operating, big trout nosing the surface,
the church reforming white frame
into handsome blue stone, and this community
going strong another hundred years.

INDEX

A bird sails from the hole in that high stone, 76
A blue stone is only one piece, 429
A brown stone if brown a certain way, 428
A field of wind gave license for defeat, 124
A gray stone does not change color wet, 427
A little guts, self drama and it's done, 185
A long freight swims upwind. Each 4 P.M., the river, 240
A small dawn, sailor. First light glints, 435
A small town slanted on a slight hill, 290
Across the street my neighbor's colored lights, 226
After a Train Trip, One Town Remains, 324
Again, Kapowsin, 230
Alki Beach, 15
All debris ends here at the north end, 399
All furniture's gone. It hits me in this light, 233
All stones have luck built in. Some, 425
All the essentials were there, the river thin, 243
Anacortes-Sydney Run, The, 74
And after forty years her flowers failed to sing, 222
And so they cheated and wandered and were loved, 379
Anna, that sea is tender but the land, 157
Announcement, 259
Antiques in Ellettsville, 88
Antisocial Easter, 17
Applause and wondrous gazes of love, 109
Approaching the Castle, 261
April in Cerignola, 118
Are these flowers paint? Back of each bouquet, 95
Argo, 26
Art of Poetry, The, 271
Ashville, 438
At last the Big Blackfoot river, 446
At Our Best, 354
At the Cabin, 336
At the Stilli's Mouth, 53
At this west-most U.S. point, 30
Aware that summer baked the water clear, 32
Ayr, 403

Back of Gino's Place, 18
Bad Eyes Spinning the Rock, 171
Bad Vision at the Skagit, 62
Ballad of the Upper Bumping, 27

Ballpark at Moiese, The, 331
Bannerman's Island, 441
Bass, 4
Bassetti's Lions, 41
Bay of Recovery, 367
Bay of Resolve, 366
Bay of Sad Loss, 365
Beachthieves, 12
Bear Paw, 215
Beaverbank, 341
Beggar in Sapri, 150
Believe in this couple this day who come, 389
Belt, 370
Between the Bridges, 60
Birds here should have names so hard to say, 191
Birthday, 338
Black from sun and the stain of hemlock bark, 34
Blond Road, The, 98
Blue Stone, 429
Bone Hunting, 371
Bouquets from Corley, 95
Braes, The, 398
Bridge of Sighs, The, 106
Brief History, 346
Brown Stone, 428
Brueghel in the Doria, 111
Burn this shot. That gray is what it is, 225

Cairn in Loch An Duin, The, 410
Camas Prairie School, 209
Cantina Iannini, 135
Cape Alava, 30
Cape Nothing, 70
Carloway Broch, 408
Caro Mimo mio: My first trip south. It's not what, 283
Castel Sant'Angelo, 112
Cataldo Mission, 190
Cattails, 248
Centuries near Spinnazola, 29
Changes at Meridian, 357
Changes in Policy at Taholah, 250
Chapel Further West than Most, A, 37
Children take longer to die, 379
Christmas with Shepherds in Brefaro, 154
Church on Comiaken Hill, The, 97
Chysauster, 182

Clachard, 381
Clams and barnacles clatter, 15
Clearances, The, 387
Cleggan, 198
Click and clatter. Water off for heaven, 59
Clouds of Uig, The, 383
Colors of a Bird, The, 76
Coming from a country where we never fail, 134
Confederate Graves in Little Rock, 440
Cornwall, Touring, 195
Cracks in light log buildings, counting sheds, 205
Cries of gold or men about to hang, 176
Crinan Canal, 199
Cripples, The, 246
Cruelty and rain could be expected, 224
Culloden, 405

Dancer at Kozani's, 72
Days she looks at floors, a thick degrading cloud, 251
Dear Albert. This is a wholesome town. Really. Cherries grow, 310
Dear An: This will be your first widow Christmas. Such a young, 285
Dear Archie: I hope the boat trip home wasn't long, 282
Dear Arthur: In a country where a wealthy handful, 313
Dear Bill: This is where the Nisei farmed, here where the blacktop, 280
Dear Bill: We don't know the new heavy kind of wolf, 289
Dear Bob: I'll be damned. The good, oh so utterly sweet, 288
Dear Bobbi: God, it's cold. Unpredicted, of course, by forecast, 291
Dear Charles: And so we meet once in San Francisco and I, 279
Dear Condor: Much thanks for that telephonic support, 275
Dear Dave: Rain five days and I love it. A relief, 292
Dear Denise: Long way from, long time since Boulder. I hope, 307
Dear Dennice: I'm this close but the pass is tough this year, 302
Dear Dick: You know all that pissing and moaning around I've, 314
Dear Ed: I get the sad news from Des Moines no doubt not sad, 305
Dear Fred: I hope this finds you, Marge and children O.K., 413
Dear Gary: As soon as you'd gone winter snapped shut again, 301
Dear Gary: The houses in Wallace are closed after 94 years, 317
Dear J.D.: One should think of Chief Joseph here, coming soft, 287

Dear Jim: The Bedfords are not to be found. Maybe, 303
Dear Jim: This is as far as I ever chased a girl, 299
Dear John: Great to see your long-coming, well-crafted book, 304
Dear John: This a Dear John letter from booze, 296
Dear Liz: Here's where I degraded myself for the last time, 295
Dear Madeline: I'm getting strange when I drink. In Solon, 277
Dear Marvin: Months since I left broke down and sobbing, 276
Dear Michele: Once, according to a native, this town, 312
Dear Mike: We didn't have a chance. Our starter had no change, 286
Dear Robert, 293
Dear Vi: You were great at the Roethke festival this summer, 298
Death in the Aquarium, 445
Death of the Kapowsin Tavern, 102
December 24, Alone, 226
December 24 and George McBride Is Dead, 87
Deep in that black water where you tossed a book, 77
Degrees of Gray in Philipsburg, 216
Dick, I went back to those rocks today, 126
Did I come from this, a hardware store, 253
Digging Is an Art, 48
Distances, 434
District in the City, A, 22
Dixon, 213
Docking at Palermo, 105
Dog Lake with Paula, 172
Doing the House, 325
Don't scream at me you God damn' wops, 113
Driving a prairie, we see a mill far off, 434
Driving Montana, 204
Druid Stones at Kensaleyre, 397
Drums in Scotland, 181
Duntulm Castle, 394
Dust that clouded your last drunk dream, 203
Dust was too thick every summer. Every winter, 346
Duwamish, 44
Duwamish Head, 65
Duwanish No. 2, 61
Dwelling, 356

Each afternoon the world goes by above it, 152
Eighteen Days in a Tuscan Wood, 117
'Eighty-nine was bad. At least a hundred, 169
Eileen, 85
Elegy, 431
End of Krim's Pad, The, 192

Even in July, from this point north, 194
Every day became a slow July. Sweat, it was clear, 340
Every good wind he hangs over the field, 385

Face the moon. Ask: is it less, now that man, 354
Fairfield, 358
Far from these stones, in my country wind shouts, 440
Farmer, Dying, 238
Ferniehirst Castle, 404
First South and Cambridge, 90
Fish swim onto sand in error, 7
Fly, crane—your wing assumes no weight, 6
Flying, Reflying, Farming, 231
For a Northern Woman, 92
For fifty years the bubbles marked, 365
For Jennifer, 6, on the Teton, 260
Forget the keep-off sign. That cow, 89
Forgive this nerve. I walked here up the long hill, 228
Fort Benton, 345
Fort Casey, without Guns, 93
Freaks at Spurgin Road Field, The, 254
From Altitude, the Diamonds, 364
From China, contra-boom-bang water, 75
From the Rain Forest Down, 59
From this hill they are clear, the people, 319
From time one I've been reading slaughter, 258

Galileo's Chair, 107
Galleria Umberto I, 129
George Stubbs at Yale, 442
Getty, 352
Ghost in a Field of Mint, 252
Ghosts at Garnet, 207
G.I. Graves in Tuscany, 115
Glen Uig, 389
Gold Man on the Beckler, The, 188
Gold Stone, 426
Good Day for Seeing Your Limitations, A, 223
Good morning. The horses are ready. The trail, 268
Good View from Flagstaff, A, 351
Goodbye, Iowa, 237
Gooseprairie, 25
Graves, 355
Graves at Coupeville, 101
Graves at Elkhorn, 169
Graves at Mukilteo, 36
Graves in Queens, 263
Graves in Uig, 384
Gray Stone, 427
Green Stone, 425
Greystone Cottage, 382
Gull Hardly Explained, The, 8
Guns at Fort Flagler, 357

Hardly a ghost left to talk with. The Slavs moved on, 368
Hawk in Uig, 385
He boots a cat, ass over claws, and laughs, 134
He crossed the country like a wire, 8
He is twice blessed, the old one buried here, 329
He loved his cabin: there, 436
He planned his course on Orinoco charts, 18
He was crude as a loon on land. His tongue, 252
He will bomb the final town, 12
He would hoard this hill, this salal, 9
Helena, Where Homes Go Mad, 176
Here at last is ending, 21
Here, but Unable to Answer, 435
Here, the nuns are rumored cruel. Beat, 46
Hideout, 64
High Grass Prairie, 346
Hilltop, The, 249
His energy did him in, came flooding, 433
History of the Sketch, A, 228
Ho. The horses can water. We are miles, 257
Holy Family, 46
Home. Home. I knew it entering, 212
Hot Springs, 214
House on 15th S.W., The, 224
Houses, 372
Houses Lie, Believe the Lying Sea, 89
How long will these graves go on, 263
How Meadows Trick You, 361
How much money would erase him in a dream, 150
How to Use a Storm, 360

I can't let it go, the picture I keep of myself, 328
I can't name those birds, black with height, 49
I can't ridge it back again from char, 102
I don't come here after June when rattlesnakes, 188
I dreamed this coast before Croatia, 151
I expected him to look dead in the casket, 431
I felt the empty cabin wasn't abandoned, 239
I forget the names of towns without rivers, 343
I got three bulls and a native cutthroat, lover, 211
I had been on the road before. The first time, 370
I imagine Druids timeless, so lacking, 397
I learned this from the old: odor of lake, 228
I like bars close to home and home run down, 249
I only dreamed that high cliff we were on, 178
I reach for you. You smile and I am male, 92
I realized early they were dying like a wall, 371
I run up the stairs too fast every morning, 137
I said the glint was thistle. It turned out tin, 361
I wake, birds flashing on my lids. The dead, 223
I wanted it depressed, one dusty road, 358
I was calling airspeed, 121
I went timid to that town, 363
I would have taken this road on sight, 398

If I painted, I'd paint landscapes. In museums, 244
If underwater and glowing, a red stone, 427
If we spend our life remembering what we love, 227
If you look at the sky, 79
If you stopped there it was only to refuel, 324
I'll call you Bedford, Ed. That's what you called me, 423
Imagining Delaware, 350
In early hymns cries came faint, 339
In gold light here a small guard, 107
In land that obviously northern, no record ever, 442
In many tongues, hawkers scream our fingers, 99
In my best dream I have crossed the border, 74
In Stafford Country, 91
In the dark a boxcar grinds, 26
In the pounding white is a man to kill, 27
In the reeds, the search for food by grebes, 64
In the stands, one old man tries to remember, 432
In this photo, circa 1934, 221
In winter, Germans gone, the sea insane, 131
In Your Bad Dream, 284
In Your Big Dream, 311
In Your Blue Dream, 294
In Your Dream after Falling in Love, 316
In Your Dream on the Eve of Success, 308
In Your Fugitive Dream, 278
In Your Good Dream, 319
In Your Hot Dream, 297
In Your Racing Dream, 300
In Your Small Dream, 290
In Your War Dream, 281
In Your Wild Dream, 304
In Your Young Dream, 287
Index, 73
Indian Girl, 251
Indian Graves at Jocko, 179
Introduction to the Hoh, 59
Invasion North, 247
Iowa Déjà Vu, 253
is now a church parking lot, the church, 430
Is this all we will know of the dark, 410
is to have an old but firmly painted name, 173
It is much like ocean the way it opens, 335
It just says 'church' on the map, 400
It promises quiet here. A green Plymouth, 205
Italian Town Abandoned, 155
It's a bad Good Friday, snow and mud, 170
It's a problem, why I'm here with amplified rock, 357
It's a rare Brueghel without people, 111
It's mystery, not wind, the men, 63
It's not you, this dead long moan from the past, 323
It's what I planned. The barbershop alone, 248
I've walked this street in far too many towns, 182

Kapowsin, 34
Keen to Leaky Flowers, 16
Kennedy Ucciso, 113
Keokuk, 266
Kilmuir Cemetery: Stone with Two Skulls and No Name, 393
Kilmuir Cemetery: The Knight in Blue-Green Relief, 391
Knock or none, that woman hears a knocking, 50

La Push, 7
Lady in Kicking Horse Reservoir, The, 201
Lake Byron, Maybe Gordon Lord, 77
Land breaks yellow south below, pale squares, 116
Landscapes, 244
Langaig, 401
Last Day There, 233
Last Words from Maratea, 139
Last Words to James Wright, 423
Late Summer, Drummond, 240
Leaving the Dream, 340
Lecture, 43
Let him pan. His sluice will rot and flake, 188
Let's take it as it is: acres flowing, 351
Letter to Ammons from Maratea, 282
Letter to Annick from Boulder, 285
Letter to Bell from Missoula, 276
Letter to Birch from Deer Lodge, 312
Letter to Blessing from Missoula, 314
Letter to Bly from La Push, 293
Letter to Gale from Ovando, 298
Letter to Garber from Skye, 413
Letter to Gildner from Wallace, 317
Letter to Goldbarth from Big Fork, 310
Letter to Haislip from Hot Springs, 304
Letter to Hanson from Miami, 283
Letter to Hill from St. Ignatius, 291
Letter to Kathy from Wisdom, 309
Letter to Kizer from Seattle, 275
Letter to Levertov from Butte, 307
Letter to Libbey from St. Regis, 295
Letter to Logan from Milltown, 296
Letter to Mantsch from Havre, 286
Letter to Matthews from Barton Street Flats, 280
Letter to Mayo from Missoula, 305
Letter to Oberg from Pony, 313
Letter to Peterson from the Pike Place Market, 288
Letter to Reed from Lolo, 287
Letter to Scanlon from Whitehall, 302
Letter to Simic from Boulder, 279
Letter to Sister Madeline from Iowa City, 277
Letter to Snyder from Montana, 301
Letter to Stafford from Polson, 289
Letter to Wagoner from Port Townsend, 292
Letter to Welch from Browning, 299
Letter to Wright from Gooseprairie, 303

Life was Greek before Greeks came. The swamp, 128
Light bangs empty barracks where, 186
Light crawls timid over fields, 213
Light from the river brightens your old room, 341
Listen, Ripley, 262
Little has changed. Six dark mornings a week, 139
Living Alone, 239
Lone Cheer from the Stands for a Bitter Crane, 6
Lone Lake, Whidbey, 71
Long and smelling good, the cemetery grass, 89
Long before I hear it, Naples bright, 106
Long day on the road, R.H., and three trips now, 318
Looking at the model of a pishkun, 174
Lord, I'd rehearsed and rehearsed your loss, 411
Lord, it took no more than the wave of a glove, 387

Making Certain it Goes On, 446
Map of Montana in Italy, A, 165
Map of Skye, A, 380
Map of the Peninsula, A, 24
Maratea Antica, 133
Maratea Porto, 131
Maratea Porto: Saying Good-bye to the Vitolos, 138
Maratea Porto: The Bitter Man, 134
Maratea Porto: The Dear Postmistress There, 137
Market this morning where dazzling rows, 108
Maybe they believed anything that solid, 381
Medicine Bow, 347
Memoirs, 41
Mendocino, Like You Said, 75
Mercy Jesus mercy, 184
Meridian, 15
Midwestern in the heat, this river's, 44
Mill at Romesdal, 396
Milltown Union Bar, The, 166
Mission in Carmel, 33
Mission to Linz, 79
Missoula Softball Tournament, 210
Montana Ranch Abandoned, 205
Montesano Unvisited, 156
Montgomery Hollow, 191
Morning at nine, seven ultra-masculine men, 284
Morning in Padova, 108
Most men are rodents clothed. After fun, 184
Most neglect this road, the concrete torn, 18
Mudhens, cormorants and teals take, 61
Museum of Cruel Days, 323
My Buddy, 269
My darling we are trolling Lake Frontal, 71
My dearest Kathy: When I heard your tears and those of your, 309
My nostrils tell me: somewhere *mare nostro*, 78
My sudden daughter, grays are latent in that sea, 330

Name the Mystery Fin and Win a Doll, 39
Napoli Again, 106
Near Kalalock, 3
Nearly all the rivers color like the sky, 59
Neighbor, 44
Ness, 407
Night at the Napi in Browning, A, 208
Night with Cindy at Heitman's, A, 193
No Bells to Believe, 51
No fish passed this way this century, 155
No gifts today. Last night no monster star, 154
No hills. Raw wind unchecked, brings word, 91
No in-between. The news is good or bad, 386
No sense of past. Did Serra, 33
No shark, the fin that scars a circle, 39
North, 12
Northwest Retrospective: Mark Tobey, 47
Not my hands but green across you now, 201
Note from Capri to Richard Ryan on the Adriatic Floor, 126
Note the stump, a peach tree. We had to cut it down, 234
Note to R.H. from Strongsville, 318
Nothing seems right, not the monument too close, 405
Now I break the mask, repeal those years, 52
Now I'm dead, load what's left on the wagon, 416
Now it's clean. The whores seem healthy, 129
Now rockets pierce the limit of our air, 43
Now the summer perch flips twice and glides, 7
Now they bury her and the clouds run scared, 48

Ocean on Monday, 21
Ode to the Trio Fruit Company of Missoula, 242
Old Map of Uhlerstown, 193
Old Scene, 243
O-Mok-See at Nine Mile, 432
On clear days here the sea is most clear, 133
On cliffs above the town, high homes disdain, 93
On Hearing a New Escalation, 258
On his sides are recreated reeds, 4
On this dishonored, this perverted globe, 352
On this map white. A state thick as a fist, 165
Once I changed my name to race the rich, 41
Once I said three gulls are often four, 158
Once more you've degraded yourself on the road, 237
One By Twachtman at the Frye, 95
One day at a time. And one barn, 327
One look at this mill and the adjacent croft, 396
One of us would spot his horse, same white, 229
One Son North to Naples, 134
One tug pounds to haul an afternoon, 5
One way of going is to bang the door your last time, 334
Only Bar in Dixon, The, 212
Only these stone hut walls record their lives, 182
Open Country, 335

Or Another Place, 13
Orcas in the Eyes, 49
Other Beaverbank, The, 336
Other Grave, The, 89
Outside: forecasts of humiliating storms, 193
Ovando, 203
Over the years these clouds have colored much, 383
Overlooking Yale, 348

Paestum, 128
Park at Villammare, The, 148
Park. Let's walk the brief path back, 408
People say his painting caught so much, 22
Phoning from Sweathouse Creek, 211
Picnic in the Saracen Ruin, The, 132
Pike Place Market, 99
Piles of rock balls used for ammo then, 112
Pipe the Gaelic back for one last dance, 387
Piping to You on Skye from Lewis, 387
Pishkun, 174
Pishkun Reservoir, 443
Pizzeria S. Biagio, 136
Places and Ways to Live, 234
Plans for Altering the River, 256
Plunking the Skagit, 63
Poem for Zen Hofman, 444
Point No Point, 194
Politely like Snakes in the Oats, 37
Popovich our guide is old and roads he knew, 153
Port Townsend, 93
Port Townsend, 1974, 352
Prado: Bosch: S. Antonio, The, 184
Prado: Number 2671, Anonimo Español, The, 185
Praise him for the place he picked, 445
Probably two thieves, but why a stone this big, 393

Quick and yet he moves like silt, 3

Rapids shake the low hung limbs like hair, 168
Reading at the Old Federal Courts Building, St. Paul, 241
Reclamation at Coloma, 175
Reconsidering the Madman, 245
Red Stone, 427
Remember Graham, 227
Remote Farm on the Dubrovnik-Sarajevo Run, 152
Repairing the House, the Church, Restoring the Music, 339
Resulting from Magnetic Interference, 14
Right Madness on Skye, The, 416
River Now, The, 368
Road Ends at Tahola, 78
Room on room, we poke debris for fun, 39

S. Miniato: One by Aretino, 109
Sailing Dalmatia, 151

Sailing from Naples, 158
St. Clement's: Harris, 411
St. Ignatius Where the Salish Wail, 170
St. John's Chapel, 399
Salt Water Story, 436
Sandbanks, The, 368
Sandbanks climb and curve until, 90
Say something warm. Hello. The world, 346
Saying Goodbye to Mrs. Noraine, 222
Say you're drunk or drugged and something hums, 369
Scene, 327
Schoolgirl at Seola, 23
Score tied in the 8th, the only fans, bison, 331
Second Chances, 328
See how the red name faded hard to sorry, 242
See them in snow under a full moon they told me, 406
See this arm, the rivers have good names, 24
Semi-Lunatics of Kilmuir, The, 379
Seven thousand acres of grass have faded yellow, 238
Shacks are brown, big where things were sold, 207
Shark Island, 196
She came to alter sky with glass, 23
Should I say, my people? I turned to stone, 138
Silver Star, 177
1614 Boren, 39
Sky was glowering so thick that day in Keokuk, 266
Skykomish River Running, 32
Small Oil Left in the House We Rented in Boulder, The, 354
Snapshot of 15th S.W., A., 225
Snapshot of the Auxiliary, A, 221
Snapshot of Uig in Montana, A, 379
Sneosdal, 390
Snoqualmie, 21
Snow air in the wind. It stings our lunch sacks, 172
Snow Poem, 362
Some days the tick of two protestant clocks, 382
Some days you're finished. Not even eels, 149
Some foreign freighter crawls a blue path north, 357
Some things you say how sweet to. A widowed aunt's, 148
Somersby, 184
Sound Track Conditional, 369
South Italy, Remote and Stone, 146
Spinazzola: Quella Cantina La, 124
Spinning hymns downstream is fun. The worm spins, 171
Spinning the Sava, 153
Squatter on Company Land, The, 96
Standing Stones of Callanish, The, 406
Starting Back, 265

Storm in Acquafredda, 147
Sun in our sails, our hooker wheels again, 196
Sung badly hymns are loaded with remorse, 37
Sweet Piece from Fontal, 71
Swimmer at Lake Edward, The, 252

Tahola, 69
Taneum Creek, 188
That girl upstream was diced by scaling knives, 65
That goose died in opaque dream, 230
That nine-foot doughboy, were the sculptor good, 88
That rock shaped like a ship might scare us now, 132
That's a place I've been. The town, 354
That's our last look at the green canal, 106
The Blackfoot bends, pools deep around, 167
The block is bare except for this five-story, 86
The castle mad with decay, intimate streets, 118
The day is a woman who loves you. Open, 204
The dead are hidden from the sea. The sea, 384
The dim boy claps because the others clap, 254
The drunk who lives across the street from us, 44
The enemy's not poverty. It's wind, 146
The flags beyond those dunes are roaring, 95
The flat year, when summer never arrived, 355
The gavel hammered. The sentence tore my ear, 241
The house you're moving from is not this house, 372
The iron doors we shut on ammo rooms, 93
The lines are keen against today's bad sky, 97
The mackerel are in. Came on the tide, 198
The man in the moon was better not a man, 271
The old man on the prison work release gang, 252
The riches we find inside will be in rich light, 261
The river seems to sour and we can't recall, 336
The rotten thing is after you've been pushed around, 391
The schoolbell rings and dies before, 209
The sea designed these cliffs. Stone is cut, 70
The sun is caked on vertical tan stone, 73
The sun, the warm man renting boats, 71
The wind at Dog Lake whispered 'stranger' 'stranger', 239
The wind is 95. It still pours from the east, 215
The writer was wrong. You can go home again, 438
There is no decision. Nothing final, 21
There was never danger in this black sad water, 199
These are strange shores. No sand, 14
These dirt mounds make the dead seem fat, 179
These graves never fit a standard hymn, 17
These Indians explain away their hair, 208
These open years, the river, 260
These shacks are tricks. A simple smoke, 60

These two cats guard the grapes. Their claws, 41
They looked soft floating down. White puffs that glowed, 247
They still seem G.I., the uniform lines, 115
They won't go away, the sea perch, 356
They're denying whites the beach. The tribe says, 250
Think how we touch each other when we sight land, 366
Think of those big trout, Bud, fifty years, 443
This is Puglia and cruel. The sun is mean, 118
This is the final resting place of engines, 177
This is the way the road bent then, wide and sullen, 347
This is where the day went slack, 29
This is where those who hate monuments, 407
This last estate of greed has been reclaimed, 175
This map defines your home. The names, 193
This river ground to quiet in Sylvana, 53
This road dips and climbs but never bends, 98
This summer, most friends out of town, 210
This then buddy is the blue routine, 269
This was our first line of defense. It held, 404
This was the last name west on the charts, 345
This water started it all. This sullen arm, 367
This will be the last time. Clearly, 325
Those knights had an eye for strategic location, 394
Those who favor our plan to alter the river, 256
Though alone, you know just over the hill, 311
Though Tuesday, 11 A.M., the shops are locked, 278
Three Stops to Ten Sleep, 257
Through the white chiffon that covered her, 72
Through those trees you traced a loud white roof, 117
Throw sand dollars and they sail alive, 3
Tiberio's Cliff, 110
Tiberio was kind according to the guard, 110
Time of day: a dim dream, probably, 127
Time to Remember Sangster, 229
Tinker Camp, The, 197
To Die in Milltown, 173
To him the window broken in the church, 245
To know expanse I read thin books, 16
To Women, 359
To write a snow poem you must ignore the snow, 362
Today, I remembered Getty, the old man, 352
Tomorrow morning at four, the women will be herded, 259
Tony, 433
Top Of The Park, Hillis. Top of the World, 348
Topographical Map, 268
Town or poem, I don't care how it looks. Old woman, 373
Towns We Know and Leave Behind, the Rivers We Carry with Us, The, 343

Tretitoli, Where the Bomb Group Was, 120
Triangle for Green Men, 9
Troubadour Removed, A, 18
Trout, 3
Trumpan, 400
Trumpets. A valley opens and beyond, 181
Turtle Lake, 239
2433 Agnes, First Home, Last House in Missoula, 205
Two cops who are really famous actors, 316
Two Graves in a Day, 52

Ugly women loud in public, 13
Uig Registrar, 386
Underwater Autumn, 7
Upper Voight's, To All the Cutthroat There, 187

View from Cortona, A, 116
Villager, 415
Viva La Resist`nza, 118

Walking Praed Street, 182
Walls were painted blue so long ago, you think, 135
Water bumps and bounces white, 25
Waves policed the sand to call, 12
Way a Ghost Behaves, The, 50
Way a Ghost Dissolves, The, 54
We are flying white air. The most pioneering, 231
We are passing it now. Our boat, 441
We are what we hear. A well known singer died, 401
We come for nothing but we read the stones, 36
We come here tourist on a bad sky day, 190
We found the sea in pieces at Pindeen, 195
We had to get him off, the dirty elf, 96
We quit that road of sad homes long ago, 262
We ripple aspen the way we move out, 336
We saw him in his powered wheelchair, 444
We went to the moon those empty Sundays, 368
We were set once. When it rained, each man, 265
We'll be confined and free. Roads end fast, 380
West Marginal Way, 5
What a walk. First mile uphill. The road, 390
What life is better—stone and stone, 47
What the Brand New Freeway Won't Go By, 86
What Thou Lovest Well Remains American, 235
Whatever they promise for money, luck, 197
What's wrong will always be wrong. I've seen him lean, 415
Wheel of Fortune, 334
When bells ring, wild rain pelts the river, 51
When hills give out, the river loses power, 62
When I came here first the lake was full, 15
When I imagine Delaware, 350
When they plan a freeway thru a city, 192

When weather shouted at us: vagabond, 101
When you find a gold stone know, 426
When you hobble, tattered through the square, 136
Where did the storm come from? No warning, 360
Where Jennie Used to Swim, 167
Where Mission Creek Runs Hard for Joy, 168
Where sea breaks inland, claiming the Quinalt, 69
Where she lived the close remained the best, 54
Where the House Was, 430
Where We crashed, 121
Where were they headed, the one winged birds, 246
White Center, 373
Who appreciates the fingers cramped, 37
Why I Think of Dumar Sadly, 228
Why Sapri Will Never Be Italian, 149
Why this day you're going so much wind, 85
Wind deserted the pond this morning. The day, 338
Windy hunks of light, not prop wash, bend, 120
With Anna at Camaldoli, 157
With houses hung that slanted and remote, 156
With Kathy in Wisdom, 178
With Melissa on the Shore, 330
With Ripley at the Grave of Albert Parenteau, 329

Yards of Sarajevo, The, 127
You a gentleman and I up from the grime, 87
You are alone on a desert. Hot blasting sand, 297
You are fishing a lake but so far no fish, 294
You are fishing but have walked away from your rod, 304
You are talking to a man named Buss. You knew Buss, 308
You are traveling to play basketball. Your team's, 287
You arrived arthritic for the cure, 214
You can always spot them, even from high up, 364
You can't weep like them, can't pound the rail, 105
You could love here, not the lovely goat, 166
You could see it way out crawling slow, 147
You curve in dandelion wine and in, 187
You hitch a ride with a cyclist. You sit in back, 300
You might come here Sunday on a whim, 216
You might die anywhere. You will die in Ayr, 403
You must fly your 35 missions again, 281
You remember the name was Jensen. She seemed old, 235
You start it all. You are lovely, 359